FATAL
FAMILIES

*For Sharon Harris-Ewing,
whose love and support
makes it all possible.*

Charles Patrick Ewing

FATAL FAMILIES

The Dynamics of Intrafamilial Homicide

SAGE Publications
International Educational and Professional Publisher
Thousand Oaks   London   New Delhi

For information:

SAGE Publications, Inc.
2455 Teller Road
Thousand Oaks, California 91320
E-mail: order@sagepub.com

SAGE Publications Ltd.
6 Bonhill Street
London EC2A 4PU
United Kingdom

SAGE Publications India Pvt. Ltd.
M-32 Market
Greater Kailash I
New Delhi 110 048 India

Printed in the United States of America

Library of Congress Cataloging-in-Publication Data

Ewing, Charles Patrick, 1949-

    Fatal families : the dynamics of intrafamilial homicide / by
Charles Patrick Ewing.
      p. cm.
    Includes bibliographical references (p.) and index.
    ISBN 0-7619-0758-0 (cloth : acid-free paper). — ISBN
0-7619-0759-9 (pbk. : acid-free paper)
    1. Homicide—United States. 2. Family violence—United States.
I. Title.
HV6529.E95 1997
364.15'23'0973—dc21   97-4798

This book is printed on acid-free paper.

97 98 99 00 01 02 03 10 9 8 7 6 5 4 3 2 1

Acquiring Editor:	Margaret Zusky
Editorial Assistant:	Corinne Pierce
Production Editor:	Sherrise M. Purdum
Production Assistant:	Karen Wiley
Copy Editor:	Joyce Kuhn
Typesetter/Designer:	Danielle Dillahunt
Cover Designer:	Candice Harman

Contents

Acknowledgments

My knowledge and understanding of "fatal families" has been enhanced by many people. Much of what I know I have gleaned from countless hours of interviews with the perpetrators and surviving victims of intrafamilial homicide. Each of these people has taught me something valuable about the subject. I have also benefited greatly from discussions with colleagues over the years, many of whom were either expert witnesses or defense counsel in family homicide cases. Among those who have most influenced my thinking are Michael Dowd, Paul Mones, Lenore Walker, Murray Levine, Mark Mahoney, Robert Geffner, Joseph McCann, and John Rowley. Others far too numerous to mention by name have also contributed to—but bear no responsibility for—the views I have expressed in this book.

As in the past, editor Margaret Zusky has encouraged my work. This time, her interest and enthusiasm gave me the much needed encouragement to finish the manuscript I started several years earlier.

Also as with past books, my family has been a great help. Sharon Harris-Ewing listened, encouraged, and gave me the time to do what I needed to do. Elaine Harris Ewing contributed her computer skills when they were sorely needed. And Ben Harris Ewing did his part by frequently knocking on my study door and giving me good reason to take a break from the often grim nature of my writing and professional work. My work with so many dysfunctional and "fatal families," although depressing at times, has given me an even greater appreciation of my own family.

Finally, I want to note—with special thanks to my friend and colleague Vice Dean Nils Olsen—that much of my work on this book was supported by summer research grants from the SUNY at Buffalo School of Law.

CHAPTER ONE

All in the Family

❖ Christine Lane, a single mother, and Aliza May Bush, her nearly 2-year-old daughter, were up early on Friday morning, February 2, 1990. Like many winter days in the rural area outside Ithaca, New York, home of Cornell University, it was cold, dark, and damp. Nearly a foot of snow covered the ground and woods outside their small, ground-floor apartment. Any groundhog who ventured forth that day would not have seen his shadow.

Mother and daughter bundled up in coats, mittens, and boots and took the garbage out at about 7:30. Walking back toward the apartment, Christine suddenly felt sick. Taking Aliza by the hand, she rushed into the apartment, hoping to make it to the toilet before it was too late.

Minutes later, when Christine emerged from the bathroom, feeling better, Aliza was gone. Christine quickly searched the entire apartment, but the child was nowhere to be found. Finally, the frantic mother stepped outside and spotted one of her daughter's tiny mittens at the end of the driveway. Moments later, she saw what looked like Aliza's footprints leading into the wooded swamp behind the apartment complex.

Assuming that Aliza had wandered into the snow-covered woods, Christine immediately called the police and reported her daughter's disappearance.

A lost child—every parent's nightmare—is one the few things in life that consistently brings out the best in people. Christine Lane could not have hoped for a better response to her early morning call for help. Police officers hurried to the scene, and, within hours, as many as 400 volunteers were combing a half-mile radius around the apartment complex. While forest rangers, firefighters, and volunteers searched every inch of the woods on foot, police helicopters scanned the area from above. Right behind the foot patrol came specially trained tracking dogs and investigators armed with sophisticated heat-sensing devices. If Aliza was out there, the searchers were determined to find her, no matter how long it took.

Unfortunately, the search team's optimistic determination did not translate into results. After almost four days and nights of fruitless searching in snow, rain, fog, and freezing cold, the authorities and volunteers gave up and admitted everyone's worst fears. If Aliza was in the woods, she was dead and probably covered with snow. Her body would not likely be found until spring or at least until a major thaw.

That was Tuesday, February 6. By Wednesday, February 7, authorities were convinced that Aliza was neither in the woods nor dead. In Wednesday's mail, Christine Lane received an envelope containing Aliza's other mitten—the mate to the one she had found in the driveway the morning her daughter disappeared. Police officials concluded that Aliza had been abducted—perhaps impulsively—by a passerby who saw her wandering outside the apartment complex and could not resist snatching the attractive little girl.

The envelope containing the mitten put an entirely new spin on the case. Investigating officers speculated that sending the mitten might be the abductor's way of telling Christine that her baby was alive and well. They rushed the mitten and envelope, which bore a local postmark, to the FBI crime laboratory for analysis. They set up a special toll-free 800 telephone line to receive tips, anonymous or otherwise. Christine Lane appealed publicly for her daughter's safe return. And, in an unprecedented gesture, the District Attorney announced that if the child was returned safely within 48 hours he would recommend leniency for the kidnapper—possibly even probation.

On Wednesday, February 12, a week after the mitten arrived, the DA's 48-hour "leniency" period expired and Aliza was still missing. Although no one came forth with the child, two people from the community did provide the police with valuable tips—information that would ultimately lead to both the victim and the perpetrator of this apparently sensational crime.

First, a local storekeeper called and said he had recently sold someone an envelope like the one that brought Aliza's mitten back to her mother. Then, another caller informed police that she had seen someone mailing something that could have been the same kind of envelope. The "someone" identified by both callers was Christine Lane.

On February 15, 13 days after Aliza was first reported missing and just hours after Christine made her final public appeal for the return of her daughter, police confronted her with these tips. Faced with a polygraph, Christine confessed that Aliza was dead.

Christine told the officers that she found Aliza dead in her crib—tangled in her blankets—on the morning of February 2. Fearing she would be accused of harming the child, she dressed her in winter clothes, wrapped her in two plastic trash bags, and buried her under heavy brush half a mile from the apartment. Then, in an effort to keep police from finding the child's body, she mailed the mitten to herself.

After confessing, Christine led investigators to the burial site, where they uncovered the toddler's body. After completing an autopsy, forensic pathologists ruled Aliza's death a homicide, and Christine Lane was charged with murder.

At trial, the prosecution was unable to establish any motive for the killing, but one witness testified that Christine Lane became angry when Aliza would not go to sleep. Although the jury rejected the state's charge of murder, they found Christine guilty of second-degree manslaughter, the reckless killing of another human being.

On January 16, 1991, almost one year after she killed her daughter, Christine Lane was sentenced to the maximum term allowed by New York law: prison for no less than 5 and no more than 15 years. ❖

❖ On October 24, 1989, anyone in the United States who read a newspaper, listened to a radio newscast, or watched network news learned that the night before, in inner-city Boston, a Black man robbed and shot Charles Stuart and his pregnant wife, Carol—a young, upper-middle-class White couple from the suburbs.

In a tragedy almost made for the electronic media, Boston police recorded a desperate 13-minute telephone conversation in which Chuck Stuart used a cellular car phone to help police locate him and his wife.

When officers finally found the Stuarts' car—listening to Chuck's call while using the sounds of sirens in the background to pinpoint the location—they found both Carol and Chuck seriously wounded. Carol had been shot in the head, Chuck in the abdomen.

Following surgery, including a cesarean section that delivered a premature baby boy, Carol died. The baby died 17 days later. Chuck also required life-threatening surgery but survived and told police what had happened.

According to Chuck's chilling account, he and Carol had just left a childbirth class at a Boston hospital when a Black man armed with a gun forced his way into their Toyota Cressida. The man, according to Chuck's extremely detailed description, was between 28 and 34 years old, stood about 5 feet–10 inches tall, weighed 150 to 160 pounds, wore a short Afro hairstyle, had shaggy facial hair, and was wearing a baseball cap and a black jogging suit with red stripes on the sleeves. Chuck was even able to describe the gunman's voice.

By Chuck Stuart's account, the gunman made him drive to a location near a public housing development in an unfamiliar, inner-city neighborhood. There the man robbed the couple, shot them both, and fled on foot with Carol's purse, her diamond ring, and $100 in cash.

The attack on the Stuarts struck both terror and outrage in a city already burdened with more than its share of street violence and racial tension. State legislators responded with a renewed call for restoration of the death penalty in Massachusetts. A Boston radio station set up a telephone hot line to take anonymous tips. A local business offered a $10,000 reward for any information leading to Carol Stuart's killer. And, day after day, the city's two newspapers romanticized the Stuarts and decried their victimization as just another awful example of the growing problem of street crime in Boston.

In the immediate aftermath of the Stuart shootings, Boston's mayor, Ray Flynn, ordered city police to give the case their highest priority. Police scoured the city's Mission Hill area, especially the public housing projects, for weeks, stopping and frisking hundreds of Black men. Finally, 19 days after the shootings, they arrested a suspect, Willie Bennett, a 39-year-old Black man who had allegedly bragged to friends that he shot the Stuarts. Chuck Stuart could not positively identify Bennett in a lineup but told police that Bennett looked most like the person who robbed and shot him.

Over the next couple of months, as Chuck Stuart recuperated and authorities searched for further evidence implicating Willie Bennett, the real story behind Carol Stuart's murder gradually emerged. Police received numerous phone calls passing along tips and rumors that Chuck Stuart was not the innocent victim he appeared to be.

Most of these tips turned out to be dead ends, but on January 3, 1990, Chuck Stuart's brother, Matthew, revealed that on the night of the killing he met Chuck near the scene of the crime. He told the police that Chuck had handed him Carol's purse, her diamond ring, and a .38 caliber revolver.

Armed with Matthew's confession, Boston police finally went after Chuck Stuart. But it was too late.

Police staked out Chuck's suburban home, but he never returned there. Apparently tipped off that the police were closing in on him, Chuck spent the night at a motel. The next morning—at the same time that prosecutors were presenting evidence against Willie Bennett to a grand jury—Chuck drove onto the highest bridge in Boston, got out of his brand-new Nissan Maxima, and jumped 145 feet into the Mystic River.

Not surprisingly, Chuck Stuart's suicide under these circumstances was widely regarded as confirmation that he had killed his wife and child. Although the full story may never be known, there is every reason to believe that Chuck Stuart killed to free himself from the responsibilities of marriage and impending fatherhood and to cash in on an estate (including life insurance) that eventually totaled nearly half a million dollars. ❖

❖ On August 20, 1989, José and Mary Menendez were found dead in their five-million-dollar Beverly Hills mansion. Their sons, Lyle, 22, and Erik, 19, told police they discovered their parents' bodies after returning from a movie theater and restaurant. Mr. and Mrs. Menendez had been repeatedly blasted at close range with a 12-gauge shotgun as they sat watching television. Police, responding to a desperate 911 call from one of the sons, found no indication of forced entry, no evidence of robbery, and no murder weapon.

José Menendez, a Cuban refugee who entered American business and rapidly became a multimillionaire, had recently taken over a major video distribution company. Police investigators initially believed the killings might be Mafia executions because they suspected the video company previously had ties to organized crime.

While police investigated this theory, Lyle and Erik, the sole beneficiaries of their parents' $14 million estate, collected $400,000 in life insurance and went their separate ways. Lyle bought a Porsche and a restaurant in New Jersey. Erik used his money to hire a coach and begin touring as a professional tennis player.

Meanwhile, as the Mafia theory led nowhere, police began to focus their suspicions on Lyle and Erik. Investigators spotted inconsistencies in the brothers' joint alibi. They found a spent shotgun shell in the pocket of Lyle's jacket. And they turned up a screenplay Erik had coauthored with a friend. The script told of a young heir who conspired to kill five people, including his own parents.

Still, it was not until seven months after the Menendez murders that authorities decided to charge the brothers with killing their parents. In March 1990, law enforcement officials seized tapes secretly recorded by a psychologist who had treated both Lyle and Erik. Based on alleged confessions contained in the tapes, police arrested both young men and charged them with capital murder. At their first trial several years later, Lyle and Erik admitted killing their parents, claiming they did so to protect themselves from abuse and/or death at the hands of their father.

Although the jury was unable to reach a verdict in the first trial, in 1996 jurors in a second trial convicted both Erik and Lyle of capital murder but spared the brothers the death penalty. ❖

At least some people suspected early on that Christine Lane, Chuck Stuart, and the Menendez brothers were all lying to authorities about the deaths of their family members. But no one really wanted to believe it.

In Christine's case, it was easier to believe that Aliza wandered off and was abducted by a stranger who just happened to be passing by. With the Stuarts, it was only too easy to believe that an affluent, young White couple driving in Boston's inner city would be kidnapped, robbed, and brutally shot by a crazed Black gunman. And in Lyle and Erik's case, it seemed at least plausible that their parents had been killed by a Mafia hit man.

People wanted to believe Christine Lane, Chuck Stuart, and the Menendez brothers because they could not believe or did not want to believe that a mother would kill her infant daughter, that a husband would murder his pregnant wife, or that two handsome, bright, and rich young men could brutally execute their parents. But, in fact, based on what we know about who kills whom in American society, Christine Lane, Chuck Stuart, Lyle Menendez, and Erik Menendez should all have been prime suspects right from the start.

The television-inspired stereotype of murder in America is that of the innocent victim shot, stabbed, strangled, or beaten to death by a total stranger—a rapist, robber, serial killer, or even mass murderer, who is drugged, deranged, sociopathic, or some combination of all three. In our

TABLE 1.1   Homicide Victims, by Relationship to Offender, 1977-1992

Year	Wife or Girlfriend	Husband or Boyfriend	Other Relatives	Other Known	Stranger	Unknown
1977	1,396	1,185	1,683	7,113	2,562	5,162
1978	1,428	1,095	1,701	6,119	2,640	5,886
1979	1,438	1,137	1,674	6,909	2,682	7,574
1980	1,498	1,129	1,797	7,304	3,064	8,248
1981	1,486	1,149	1,869	7,837	3,491	6,666
1982	1,408	1,008	1,807	7,290	3,551	5,904
1983	1,487	1,043	1,796	6,681	2,897	5,445
1984	1,420	897	1,701	6,542	3,289	4,822
1985	1,480	835	1,708	7,099	2,752	5,106
1986	1,525	866	1,690	7,708	2,679	6,142
1987	1,508	824	1,729	7,377	2,653	5,950
1988	1,592	765	1,613	7,383	2,564	6,783
1989	1,441	817	1,741	7,568	2,817	7,117
1990	1,524	797	1,688	7,946	3,375	8,134
1991	1,528	714	1,703	7,567	3,716	9,472
1992	1,510	657	1,531	7,550	3,218	9,295
Total:	23,669	14,918	27,431	116,073	47,950	107,706

SOURCE: U.S. Department of Justice, *Violence Between Intimates,* 1994.

fears, murderers are nameless, faceless, hardened criminals lurking somewhere "out there," ready to strike and kill randomly. Thus, the way to avoid becoming a murder victim is to stay away from the wrong places, mainly "bad" neighborhoods in tough, blighted urban areas, where drugs, craziness, criminality, and the other ingredients for homicide flourish openly.

There is, of course, some basis in fact for these stereotypes. In some geographic areas, mainly decaying inner-city neighborhoods, life is cheap, death comes all too easy, and the risk of being randomly murdered by a total stranger cannot be dismissed lightly. But for most Americans—regardless of where they live but especially for those who make it a point not to frequent the inner city—the risk of being murdered is much greater in their own homes than on any mean street they are ever likely to traverse. And the risk of being slain by an acquaintance or family member far exceeds any risk of dying at the hands of a homicidal stranger.

Annually, nearly half of the 20,000-plus homicide victims in the United States are related to or acquainted with their killers. As indicated in Table 1.1,

TABLE 1.2   Relationship of Murderer to Murder Victim in the United States, 1994

Victim	Percentage
Husband	1.56
Wife	3.73
Mother	0.54
Father	0.85
Daughter	0.96
Son	1.48
Brother	0.78
Sister	0.18
Other family member	1.76
Friend	3.32
Boyfriend	1.03
Girlfriend	2.38
Acquaintance	27.75
Neighbor	0.78
Stranger	13.08
Employee	0.03
Employer	0.06
Relationship unknown	39.72

SOURCE: Federal Bureau of Investigation, *Crime in the United States: Uniform Crime Reports*, 1995.

the number of Americans killed by family members has remained relatively stable over the past couple of decades. Between 1977 and 1992, there were 337,747 reported homicide victims in the United States, 66,018 of whom (19.5 percent) were killed by relatives, including "boyfriends" and "girlfriends." The only substantial year-to-year variation has been in the number of men killed by their wives and girlfriends, which dropped by nearly 50 percent between 1977 and 1992.

FBI data from 1994 illustrate the pattern of relationships found among victims and offenders in homicide both in and outside the family. As seen in Table 1.2, wives are the most common victims of intrafamilial killings, followed by husbands, sons, daughters, fathers, brothers, mothers, and sisters.

Among intrafamilial killings, the most common relationship between killer and victim is husband-wife. In a recent analysis of more than 8,603 homicides in the nation's 75 largest counties,[1] the U.S. Justice Department found that among the 16 percent that were intrafamilial, 40.9 percent involved one spouse killing another. Among White victims murdered by their spouses, 62 percent were wives. Among Blacks murdered by their spouses, 53 percent were wives.

Those data are in keeping with others compiled by the U.S. government. Annually, in recent years, more than a third of all female homicide victims in the United States have been killed by family members, most often their husbands, and women have been the victims in roughly 60 percent of all interspousal killings. In 1990, for example, 62.5 percent of the victims of interspousal homicides were wives.[2] More recently, in 1993, among those killed by spouses, 62 percent of White victims and 53 percent of Black victims were female.[3]

Many other women, of course, are also slain by their "boyfriends," "lovers," and "common-law" husbands—men with whom they share intimate relationships but to whom they are not "related" in the eyes of the law. In 1990, women were the victims in roughly two of every three "boyfriend-girlfriend" slayings in the United States.[4] Overall, on average, every six hours an American woman is killed by her husband or boyfriend.[5]

When children are killed, their killers are usually relatives, most often parents. For example, in the U.S. Department of Justice study of urban homicides, parents were the perpetrators in 57 percent of the killings of children under the age of 12.[6]

In recent years, documented child abuse deaths in the United States have reached record highs. Annually, more than 1,000 children are victims of fatal child abuse and/or neglect. In 1992, the U.S. Department of Health and Human Services put the number at 1,068, with 44 states reporting.[7] In 1993, according to the American Psychological Association, roughly 1,300 American children died as a result of abuse and/or neglect.[8] Since cause of death is often especially difficult to document in child abuse fatalities, experts say these verified cases probably represent only about half the actual number of children killed by child abuse annually in the United States.[9] The vast majority of these child abuse killings are committed by parents or parent surrogates.

Although children of all ages are among those killed by abusive parents and relatives, the problem is much greater for very young children, who are more physically vulnerable and thus more likely to die when exposed to severe physical abuse. Levine and his colleagues estimate that "75 percent or more of maltreatment-related fatalities occur in children under the age of four" while approximately 40 percent of all such fatalities "involve children under two."[10]

Children are also often killed by their siblings. In a recent U.S. Department of Justice analysis, sibling homicides accounted for 9.4 percent of all intrafamilial killings.[11]

People also frequently kill their parents. In the Justice Department's survey of urban American homicides, 11.7 percent of the intrafamilial homicides involved one or more offspring killing a parent.[12]

In addition to relationship, gender and age seem to make a substantial difference in intrafamilial killings. Killings of any sort committed by women are rare—generally less than 15 percent of all criminal homicides— but when women do kill, they most often kill family members.[13] Among juveniles who kill, almost 90 percent are boys, but girls are more than three times as likely to kill family members.[14]

Data from the Department of Justice suggest that females are the perpetrators of roughly one-third of all intrafamilial killings.[15] These same data also indicate that when a parent kills a child the perpetrator is female in 55 percent of cases.[16]

Finally, it is worth noting that alcohol abuse, mental illness, and criminality also bear strong statistical relationships to intrafamilial homicide. Among the intrafamilial killings examined by the Justice Department, nearly half of the perpetrators and roughly a third of the victims had been drinking at the time of the killing; 14 percent of the killers had a history of mental illness; and 56 percent of the perpetrators had records of arrests or convictions.[17]

Intrafamilial homicide takes many forms. Husbands kill wives; wives kill husbands. Parents kill children; children kill parents. Siblings kill siblings. Even grandparents, aunts, uncles, and cousins are both the victims and perpetrators of killings within their own families. Some family killers kill only a single relative. Others kill more than one. Some kill their entire families. Still others add to the carnage by killing themselves.

Some who kill family members are motivated by greed—for example, speeding up inheritance of their parents' fortune, however large or small it might be. Others, such as battered women and children who kill their abusers, kill in self-defense. Still others kill family members impulsively in what appear to be normal—or at least understandable—human responses carried to fatal extremes or, in some cases, pushed to lethal proportions by some combination of stress, drugs, and/or alcohol. Finally, a small percentage of those who kill family members are seriously disturbed—mentally ill and/or legally insane.

Whatever its origin, homicidal violence directed toward a family member is widely regarded as the most dreadful and frightening of all crimes. Killing a family member seems especially horrible because families are—at least according to popular myth—warm, loving, peaceful social units, the members of which loyally defend, protect, and nurture one another.

Growing public awareness of divorce, domestic violence, and other forms of family strife has, to some extent, undermined this idealized stereotype of the family. However, for the most part, the family continues to be revered as both a sacrosanct and vital institution in modern society. Thus, the killing of a relative threatens not only the viability of the family in which the homicide occurs but symbolically strikes a severe blow against the institution that is at the very core of our social order.

Family homicide is particularly frightening because it is a phenomenon to which virtually all of us are vulnerable. For better or worse, we are a society of families. Every one of us is someone's son or daughter. Most of us also have siblings, children, spouses, or at least one or more "significant other" with whom we share family-like intimacy. We can and do take all sorts of steps to minimize the risk of being murdered by strangers (e.g., staying away from "bad" neighborhoods; installing and using locks and alarm systems; and carrying whistles, mace, and even guns), a risk that for most of us is already infinitesimal. Yet there is very little if anything we can do to reduce what is for most of us the much greater risk of being killed by members of our own families.

Thus, in a very real sense, every intrafamilial homicide is a reminder that—even in safe neighborhoods, behind locked doors, and protected by alarms and weapons—we are all vulnerable.

This book examines the nature, causes, and consequences of family homicide in modern American society. Much of its content is unpleasant, disturbing, and perhaps even shocking to some. The chapters that follow contain explicit details of dozens of cases of intrafamilial homicide.

The intent, however, is not to shock readers, exploit their fears and feelings of vulnerability, or sensationalize what is already almost an inherently sensational topic. On the contrary, the purpose of this book is to combat fear, myth, and sensationalism with understanding and facts; to examine objectively the social, cultural, and psychological forces that lead people to kill members of their own families. Such an examination, it is hoped, will not only lead to a better understanding of this problem but perhaps also point the way to potential solutions.

CHAPTER TWO

Batterers Who Kill

✦ Lisa Bianco was just 18 when she married 27-year-old Alan Matheney in 1978. When the couple met and dated, Lisa thought Alan was a perfect gentlemen. But by the time they married, she knew better. Alan Matheney was a brute, a batterer who spent the next 7 years using Lisa as a punching bag. Matheney, who stood a full foot taller than Lisa, beat her literally hundreds of times.

Like most battered women, Lisa found it difficult if not impossible to break away from Alan. Helpless and hopeless, she simply endured, living life one awful day at a time, from one beating to the next.

Alan Matheney might still be beating Lisa Bianco but for the advice she received one night in 1985. Her face beaten beyond recognition and her clothes virtually ripped from her body by her husband, Lisa fled to an Indiana battered women's shelter. When Lisa refused to say what happened to her, Sandy Money, a counselor at the shelter, told Lisa about how another battered woman had made the break and escaped from her batterer. Sandy told Lisa that with a lot of help she could do the same thing.

It was not easy, but Lisa Bianco took the counselor's advice. By the end of the year, she had divorced Alan and secured custody of their two children, who were then 3 and 7. But as many battered women find out quickly, divorce, by itself, offers no real escape from a batterer. Alan Matheney had warned Lisa that he would never let her go, and he made good on that promise.

Alan followed Lisa, accosted her, and continued to beat her every chance he got. Lisa sought protection in court orders, disguises, and even bodyguards, but nothing stopped Matheney's relentless efforts to control and intimidate her. When the divorce was finalized, he responded by kidnapping the couple's two children and taking them more than 650 miles to North Carolina. Lisa filed charges, and Alan was arrested, extradited, and prosecuted. Lisa's children were returned, but that was not the end of it.

Released on just $1,000 bail, Alan broke into Lisa's home and beat, raped, and tried to strangle her. Telling authorities she knew that if she did not take a stand she would continue to be victimized, Lisa filed additional charges against her ex-husband. Again, she faced an uphill battle.

Criminal justice authorities were neither sympathetic nor helpful. Some said flatly that, as a matter of principle, Alan Matheney should not be locked up. The rape charge was dropped after one official wrote a memo to the court saying that for all he knew the alleged rape and beating had been just a "wonderful social affair with sex involved." Lisa, he told the court, now seemed to be using the criminal justice system to "whip her husband to death." This official closed his report to the court with one word followed by an exclamation point: "Ugh!"

Nevertheless, Lisa persevered, and Alan Matheney was finally jailed. Convicted of assault and kidnapping, he was sentenced to serve eight years in prison.

But Lisa had no time or reason to rejoice. She knew that even the walls and bars of a state prison could not protect her for long. Alan Matheney told her that, whatever it took, he would get out and kill her. And, from years of experience with him, Lisa knew he would do just that.

Lisa Bianco could have run. It occurred to her to get herself and her children as far away from Indiana as possible. But then Alan had also promised that no matter where she went he would track her down and kill her.

Knowing that once she started running she would be looking over her shoulder for the rest of her life, Lisa decided to stand her ground. Instead of fleeing, she educated herself and became a highly visible, widely known advocate for battered women in the state of Indiana. Perhaps she felt that hiding in plain sight was the best—if not the only—strategy to save her life. In a self-help brochure she wrote for other battered women, Lisa advised that if a woman's batterer hunted her down, she should run outdoors, scream, and make herself known to others.

Staying in public places might provide some measure of protection, Lisa counseled others in her predicament.

The test of Lisa's ability to follow her own advice and the usefulness of that advice came earlier than she expected, even in her worst fears. Incredibly, in January 1989, before he had served even two years in prison, model inmate Alan Matheney was offered a furlough—the chance to leave prison for a day without official supervision.

Fortunately, Alan's mother called Lisa and warned her just in time for Lisa to contact the county prosecutor, who saw to it that the day pass was canceled. Prison officials agreed to notify both Lisa and the prosecutor in advance of any other furloughs Matheney might be granted.

Less than two months later, however, prison authorities failed to keep their word. On March 4, 1989, without notice to anyone, Alan Matheney was allowed an 8-hour pass in the custody of his mother. Alan was by then actually eligible for a 48-hour pass, but prison authorities had cautiously decided to test him first on an 8-hour furlough.

Once outside the prison gates, Matheney talked his mother into driving him to his old neighborhood—a clear violation of the terms of his furlough. Once back in Mishawaka, Indiana, Alan got rid of his mother, stole a gun from a friend's home, and drove to Lisa's house.

Matheney knocked the glass out of the back door and broke into the house. His 10-year-old daughter realized it was him, screamed, and ran to a neighbor's home for help. Moments later, Lisa, wearing only panties, ran from the house with Alan following close behind. Neighbors—along with Lisa's two daughters—watched in horror as Matheney quickly caught up to his ex-wife, knocked her to the ground, and, with some 20 blows, used the butt of a shotgun to beat her head in. The gun butt broke into pieces as it shattered Lisa's skull.

Alan Matheney was charged with capital murder. A jury quickly rejected his insanity plea as contrived, convicted him, and recommended the death penalty. The judge who heard the evidence then sentenced Matheney to die in the Indiana electric chair. Although the Indiana State Supreme Court affirmed Matheney's conviction and death sentence, one of the court's judges dissented, urging that Matheney should have been spared capital punishment because he had killed Lisa Bianco "under the influence of extreme mental and emotional disturbance" and because "in his relations with neighbors, fellow workers, his children, and the children of others, [he] was useful, generous and kind."

Meanwhile, Indiana Governor Evan Bayh had approved a settlement to the lawsuit brought against the state on behalf of Lisa Bianco's two children. Admitting the state's failure to protect Lisa, Governor Bayh authorized the state treasury to pay $900,000 to the children plus additional funds to their maternal grandmother, who took over the task of raising them. ❖

❖ Although it took Lisa Bianco years to seek legal help in her struggle to be free of her husband's violence, Pamela Nigro Dunn was married just two months before she went to court. On March 14, 1986, Pamela appeared in a Massachusetts District Court to ask for an order of protection as well as for police protection so she could return to her apartment and collect her belongings.

Pamela explained to Judge Paul P. Heffernan that her husband, Paul, had locked her in their apartment and beaten, choked, and threatened to kill her. She asked the judge to order Paul to stay away from her and to have police escort her home so she would not be beaten or killed while she moved out. Judge Heffernan told Pamela Dunn that she did not need police protection when she went back to the apartment. He told her to go home and act like an adult.

As for the order of protection, Judge Heffernan granted Pamela's request, forbidding Paul to go near her. But before issuing the requested order, Judge Heffernan castigated Pamela for wasting the court's time with such a trivial matter when he had many more serious concerns to deal with.

Finally, the judge told Pamela that her request for a protective order was a waste of public funds. If the couple wanted to fight with each other, the judge said, they should do so without putting a burden on the taxpayer.

Although Pamela got her order of protection, she found out quickly what an order of protection really is: simply a piece of paper. Such an order becomes "protection" for a battered woman only when and if (1) her batterer violates the explicit and particular terms of the order; (2) she calls the police; (3) the police come; and (4) the police actually enforce the order (i.e., force the batterer away from the woman).

Pamela Dunn's order of protection may have helped keep her estranged husband away from her for awhile, but not for long. Faced with Paul's continued harassment and threats, Pamela moved in with her parents. When Paul started following Pamela, her mother began walking her to and from the bus stop, hoping to deter any confrontation. That strategy worked briefly. But on August 16, 1986, less than a month before the 6-month order was due to expire, Pamela and her mother were walking down a street near their home in Arlington, Massachusetts when they were accosted by Paul Dunn.

Paul jumped from his car, yelled at both women, and then sprayed mace into Pamela's eyes. When Pamela—who was 5 to 6 months' pregnant—struggled to free herself from Paul's grasp, he pulled out a .45 caliber commando rifle, shot her in the abdomen, forced her into the car, and drove away.

The next day police found Pamela Dunn's body lying face down in a puddle at the town dump. In addition to being shot, she had been severely beaten, stabbed, and strangled.

In the aftermath of Pamela Dunn's tragic death, the justice system turned its attention to two culprits: Paul Dunn and Paul Heffernan.

Paul Dunn pleaded insanity but was convicted of first-degree murder and sentenced to life in prison.

The other Paul—Judge Heffernan—fared much better. After finding that Heffernan's treatment of Pamela Dunn was not an isolated instance and that other battered women had complained about his conduct toward them from the bench, the State Judicial Conduct Commission urged the State Supreme Court to censure the judge.

Although finding it "clear beyond serious dispute" that Judge Heffernan had violated canons of judicial conduct by treating Pamela Dunn with "discourtesy, rudeness and sarcasm," the Massachusetts Supreme Judicial Court—the state's highest tribunal and one of the most respected courts in the United States—issued only a private reprimand, a letter urging the judge to improve his behavior. ❖

❖ On August 27, 1989, at 10:45 p.m., Maria Navarro picked up the telephone in her home and dialed 911. The conversation between Maria and the Los Angeles police operator was brief:

Operator: 911. What's your emergency?

Maria: I was just—I have a restraining order on my husband and he just threaten[ed] me. [He said,] "I'm coming over there with a .35, some kind of gun, and shooting everybody." I'm having a party and it's my birthday . . .

Operator: Who did he shoot at?

Maria: No. He didn't shoot at nobody, but he's threatened of coming
over here and . . .

Operator: But he hasn't come over there?

Maria: No, he hasn't.

Operator: But he's just threatening to do so?

Maria: Yes, and I'm sure he will.

Operator: Okay, well the only thing to do is just call us if he comes over
there. I mean, what can we do? We can't have a unit sit there and
wait and see if he comes over.

Maria: Oh, my God.

Operator: So if he comes over, don't let him in. Then call us.

Maria: Okay, thank you.

What Maria Navarro was trying to tell the officer who answered the
police emergency line was that her brother-in-law had just called to say
that her estranged husband, Raymond Navarro, Jr., was on his way to kill
her. A party, celebrating Maria's 27th birthday, was going on in the
converted garage she called home. Her children and many of her relatives
and friends were there. She feared for herself and for all of them.

Maria had good reason to fear that Raymond Navarro would show up
and kill her. For years, he had beaten Maria and the children, threatened
them, and trashed their belongings. Seventeen months earlier, Maria had
decided she could take no more of Raymond's abuse. After filing for
divorce, she secured custody of the children and obtained a protective
order directing her husband to stay at least 100 yards away from her.

Since the filing of the divorce papers, Raymond had followed the letter
of the order but not its spirit. Although he managed to remain a football
field's length or more away from her physically, he was constantly on top
of her psychologically. He followed her wherever she went, tracked her
every move, and always seemed to be waiting for her to come or go.

When Maria hung up the phone after talking to the 911 operator, she
was weeping and trembling. She had never expected that the police might
not respond to her frantic call.

Maria and her guests feared staying in the small apartment, but they
also feared leaving. As a precaution, one relative was posted at the door to
serve as a lookout. Still, 15 minutes later, Raymond Navarro scaled a wall
behind the converted garage and took Maria and her guests by surprise.

Crashing though the door, armed with a handgun, Navarro started shooting. Family members and friends scattered; some ran out the door; the
children ducked under a bed.

When the shooting stopped just a few minutes later, Maria Navarro,
two of her aunts, and one friend of the family were dead. A third aunt as
well as another family friend were seriously wounded, one shot in the head,
the other in the abdomen. After shooting six people, Raymond fled to his
father's home where he held a SWAT team at bay until 4 a.m., when he
finally surrendered.

Raymond Navarro was charged with four counts of murder. Convicted
on all counts and eligible for the death penalty, he was sentenced to life in
prison with no possibility of parole. The 911 operator/dispatcher was
cleared of any wrongdoing and even defended by Los Angeles County
Sheriff Sherman Block.

Concluding that the operator had responded properly to Maria
Navarro's urgent call and did not violate any departmental procedures,
Sheriff Block said it was impossible to respond to every single threat.

Two months later, in a *Los Angeles Times* "op-ed" piece, Susan Yocum,
a Los Angeles police officer, further defended the 911 operator, warning
readers that they were deluding themselves if they thought the police could
be counted on to stop someone determined to kill.[1] ❖

Cynical as it may sound, Officer Yocum's assessment is undoubtedly
accurate, especially when applied to battered women whose batterers
threaten to kill them. Even where the police take extraordinary care to
protect such women, they generally cannot prevent their batterers from
killing them. Consider the case of April and Tony Lasalata.

❖ High school sweethearts from New York's Long Island, April and Tony
were married in 1975. Tony was a drug abuser, and April's parents warned
her not to marry him. But April, a high school girl in love, refused to listen.

Surprisingly, the marriage went reasonably well for the first few years.
Tony never struck April until after they bought their first house in the late
1970s. From that time on, the relationship went slowly but steadily downhill.
The Lasalatas had two children and were apparently both good parents. But
their parenting did little to overcome the growing rift between them.

Tony would come home drunk, beat April, and then smash her
belongings, especially those items he knew had great sentimental value to

her. Anything or nothing could set off one of his violent temper tantrums. One night in 1982, Tony came home to find April alone in the house with a former classmate—a man who had brought her home early from a wedding when she became ill. Thereafter, Tony became obsessed with the idea that other men, even his closest friends, were conspiring to have sexual relations with April.

In December 1987, April finally managed to divorce Tony but not get rid of him. As the divorce proceedings wore on, Tony became increasingly violent and out of control. In one 10-month period, April had to call the police eight times to remove Tony from the home after he had abused her. Finally, she obtained a court order directing Tony to stay away from her, her home, her workplace, and the couple's children.

Once the divorce was finalized, April got custody of the children and was able to limit their contact with Tony. That seemed to help the children, but for April and Tony things got even worse.

April and Tony owed about $5,000 on their $130,000 home. Tony wanted to sell the house and split the proceeds. Instead, April got the court to allow her and the children to continue living there while Tony paid $130 a week (17 percent of his gross weekly income) in child support. As a result, Tony was reduced to living in a $90-a-month mobile home.

To make matters worse, from Tony's perspective, April took advantage of her newly gained freedom by developing a romantic involvement with the tenant who rented the basement apartment in the Lasalatas' home.

On February 26, 1988, Tony went to the house, cut the telephone wires, and broke in. When April arrived a short while later with one of the couple's sons, Tony grabbed the boy, locked him in his bedroom, and then turned on April with a knife and a shotgun. After dragging April to the basement by her hair, Tony stabbed her three times and fled.

In the aftermath of the attack, Tony was charged with attempted murder and released on $25,000 bail to await trial. He spent several months in a private psychiatric hospital but was discharged to the community, presumably no longer dangerous.

Once she heard that Tony was back on the streets, April turned to the local police for protection, and they gladly complied, giving her the kind of protection most battered women dream about but never get. Police officers installed a special burglar alarm in April's home, attached a recording device to her telephone, and gave her an electronic "panic button" to wear at all times. The button, if pressed, would summon police immediately.

As it turned out, however, all the high-tech security hardware and police surveillance in the world probably would not have been enough to protect April. Tony Lasalata simply would not let go. He had to control April. Nothing would deter him.

In April 1989, just two weeks after doctors released him from the psychiatric hospital, Tony ambushed and murdered April. Jumping from behind a bush as April stood on her doorstep, Tony shot and killed his ex-wife. He then drove to a nearby highway rest stop and shot and killed himself with the same gun. ❖

Although Lisa Bianco, Pamela Dunn, Maria Navarro, and April Lasalata had all been married to the battering men who killed them, lack of a legally recognized marital relationship is no barrier to domestic violence or homicide.

❖ Like many battered women, including many who are murdered, Anna Alfaro, a 22-year-old Los Angeles secretary, was not married to the man who battered her. Anna had been dating Ruben Garcia, a 20-year-old L.A. street-gang member, on and off for about a year when she decided she would no longer tolerate being beaten by him.

By September 1989, she had managed to break away from Garcia. She had even made plans to marry another man. But none of that stopped Garcia from continuing to abuse her or from eventually killing her.

During the last 4 months of her life, Anna Alfaro repeatedly called the police to complain that Garcia was threatening and/or assaulting her. The police faithfully responded, but each time they were too late. Garcia had already taken off.

On one occasion in September, criminal charges of battery were lodged against Garcia, but he was never arrested. Amazingly, because the case was characterized as domestic violence and the charges were considered minor, prosecutors simply mailed Garcia, a transient gang member, a notice to appear in court. Whether Garcia ever received the notice—sent to his last known address—or simply ignored it is not known. In any event, he never showed up in court.

Finally, a warrant was issued for Garcia's arrest, but police never served it. The warrant was simply filed, to be served if and when police ever happened to stop Garcia and run his name through their computers.

That never happened, but Garcia did surface again. On November 16, he showed up at the home of Anna's parents and assaulted her. Anna called the police and they investigated, but she refused to press charges. Small wonder, given what little good it had done to press charges the last time he had beaten her.

On December 11, Garcia again assaulted Anna. Again she called the police, they came, and she declined to press charges. Instead, Anna decided to do two things to protect herself: move to a new address and seek a court order of protection that would enable police officers to arrest Garcia if he even came near her.

Eleven days later, Anna had moved, but that did not stop Garcia. He learned her new address, showed up there, and threatened her with a knife. As usual, the police were called but arrived after Garcia was gone. No charges were filed, and the officers did not bother to go after Garcia. Ironically, Garcia was on parole and could have been taken in for violating the conditions of his parole. But this was Friday night, December 22, detectives were off duty for the holiday weekend, and the necessary paperwork could not be processed until after Christmas Day.

Two days later, on Christmas Eve, Ruben Garcia again confronted Anna as she arrived at her parents' home. Anna was loaded down with gifts for her family when Garcia ambushed her, forced her at gunpoint into an alley behind a nearby apartment building, and then raped, shot, and killed her before fleeing.

But even after he had killed Anna Alfaro, Garcia would not give up. Over the next two days, he called members of Anna's family and threatened to kill them. On the same days, Garcia was spotted four times near the Alfaros' home in Van Nuys. Once he was seen hiding in the bushes outside the house. Other times, he drove by in a yellow car. Once he even got out of the car and taunted the grieving family members.

Although charged with murder, Garcia remained at large. Finally, police were posted outside the Alfaro home and at Anna's memorial service, where they wore bulletproof vests, screened the mourners, and directed them to the back door of the funeral home, all the while watching for Ruben Garcia, who never showed up.

After the service at the heavily guarded funeral home, Anna Alfaro, dressed in the white gown she was to have worn in her wedding, was buried in El Salvador, her birthplace.

Nearly 2 years after Anna's death, Garcia was finally captured by police in New York City, where he had already been arrested several times while using various aliases. ❖

WHY BATTERERS KILL

Each year in the United States, more than 1,000—and sometimes as many as 1,300—battered women are murdered by their batterers.[2] On average, three or four battered women are killed every day. The vast majority of women killed by their abusive mates have previously turned—without success—to the police and/or the courts for help. Indeed, it has been estimated that in more than 80 percent of spousal homicides the police had been called to the marital home at least once in the 2 years preceding the killing.[3]

Why are so many battered women killed by their abusers, and why doesn't the law do more to prevent these killings?

The overall likelihood that a battered woman will be killed by her batterer is directly proportional to the degree she resists being abused. Battered women who resist abuse or fight back are much more likely to be killed than battered women who suffer in silence. Battered women who leave or even try to leave their batterers are the most likely of all to be killed.[4]

Research consistently finds that violence against battered women escalates significantly, often to fatal or potentially fatal proportions, any time these women try to take any control over their lives or the battering relationship.[5]

It is interesting, although not surprising, that as the number of alternatives for battered women (e.g., shelters and other community resources) has increased in recent years so has the number of battered women killed by their batterers. Ironically, giving a battered woman a place to go makes it more likely that she will leave—or at least try to leave—her batterer, but that also increases the likelihood that she will be killed by him.

The explanation lies in the dynamics of the battering relationship. Control is the ultimate issue in most of these relationships. Batterers have an obsessive if not a pathological need to control the lives of the women with whom they share intimate relationships. Indeed, much if not most abuse in these relationships (whether physical, psychological, or sexual) seems to be an expression of that need.

For example, batterers routinely tell battered women that they would not be beaten if only they did what their batterers wanted. Moreover, most batterers do all they can to socially isolate battered women and keep them from developing or maintaining relationships with family or friends. Many batterers even go so far as to deny abused women access to money, cars, phones and even the mail, virtually imprisoning them in efforts to prevent meaningful interaction with the world outside the battering relationship.[6]

Finally, virtually all batterers make it clear both implicitly and explicitly that "their" women are not free to leave the relationship. Not infrequently, batterers threaten to kill not only battered women but their children and their families if they try to leave. Other more subtle but effective ways a batterer conveys the same message include constantly berating the battered woman and telling her she could not make it on her own, that no other man would have her, and that she is lucky that he puts up with her.[7]

The control aspect of battering relationships also becomes apparent upon close examination of batterers themselves. Men who batter come from all walks of life, but they have many things in common—not only with other batterers but with battering victims as well.[8] Typically, batterers have low self-esteem and have witnessed or been directly victimized by abuse in the families in which they grew up. They are generally insecure men who feel they have no real power or control in other aspects of their lives. Home is the one arena where they feel dominant and in control, but even there they are insecure and feel a continual need to prove they are really in charge. The thought that they might lose "their" women or children is a constant, nagging threat.

As Holmes and Holmes have explained,

> Perhaps men who feel unable to control their lives outside the family are particularly likely to exert control within the family. One person such a man may be able to control is his female partner. . . . If such a man is placed in a situation where his partner is striving for personal autonomy . . . he may see violence as the sole answer to the problem. Killing, here, may be seen as an act of control.[9]

Although the barriers to freedom are clearly different—and more tangible for battered women—batterers, like the women they abuse, are also often "trapped" in battering relationships. To put it another way, batterers need the women they batter. Indeed, researchers and clinicians consistently find that when battering relationships end, most batterers move on to other relationships in which they batter their new mates.[10]

Once battering is viewed as an expression of the batterer's obsessive and distorted need to control the battered woman, it should come as no surprise that most battered women killed by their batterers are those who—like Lisa Bianco, Pamela Dunn, Maria Navarro, and April Lasalata—not only tried but succeeded in leaving their batterers. Their mates—men like Alan Matheney, Paul Dunn, Raymond Navarro, and Tony Lasalata—could not accept the loss of control they experienced when "their" women left them. Unable to regain that control by any other means, they resorted to the ultimate form of control: murder.

THE FAILURE OF THE LEGAL SYSTEM

Although much of the blame for spousal abuse and the killing of battered women lies with batterers, the fault is not theirs alone. Every instance in which a woman is beaten or killed by her batterer is also a reflection of the failure of the legal system to protect battered women. The law's response to battered women varies from case to case, time to time, and place to place, but rarely is that response anywhere near adequate.

The experiences of Maria Navarro and Pamela Dunn may seem extreme, but they are not unusual. Sadly, the responses they received from the legal system are still more the rule than the exception when a battered woman looks to the law for help.

Although many, perhaps most, battered women suffer in silence, a growing number are turning to the legal system for help. And when they do, they turn first to the police—the one legal agency that is open 24 hours a day, 365 days a year, and makes house calls. But what response do battered women get when they call the police?

Those, like Maria Navarro, who call to report a "mere" threat of injury or death are likely to get no response at all. Unless a battering is ongoing or has just concluded, a battered woman who calls the police will almost always be told to "let us know if he does anything." Of course, as the case of Anna Alfaro dramatically illustrates, by then it is usually too late for effective police intervention.

But even when a battered woman calls the police to report an ongoing battering incident, the police response is often not much better. Leaving aside the low priority that many departments assign such calls, frequent delays in response time, and the occasional failure to respond at all, police responses to domestic violence calls are almost always woefully inadequate.

Typically, by the time the police arrive, the batterer has stopped beating the woman. Since they do not witness the crime, the responding officers are, in most states, powerless to make an arrest or even remove the batterer from the home. Even in jurisdictions where they have that authority, officers are often unlikely to exercise it, preferring instead to quiet the situation and leave as quickly as possible. At best, they advise the battered woman that she has several options, including seeking an order of protection, filing charges with the local prosecutor's office, or simply leaving her batterer.

As noted earlier, the first of these options is frequently illusory. An order of protection is simply a piece of paper. Lisa Bianco, Pamela Dunn, Maria Navarro, and April Lasalata all sought and obtained orders of protection, but in no case did that stop their batterers from killing them. In theory, a batterer who violates an order of protection is in contempt of court and subject to summary incarceration. In reality, however, judges almost never back up these orders by locking up the men who violate them. Knowing that, police officers rarely bother to respond to, much less try aggressively to enforce, orders of protection.

Filing formal complaints against a batterer sounds easier and more effective than it is. Unfortunately, battered women, in general, have a reputation for filing and then dropping charges against their batterers. Some are talked out of the charges by their batterers, some realize that they cannot afford to have the family's breadwinner locked up for long, and others are intimidated and coerced into dropping the charges. Aware of all this, prosecutors are often reluctant to even allow a battered woman to file charges.

For the same reason, when a woman insists on charging her batterer, prosecutors rarely press the case with any vigor. Indeed, prosecutors often refuse to prosecute these cases at all. In one recent study reported by Walker, 90 percent of the battered women interviewed not only called police but actually filed complaints against their batterers. Fewer than 1 percent of these complaints were ever prosecuted.[11]

CHAPTER THREE

Battered Women
Who Kill

✦ From 1978 until 1983, Leslie Emick lived with Marshall Allison in a scenic but impoverished rural area in western New York. The couple had two children and lived a generally uneventful life until 1981. It was then, after the birth of their second child, that Marshall began to abuse Leslie. Often, he accused her of infidelity. Unsatisfied with her denials, he began to beat her. He knocked her head against a tree, stabbed her with a pencil, and clubbed her with a piece of firewood.

Later, Marshall took to tying Leslie up and bullwhipping her. From the whip, he moved on to using other devices against her. Insisting that Leslie refer to him as "master," he abused her sexually and physically with ropes, belts, needle-nosed pliers, a vacuum cleaner attachment, a hunting knife, and a homemade wooden dildo.

By February 1983, the abuse had escalated even further. On February 22, Marshall told Leslie he intended to keep her from having sex with other men. His method was to jam an electric immersion coil into her vagina and then use it to burn other parts of her body. That same day, Marshall tried to hang Leslie. While she struggled to keep from being strangled, Marshall used a mallet to beat her into unconsciousness.

Two days later, Marshall punched Leslie and knocked her head against a cupboard. Later that day, Marshall told Leslie he planned to kill her and the children and then himself. He gave her the choice of killing herself or having him do it the next day.

At approximately 4 a.m. the following morning, 22-year-old Leslie picked up Marshall's .22 caliber rifle and shot him five times in the head as he lay sleeping.

A medical examination of Leslie, conducted after the killing, revealed multiple puncture wounds, burns, welts, bruises, and abrasions, including a contusion and abrasion inside her vagina. A psychiatrist who examined Leslie concluded that she suffered the classic symptoms of battered woman syndrome. Later, the psychiatrist would testify that there was no doubt that when Leslie killed Marshall she was reasonably in fear for her life and the lives of her children.

Despite this medical and psychiatric evidence, a jury rejected Leslie Emick's self-defense claim and found her guilty of first-degree manslaughter. Although she was sentenced to serve from 2 to 6 years in prison, Leslie's conviction was reversed on appeal. Although the appeals court ordered a new trial, the case was never retried because Leslie agreed to plead guilty to the lesser offense of involuntary manslaughter and to accept a sentence of 5 years' probation and 3,000 hours of community service.

Marshall Allison's family denied that he had abused Leslie and decried the plea bargain as unjust. ❖

❖ Although just 39 years old, Judy Norman had been married 25 years when she shot and killed her sleeping husband. For the last 20 of those years, John Norman brutally abused her. He slapped, punched, and kicked her. He struck her with fists, shoes, baseball bats, beer bottles, ashtrays, and glasses. He smashed a glass in her face, doused her with hot coffee, and put out cigarettes on her skin.

In addition to this physical abuse, John terrorized Judy psychologically. He forced her into prostitution, demanded that she earn a minimum of $100 a day, and beat her if she failed to make that quota. He threatened to kill her, constantly referred to her as a "dog," "bitch," and "whore," and joked with family and friends about her status as a prostitute. At times, he denied her food for days at a time. Other times, he demanded that she bark like a dog and beat her if she refused. He also made her eat cat and dog food from their pets' bowls and forced her to sleep on a concrete floor, telling her that "dogs don't lay in the bed."

On June 10, 1985, John dropped Judy at a highway rest stop where he demanded that she engage in prostitution. When he returned to the rest area later that day, he was drunk. He punched Judy in the face, slammed the car door on her, and threw hot coffee at her. Driving home, John was arrested for operating a vehicle while under the influence of alcohol.

When John was released from jail the next morning, he went home and started beating Judy. Throughout the day, he slapped her and threw glasses, ashtrays, and bottles at her. After demanding that she make him a sandwich, he smeared it in her face.

By evening the abuse had become so bad that the police were summoned to the Norman home. The officer who responded at about 8 p.m. found Judy bruised and crying. She told him John had been beating her all day and that she could no longer stand the abuse. The officer advised swearing out a warrant for John's arrest, but John threatened to kill Judy if she did so.

The officer left the Norman home but was called back a short time later, this time to find that Judy had taken an overdose of "nerve pills." When the officer arrived, John was trying to keep emergency personnel from attending to Judy, telling them to "let the bitch die. . . . She ain't nothing but a dog. She don't deserve to live." Over John's resistance, Judy was taken to a nearby hospital, where she was evaluated and released after telling a therapist she felt depressed, angry, and hopeless. Taking the therapist's advice, Judy spent the night at her grandmother's house instead of returning home.

The next day, June 12, the day John Norman would die, Judy returned home and was again beaten by her husband. At one point during the day, Judy drove John on an errand. Displeased with her driving, he slapped her, kicked her in the head, poured a bottle of beer over her, and threatened to "cut your breast off and shove it up your rear end."

When the couple returned home, the beatings and verbal abuse continued. John threatened to cut Judy's throat, threatened to kill her, smashed a donut in her face, and put a cigarette out on her chest.

Finally, John decided to take a nap. While he slept, one of Judy's daughters came by and asked Judy to care for her baby. Judy agreed to baby-sit. But when the child began to cry, Judy feared that John would awaken. To avoid that, she took the baby to her mother's house.

While at her mother's home, Judy found a .25 caliber automatic pistol. Returning home, she aimed the pistol at her sleeping husband and shot him three times in the back of the head.

Judy Norman was charged with first-degree murder. Despite extensive evidence that she was a battered woman who felt she had no choice but to kill her abusive husband, Judy was convicted of voluntary manslaughter and sentenced to 6 years in prison. Although an appeals court reversed Judy's conviction and remanded the case for a new trial, the North Carolina Supreme Court overruled that decision and reinstated the original verdict, concluding that "there was no evidence that at the time of the killing defendant reasonably believed herself to be confronted by circumstances which necessitated her killing her husband to save herself from imminent death or great bodily harm." ❖

❖ When Evelyn Humphrey was 7 years old, her father began giving her alcohol and drugs. He also started raping her. When she revealed the abuse, she was met with disbelief. When she ran away from home, she was forced back.

Evelyn was sexually abused by her father until she was 15, when she escaped her family of origin by marrying one of her mother's friends. Within 3 months, Evelyn's husband had forced her into prostitution, beaten her, and assaulted her with a knife. When she ran away from him, he found her and dragged her back. Although he made it clear that he did not want her, he also told her that he would make sure no one else would ever have her.

At age 22, Evelyn escaped this abusive relationship when her husband divorced her. A divorced woman with a 15-year history of abuse, an eighth-grade education, and few prospects, Evelyn quickly married another abuser, whom she left after he shoved her head through a window. Six months later, she took up with yet another abusive mate. This man forced her back into prostitution and threw her down a flight of stairs. She left him at one point but quickly returned and remained with him until he died.

At age 30, Evelyn became involved with still another abuser, Albert Hampton. For the next 2 years, Hampton (who was 5 inches taller and 150 pounds heavier than Evelyn) repeatedly beat her, broke her nose, knocked her teeth out, tormented her with a gun, and threatened to kill her.

This relationship came to an abrupt end on March 18, 1992. After a daylong argument, Evelyn could take no more of Hampton's abuse. After he hit her twice and shot at her, she seized his .357 magnum and shot him dead. When the police arrived at the couple's Fresno, California home,

Evelyn told them, "I shot him. That's right, I shot him. I just couldn't take him beating on me no more." Later, Evelyn explained,

> He deserved it. I just couldn't take it anymore. I told him to stop beating on me. . . . He was beating on me, so I shot him. I told him I'd shoot him if he ever beat on me again. . . . I'm just tired of him hitting me. He said, "You're not going to do nothing about it." I showed him, didn't I? I shot him good. He won't hit anybody else again. Hit me again, I shoot him. . . . I warned him. I warned him not to hit me. He wouldn't listen.

Convicted of voluntary manslaughter, Evelyn Humphrey was sentenced to 8 years in prison. In 1996, however, her conviction was overturned on appeal, and she was released from prison after serving 4 ½ years. ❖

❖ Donna Bechtel, a former aide to a U.S. congressman, was in her late forties when she met Ken Bechtel, a prominent Oklahoma businessman roughly the same age. Ken was in the process of divorcing. The couple dated while Ken's divorce was pending. On July 4, 1982, Donna experienced his abuse for the first time.

In a drunken rage, Ken grabbed her by the hair, threw her into the windshield of his boat, and then pelted her with canned goods. Donna managed to get away, but Ken caught up with her, forced her into his car, grabbed her by the hair, and repeatedly slammed her head into the car window. When he finally drove her home, she ran inside, locked the doors, and got him to leave by telling him she had a gun.

Despite this incident, on August 25, 1982, Donna married Ken, whose divorce had recently been finalized.

Thereafter, until his death 2 years later, Ken abused Donna on approximately 23 occasions. The abuse, which took place primarily when Ken was drunk, involved grabbing Donna by the ears or hair and pounding her head on the ground or into doors and walls. Three times Donna had to be treated in a hospital emergency room, and five times she called the police to their home. Several times, Donna fled from Ken and spent the night in a hotel or with a family member or friend.

On September 23, 1984, at about 5:30 a.m., Ken returned home unexpectedly from a hunting trip. He was quite intoxicated and awakened Donna to tell her he had just been ticketed for driving under the influence of alcohol. Ken continued to drink, and after several hours of listening to him, Donna went back to bed. A short while later, she heard Ken open a drawer. When she looked up she saw a gun in his hand and heard him say she would not be needing the weapon anymore.

Donna got up, ran to a closet, and tried to locate her purse and keys. Naked, Ken grabbed her before she could escape. He threw her onto the bed, pressed his arm into her throat and told her he was going to "fuck you and kill your ass." Ken then pounded Donna's head on the floor, picked her up, and forced her back onto the bed.

On the bed, he pulled off her nightgown and jammed his fingers into her vagina. Then—after climbing on top of her, holding her down with his knees, and banging her head against the back of the bed—he ejaculated on her face and stomach.

Although Ken allowed Donna to get up to wash off, he attacked her from behind as she stood in the bathroom. After throwing her to the floor, he forced her back to the bed, knocked her head against the bed board, and then slumped on top of her. Donna eased herself out from beneath her husband and lit a cigarette. She then retrieved his gun from beneath the bed and shot him.

Twice, Donna Bechtel was tried for murder, convicted, and sentenced to life in prison. Both convictions were overturned on appeal. ❖

BATTERED WOMEN AND BATTERED WOMAN SYNDROME

The cases of Leslie Emick, Judy Norman, Evelyn Humphrey, and Donna Bechtel are not unusual. Each year, an estimated 4 million women are seriously assaulted by the men with whom they share intimate relationships.[1] A small proportion of these battered women ultimately respond by killing their abusers. When they do, they are almost invariably charged with murder or manslaughter and plead self-defense. Despite abundant evidence that they were severely abused by the men they killed, most of these women are convicted and sentenced to prison.[2]

Who are these women? Why do they kill? And why does the law treat them so harshly?

A rather consistent picture of battered women has emerged from empirical studies, clinical reports, and other sources. These women are repeatedly abused physically, sexually, and/or psychologically by the men with whom they share intimate relationships. They have been punched, kicked, strangled, burned, scalded, shot, and stabbed; attacked with guns, knives, clubs, iron bars, straight razors, broken bottles, and automobiles; and beaten with whips, belts, chains, clubs, lamps, chairs, wrenches, and hammers. They have suffered bruises, lacerations, cuts, broken noses, fractures (including broken ribs, backs, and necks), dislocations, miscarriages, internal bleeding, concussions, and subdural hematomas.[3]

Many—60 percent according to some studies—have also been sexually abused by their batterers. They have been raped, sodomized, and compelled to engage in group sex, bestiality, bondage, and numerous other sadomasochistic sexual acts. Many of these women have been sexually abused in front of their children.[4]

Along with describing the nature and extent of the abuse inflicted upon battered women, researchers and clinicians have attempted to explain why these women remain in relationships where they are so severely abused. Together, these explanations have come to be referred to loosely as "battered woman syndrome." Dr. Lenore Walker, the psychologist who pioneered this field of study and practice, has identified the key features of the syndrome.[5]

Walker posits a three-phase "cycle theory" of violence in battering relationships.[6] Phase 1, "tension building," includes verbal and minor physical abuse as well as attempts by the woman to placate the batterer and prevent more serious abuse. In Phase 2, the mounting tension culminates in what Walker calls an "acute battering incident"—usually a severe beating. In Phase 3, "loving contrition," the abuser becomes remorseful, apologetic, and loving and assures the woman that the battering will not be repeated.

In some relationships, "loving contrition" may last for an extended period of time, but invariably it wanes, tension mounts anew, and another acute battering incident occurs. As this cycle is repeated, the violence often escalates. Yet with the completion of each cycle, the woman is again encouraged to believe that the abuser will change and the battering will cease. In short, she receives positive reinforcement for remaining in the relationship.

Walker adapted Seligman's theory of "learned helplessness" to explain why many battered women fail to leave their abusers. Seligman discovered that laboratory animals previously subjected to inescapable electric shocks continued to behave in a passive, helpless manner even when given opportunities to avoid being shocked. According to Seligman, these animals have "learned" that they are helpless: "Organisms, when exposed to uncontrollable events, learn that responding is futile."[7]

Similarly, when repeatedly exposed to painful stimuli over which they have no control and from which there is no apparent escape, battered women respond with the classic symptoms of learned helplessness. They come to believe that nothing they do will alter or affect any outcome in their lives. Like Seligman's laboratory animals, they eventually cease trying to avoid the painful stimuli and fail to recognize or take advantage of available opportunities for escape.

Finally, Walker and others have identified several additional factors that help keep battered women trapped in abusive relationships. Many of these women lack the financial resources to leave their abusers. But many face other serious obstacles as well: Family and friends disbelieve them and/or encourage them to remain with their abusers. Aside from battered women shelters (which, when available, provide only temporary refuge), battered women often simply have no place to go. Police and other criminal justice officials often provide little or no help even though battered women are clearly crime victims. Finally, and perhaps most significantly, many abusers threaten battered women (and/or their children) with more severe abuse, even death, if the women leave.

BATTERED WOMEN WHO KILL

Battered women who kill their batterers have not been the subject of much systematic research. Most of what is known about them is derived from clinical and anecdotal reports. But these reports all paint a remarkably similar picture of the battered woman who kills her abuser.

Battered women who kill have invariably been abused both physically and psychologically by the men they killed.[8] Many have also been raped and/or sexually abused by their batterers. Although battered women who kill have much in common with other battered women, and it is difficult to generalize from the limited data available, it appears that those who kill have been subjected to more severe abuse, are somewhat older and less well educated, and have fewer coping resources than battered women in general.[9]

Battered women who kill their abusers seem to have been more frequently beaten, threatened with weapons, and subjected to death threats, particularly

threats of retaliation for leaving. Those who kill also appear to have
suffered more serious injuries than other battered women. Finally, battered
women who kill seem more likely to have been socially isolated by their
abusers.[10]

The actual number of battered women who kill their abusers is
unknown but not impossible to estimate. Women rarely kill others, but
when they do, their most common targets are male intimates. In 1994, for
example, in cases where the gender of the perpetrator was known, fewer
than 10 percent of those arrested for nonnegligent homicide in the United
States were women.[11] Of these women, 346 killed their husbands, and
another 228 killed boyfriends. Various estimates suggest that between 40
percent and 90 percent of these 574 women were battering victims who
killed their batterers.[12]

It is also possible to draw at least rough generalizations about the
circumstances under which battered women kill. Ewing collected data on
100 cases in which allegedly battered women killed their batterers.[13] In 87
of these cases, there were sufficient data to reconstruct the homicidal
incidents. Only a third of these killings (29 of the 87) took place during
the course of a battering incident. The others occurred sometime after
battering incidents, arguments, or threats, while the abusers were asleep or
otherwise preoccupied.

Like many other battered women who kill, the 100 women in these
cases were all charged with murder, manslaughter, or another form of
criminal homicide.

Three of the 100 were acquitted by reason of insanity; 3 had the
charges against them dropped; and 9 pleaded guilty. The remaining 85
went to trial, claiming self-defense. Of these, 63 were convicted, 12 of them
sentenced to life in prison, including 1 without parole for 50 years. Others
received sentences ranging from 4 years' probation to 25 years in prison.
Seventeen of these women received prison sentences potentially longer
than 10 years.

Many if not most battered women who kill their batterers (regardless
of the circumstances of the homicide) now seek to introduce expert
psychological or psychiatric testimony regarding battered woman syndrome. Typically, the expert explains the syndrome and testifies that the
defendant was suffering from it at the time of the killing. Such testimony
is aimed at helping jurors understand why the woman endured such
allegedly serious abuse for so long, why she did not leave her abuser, and

why she felt it was necessary to use deadly force at a time when she was not being battered.[14]

Virtually all legal commentators and courts now agree that such testimony should be admissible in homicide prosecutions of battered women who kill their alleged batterers. Unfortunately, however, in many cases this testimony does not appear to be as helpful as some would hope. For example, expert testimony on the battered woman syndrome was offered in 44 of the 100 cases examined by Ewing and admitted in 26 of the 85 cases that went to trial. Yet in 17 of those 26 cases, the battered woman defendant was still convicted.[15]

That result, although striking, is not surprising. The legal test for self-defense is whether the user of deadly force acted to avert what reasonably appeared to be an imminent threat of death or serious bodily injury.[16] Expert testimony regarding battered woman syndrome helps explain why, despite the claimed abuse, the woman did not leave her batterer before killing him, but such testimony frequently offers little explanation of the reasonableness of the woman's ultimate homicidal act.

Such testimony may help the jury understand why, because of the beatings she has suffered in the past, the battered woman is better able to predict the likely degree of violence in any particular battering incident.[17] But, even to the extent that expert testimony serves this function, it does so, primarily if not exclusively, in what appear to be the minority of cases—those in which battered women kill during the course of a battering incident. In what appear to be the majority of cases—those where the killing took place after a battering incident or while the batterer was asleep or otherwise preoccupied[18]—the battered woman defendant's ability to predict the likely extent of violence involved in any given battering incident is not immediately relevant to her legal claim of self-defense.

WHY BATTERED WOMEN KILL

Despite the law, the fact that a battered woman who killed her batterer did not do so in response to what reasonably appeared to be the threat of imminent death or serious bodily injury does not necessarily mean she did not act in self-defense. Many battered women who kill, including those who kill outside direct confrontations with their batterers, undoubtedly do so in self-defense, although not in the narrow legal sense of that term.

The law of self-defense equates "self" with only the corporeal aspects of human existence—physical life and bodily integrity. But outside the law, "self" is commonly understood to encompass not only those corporeal aspects of existence but also the psychological functions, attributes, processes, and dimensions of experience that give meaning and value to physical existence.[19] "Self" clearly refers to both the physical and the mental being and thus includes such recognized and socially valued psychological attributes as security, autonomy, identity, consciousness, and spirituality, among others. Furthermore, it has long been understood that harm to the psychological aspects of the self may be just as detrimental as injury to the physical or bodily aspects of the self. Indeed, many mental health experts regard serious psychopathology as largely a product of injury or threat to the psychological components of the self.

If "self" is viewed in this broader and more commonly accepted manner, it appears that many, probably most, battered women who kill their batterers do so in self-defense. They kill to prevent their abusers from seriously damaging, if not destroying, psychological aspects of the self that give meaning and value to their lives.[20]

CHAPTER FOUR

Munchausen Mothers

❖ Charles was born prematurely but otherwise healthy in 1946. When he was 1 month old, his mother, Martha, took him to an Ohio hospital, complaining that he had suddenly stopped breathing and turned blue while she was holding him. Upon admission to the hospital, baby Charles seemed undernourished but otherwise well developed.

Admitted with a diagnosis of malnutrition, he spent 7 days hospitalized. Physical examinations and lab tests were all normal. Charles gained 6 ounces in a week and was discharged.

Two days later, he died at home after suffering what Martha said was a coughing and choking spell. No autopsy was done. Cause of death was listed as "enlarged thymus"—a normal condition in infants—and "status lymphaticus"—a nonexistent disorder.[1]

Later the same year, another tragedy struck Martha and her family. Martha's 3½-year-old nephew, John, died while in bed with Martha. Since three other children in the house had diphtheria, it was assumed, without any specific autopsy findings, that John died from that illness.

In 1950, Martha gave birth to her second child, Mary. Like Charles, Mary was born prematurely. After spending the first few weeks of her life in an Ohio hospital, she was discharged, and her mother took her home.

Within a week, Mary was readmitted to the hospital after Martha complained that the baby had stopped breathing and turned blue. Physical examination was essentially normal, a 2-day hospital course was uneventful, and Mary was sent home.

Eight days later, Martha brought Mary back to the hospital, again with complaints of apnea and cyanosis. Martha told physicians and nurses that after Mary stopped breathing and turned blue, she had revived the baby with mouth-to-mouth resuscitation. Again, the baby showed no symptoms while hospitalized. Again, physical examinations were normal, laboratory tests all came back negative, and no medical cause for Mary's condition was ever diagnosed.

Ultimately, at 1 month and 27 days of age, Mary died in her mother's arms.

On June 22, 1952, Martha gave birth again. This time, the baby, named Carol, was a normal, healthy, full-term infant. But, like her siblings before her, she did not live long. Carol was 3 months and 21 days old when, alone with her mother, she reportedly had difficulty breathing, choked, turned blue, and died in Martha's arms.

No autopsy was done. The cause of Carol's death—based solely on what Martha told the certifying physician, and not on anything he personally observed—was listed as "epiglossitis" and "bronchopneumonia."[2]

All of these deaths puzzled the physicians who investigated them. All sorts of medical tests were done in efforts to say just why these children had suddenly become ill, but the medical investigations were hindered by two factors. First, Martha seemed like such a caring, loving mother that no one ever really suspected foul play. Second, and perhaps most important, Martha was a military wife who frequently moved from base to base with her husband, an Army officer. Consequently, none of the medical authorities ever had the full story.

Having lost so many babies of her own, Martha Woods eventually took to caring for other people's children. The results were equally fatal. First, Martha helped care for her 14-month-old niece, Lilly. One night in 1958, Lilly's parents woke up to find Martha holding Lilly. Martha said Lilly had seemed to be choking and turning blue, so she administered mouth-to-mouth resuscitation. Rushed to the hospital, Lilly was dead on arrival. No autopsy was ever performed, but cause of death was listed as "acute fulminating pneumonia."[3]

Next, while baby-sitting three children, Martha rushed the youngest, 18-month-old Eddie, to the hospital. Although Martha said Eddie had become cyanotic and she had been forced to perform mouth-to-mouth resuscitation to restore his breathing, he appeared normal and healthy and was released. Later that day, Eddie's mother noticed a bruise on the boy's neck that had not been there when she bathed him the night before.

In January 1964, Martha began baby-sitting for Marlan, a boy about 1 year old. Over a 5-month period, Marlan suffered three attacks of cyanosis while in Martha's care. Each time, according to Martha, the boy simply stopped breathing, turned blue, and required mouth-to-mouth resuscitation. After the first attack, Marlan was hospitalized for 5 days, during which he showed no symptoms, all examinations and tests were within normal limits, and no cause was found for the claimed incident of apnea and cyanosis. Four months later, after the second attack, he was rehospitalized. Again, no cause was found for the reported cyanosis.

On the day he was released from the hospital, Marlan was returned to Martha's care. That very day, while alone with her, he died. According to Martha, the boy's breathing became shallow and he turned blue. She said she tried unsuccessfully to save him with mouth-to-mouth resuscitation. An autopsy was done but revealed little. Marlan's death certificate said simply "death sudden, cause unknown."[4]

Having struck out as a natural mother and baby-sitter, Martha Woods found one more source of children. In the late 1960s, she and her husband adopted one child and started to adopt another. The first child, Judy, was adopted by the Woods when she was 3 days old. Between the ages of 5 months and 2½ years, Judy reportedly suffered at least six episodes of apnea and cyanosis. Each episode occurred while Judy was alone with Martha, and no one else ever witnessed any of these attacks.

Although baby Judy was repeatedly hospitalized and subjected to numerous tests, she never demonstrated any symptoms while in the hospital, and medical professionals never found any cause for the symptoms Martha claimed to have observed. Upon her final discharge from the hospital at age 2½, Judy was removed from Martha's custody and never again suffered from apnea or cyanosis.

Amazingly, despite her track record, Martha was allowed to care for one more child after adopting Judy. In the summer of 1969, just a couple of months before Judy's last attack of apnea and cyanosis, Martha and her husband were given preadoption custody of a 5-month-old baby boy.

Paul, who had spent the first 5 months of his life in foster care, was a normal and healthy infant when he came to live with the Woods. But within a month, his health failed; five times, Martha said, she found him blue and blue and gasping for breath. The first four times she revived him with mouth-to-mouth resuscitation and rushed him to the hospital, where he was examined, pronounced healthy, and released. The fifth time, on August 20, 1969, Paul lapsed into a coma from which he never recovered. On September 21, 1969, 7-month-old Paul David Woods died.

When Paul suffered his final and fatal attack, the Woods were living at the Aberdeen Proving Grounds, an Army base in Maryland. Paul was initially hospitalized at Kirk Army Hospital but later transferred to Johns Hopkins Hospital in Baltimore, one of the nation's leading medical centers. Despite a multitude of medical tests, doctors there never isolated any natural cause for Paul's coma.

At one point, Martha suggested that Paul may have fallen victim to chemical poisoning, since there had recently been extensive insecticide spraying at the Army base where the Woods lived. That theory was rejected when toxicological tests failed to find any evidence to support it.

When federal authorities finally pieced all the evidence together, they found more than enough reason to suspect that Martha Woods had killed baby Paul. Dr. Vincent DiMaio, a forensic pathologist who studied Paul's medical records and autopsy report, concluded that Paul's death was neither suicide nor accident and was not the result of any natural cause.

Dr. DiMaio said that, based solely on his review of the medical records and autopsy, he was "seventy-five percent certain that Paul's death was homicide caused by smothering."[5] His "twenty-five percent degree of doubt," he said was based upon "the possibility that Paul died naturally from a disease currently unknown to medical science."[6] If he also considered what happened to Martha Woods' other children, Dr. DiMaio said, his "opinion would be that Paul was a victim of homicide beyond a reasonable doubt."[7] As Dr. DiMaio later explained,

> With some slight variations a pattern to these deaths was apparent. The children were all very young—all but one under two years of age. They had breathing difficulties and became cyanotic. Mouth-to-mouth resuscitation was applied, usually by Mrs. W., and recovery would take place. . . . On admission to a hospital their course would be uneventful with a negative physical examination and laboratory tests. No attacks of respiratory difficulty and cyanosis would occur while hospitalized. Episodes of cyanosis occurred only when [Mrs. W.] was present or in the vicinity.[8]

Ultimately, Martha Woods was charged with murdering Paul. She was also charged with assaulting, mistreating, and attempting to murder Judy. Psychiatric examinations found her to be both sane and competent to stand trial. After a 5-month trial in federal court, the judge acquitted Martha of the charges related to Judy but let the other charges go to the jury. The jury convicted Martha of eight charges stemming from Paul's death, including first-degree murder, assault with intent to murder, attempted murder, and mistreatment of a minor.

The judge then sentenced Martha to a term of life imprisonment for murder plus 75 years for the other convictions. Martha's appeals were rejected by both the Court of Appeals and the U.S. Supreme Court. ❖

❖ Just as the sad saga of Martha Woods was coming to an end in Maryland, the case of Marybeth Tinning was beginning in Schenectady, New York. Whereas Martha Woods was implicated in the deaths of seven children, including three of her own, Marybeth Tinning, a former pediatric nurse's aide, apparently killed eight children—seven of her natural offspring and one who was adopted.

Marybeth's children started dying in 1972. On December 26, 1971, she gave birth to her third child, Jennifer. It had been a difficult and stressful pregnancy. Jennifer was born with a raging brain infection and died a week later without ever leaving the hospital.

Two weeks after Jennifer's death, Marybeth rushed her second-born child, 2-year-old Joseph, Jr., to the emergency room, complaining that he had suffered a seizure after choking on his own vomit. Joey was admitted but released after a few days of observation. The day Joey was discharged from the hospital, January 20, 1972, Marybeth brought him back within hours. This time Joey was dead. Marybeth said she had found him cyanotic and tangled in his crib sheet. No diagnosis was made and no autopsy was done.

Less than 2 months later, Marybeth was back in the emergency room—this time with her firstborn, 4½-year-old Barbara. As Marybeth explained, Barbara had gone to bed, started having difficulty breathing, and then began convulsing. Marybeth rushed the child to the hospital and was urged to leave her there for overnight observation. Marybeth refused and took Barbara home.

Within hours, mother and child were back; this time Barbara was unconscious. The ER staff resuscitated Barbara and placed her in intensive care, where she died the next morning without ever regaining consciousness. After a hospital autopsy failed to reveal any specific cause of death, a "diagnosis" of Reye's syndrome was made based solely on the fact that Barbara had suffered from a fever before her death.

In fall 1972, while recovering from the deaths of their three children, Marybeth Tinning and her husband applied to become foster parents. After a quick investigation into the Tinnings' background, the Social Services Department granted their request. The Tinnings were first given a boy who stayed with them only very briefly. Then, in early 1973, they were granted custody of a 10-year-old girl. In February, Marybeth became pregnant and immediately gave her foster daughter back to the Social Services Department.

On November 21, 1973, Timothy Tinning—a small but healthy, full-term baby—was born. He lived less than 3 weeks. On December 10, Marybeth rushed him to the ER, where he was pronounced dead on arrival. According to Marybeth, he had died mysteriously in his crib.

No autopsy was performed on Timothy. A physician, unaware of the other Tinning children's deaths, filled out the death certificate, listing sudden infant death syndrome (SIDS) as the cause of death.

Almost a year and a half went by before Marybeth had another baby. Nathan Tinning was born on Easter Sunday, March 30, 1975 and died September 2 the same year. As Marybeth told it, she had been driving in the car with the baby when he made a funny noise and started turning blue. According to Marybeth, she then drove several miles to seek help at the restaurant where she worked.

By the time help was summoned, Nathan was beyond saving. He made it to the ER but died the same day without regaining consciousness. A limited autopsy was done by another physician who did not know the Tinnings' history. No cause of death was established.

When Marybeth did not become pregnant in more than 2 years following Nathan's death, she and her husband decided to adopt. While the adoption was being worked out through a baby broker, Marybeth learned that she was pregnant. Although she could have declined to complete the adoption, she did not.

Michael Raymond, Marybeth's adopted son, was born on August 3, 1978; Mary Frances, her daughter, was born on October 29, 1978. Mary Frances lived for 4 months, Michael made it to age 2½.

On January 20, 1979, Marybeth rushed Mary Frances to the emergency room. The baby was unconscious, and Marybeth said that was how she had found her in her crib. The ER staff revived Mary Frances, but a month later she was back. Marybeth's story was the same, but this time

Mary Frances did not recover. After 2 days, the Tinnings agreed to remove Mary Frances from a respirator, and she died. An exhaustive autopsy found "no anatomic cause of death."[9] The investigation went no further.

Although Marybeth claimed she had a tubal ligation after Mary Frances was born, it was not long before she was pregnant again. Adopted son Michael was just 15 months old when, on November 19, 1979, Marybeth gave birth for the seventh time. Jonathan, Marybeth's fourth natural son, was born a month prematurely and suffered from several relatively minor genito-urinary abnormalities. But when he went home with his mother a couple of weeks later, he was healthy and doing well. Four months later he was dead.

Jonathan Tinning's short life paralleled that of his late sister, Mary Frances. Twice Marybeth said she found him unconscious. Both times she rushed him to the ER. The first time he was revived. The second time, he was brain damaged beyond hope for survival. Four weeks later and still comatose, he died. Autopsy revealed no apparent cause of death, so the medical examiner simply wrote "etiology undetermined."[10]

Before Jonathan died, he was flown to Children's Hospital in Boston, a renowned medical center affiliated with Harvard Medical School. There, he was subjected to various genetic tests on the theory that perhaps some exotic genetic abnormality was killing Marybeth Tinning's children. Every test came back negative—doctors could find no genetic abnormality, let alone one that would account for his symptoms.

As it turned out, there was no need to rule out something in the Tinning children's genes. Michael, who was adopted and thus shared none of the those genes, died less than a year after Jonathan. When Michael was 2½, Marybeth took him to the emergency room with a banged-up forehead. She told the ER staff that Michael had fallen down half a flight of steep stairs. They bandaged his head, said he might have a slight concussion, and sent him home.

For the week afterward, according to Marybeth, Michael was ill— vomiting, screaming, and having difficulty keeping his balance. Then, as these symptoms abated, he developed a bad cold.

On March 1, 1981, Michael visited his grandparents and seemed energetic and in good spirits. The next morning after her husband left for work at about 7:30, leaving Marybeth alone with Michael, Marybeth called a friend to say that she could not awaken the child. Marybeth asked her friend what to do; the friend said to take him to the emergency room right away.

Marybeth was then living right across the street from a hospital, but instead of rushing her son to the ER, Marybeth called the office of Michael's pediatrician and arranged to take the boy in to be seen during the doctor's 10 a.m. sick call—a time he set aside each day for seeing sick children.

At 9:45 a.m., Marybeth showed up at the pediatric office across town, carrying Michael in a blanket. The office nurse unwrapped the blanket, called an ambulance, and administered CPR; a doctor arrived and tried to revive Michael, but it was too late. Michael died before he reached the hospital. An autopsy showed that Michael was suffering from acute pneumonia but reached no conclusion as to the cause of his death.

For the next 4 years, from 1981 to 1985, the deaths in the Tinning family stopped because Marybeth Tinning had run out of children. On August 22, 1985, Marybeth gave birth to her last child, Tami Lynne. By December 19, 1985, Tami Lynne Tinning was dead.

Marybeth told her husband, family, and friends that she had gone to bed but gotten up and found Tami Lynne tangled in her crib blanket and not moving or breathing. According to this account, Marybeth called an ambulance and administered CPR; Tami Lynne was rushed to the hospital, but doctors were unable to save her.

Tami Lynne's death triggered a massive and long overdue investigation into the deaths of Marybeth Tinning's children. After an autopsy failed to reveal any conclusive cause of death, and Tami Lynne's demise was attributed to SIDS, Dr. Michael Baden was called into the case. Dr. Baden, director of the New York State Police Forensic Science Unit and former Chief Medical Examiner for New York City, reviewed the records of all nine deaths and concluded that all of Marybeth's children, except Jennifer, had been suffocated.

A State Police task force was created to investigate the deaths further. Task force members created a psychological profile of Marybeth. They also learned that physicians, nurses, social workers, police officers, funeral directors, neighbors, family, and friends had long suspected that Marybeth Tinning was killing her children. And they discovered how, through a lack of communication and centralized record keeping, these suspicions went largely uninvestigated.

Dr. Baden's findings, combined with the work of the State Police task force, led authorities to confront Marybeth Tinning on February 4, 1986. After lengthy interrogation, Marybeth broke down and confessed. First she admitted having poisoned her husband with an overdose of prescription drugs. Then, she admitted killing three of her nine children.

"I killed them. I killed my children," Marybeth initially blurted out.[11] But when police officers pushed Marybeth for details, she admitted killing only Tami Lynne, Timothy, and Nathan. In her words, "I did not do anything to Jennifer, Joseph, Barbara, Michael, Mary Frances, Jonathan. Just these three—Timothy, Nathan, and Tami. I smothered them each with a pillow because I'm not a good mother. I'm not a good mother because of the other children."[12]

Describing Tami Lynne's killing, Marybeth said that after trying several times to get the baby to stop crying "I finally used the pillow from my bed and put it over her head. I held it until she stopped crying. I didn't mean to hurt her. I just wanted her to stop crying."[13]

Charged with second-degree murder—the highest charge possible under New York law—Marybeth recanted her confession and claimed that the police had forced it out of her. After a lengthy hearing, the judge refused to throw out the confession.

At trial, Marybeth's attorney contended that Tami Lynne died of a rare hereditary disorder that may have also taken the lives of the other Tinning children. Marybeth was tried and convicted of murdering Tami Lynne. Although the jury found reasonable doubt that Marybeth had intentionally killed her baby, they concluded beyond a reasonable doubt that she acted recklessly and with depraved indifference to human life when she smothered Tami Lynne.

Conviction of second-degree murder in New York carries a minimum term of 15 years and a maximum sentence of 25 years to life. Marybeth was sentenced to serve 20 years to life in prison. She will be 66 years old before she is eligible for parole.

Although the district attorney threatened to bring additional murder charges, plans to prosecute Marybeth for the deaths of her other children were eventually scrapped. Citing other pressing prosecutorial concerns such as drugs and handguns, the prosecutor announced on April 17, 1990 that he would not pursue further charges against Tinning. Such prosecution, he said, would be neither practical nor worthwhile given that even if he successfully prosecuted Marybeth for the other deaths, her 20-year sentence would be increased by 10 years at most. ❖

WHY THEY KILLED: MUNCHAUSEN SYNDROME BY PROXY

How could a mother kill infant after infant and get away with it for as long as Martha Woods and Marybeth Tinning apparently did? And how could any mother do such a thing to so many of her own children?

The first question is perhaps easier to answer. Both Martha Woods and Marybeth Tinning seem to have escaped prosecution for so long in part because it was so hard to believe that any mother would do such a thing. In both the Woods and Tinning cases, there were suspicions of homicide all along. Indeed, after all but the first of the Tinning deaths, child abuse and law enforcement authorities were contacted by numerous people—some merely raised suspicions, but others directly accused Marybeth Tinning of killing her children.

In both cases, even as the evidence of foul play mounted, authorities were extremely reluctant to charge an apparently loving and bereaved mother with repeatedly killing her own children.

The second question—why a mother would repeatedly kill her children—is not as easy to answer. Insanity comes quickly to mind, but neither Martha Woods nor Marybeth Tinning were found insane or even incompetent to stand trial. There was no evidence that either woman was psychotic or out of touch with reality. Undoubtedly, any person who repeatedly kills his or her own offspring is psychologically disturbed but not necessarily in the sense—or to the degree—one might expect.

There is good reason to believe that both Martha Woods and Marybeth Tinning were not psychotic but, instead, suffered from an extremely rare and bizarre mental illness called Munchausen syndrome by proxy.

Munchausen syndrome, first described in the medical literature some 40 years ago, is named for the 18th-century German baron Karl von Munchausen, whose propensity for telling far-fetched tall tales was chronicled in the 1989 Hollywood movie *The Adventures of Baron Munchausen*.[14] Persons suffering from Munchausen syndrome repeatedly produce in themselves symptoms of physical illness and then present themselves for medical treatment in apparent efforts to get attention.

Some Munchausen sufferers feign symptoms of illness, but many intentionally create these symptoms by injecting themselves with toxic substances (e.g., drugs, poisons, and even their own urine and feces) or by creating bruises, lesions, and other bodily injuries consistent with illness.

In formal psychiatric terminology, "Munchausens" present a form of Factitious Disorder, which the latest edition of the *Diagnostic and Statistical Manual of Mental Disorders* (*DSM-IV*), used by virtually all mental health professionals, classifies as a mental illness and distinguishes the disorder from mere malingering.[15] According to the *DSM-IV*,

Malingering differs from Factitious Disorder in that the motivation for the symptom production in Malingering is an external incentive, whereas in Factitious Disorder external incentives are absent. Individuals with Malingering may seek hospitalization by producing symptoms in attempts to obtain compensation, evade the police, or simply "get a bed for the night." However, the goal is usually apparent, and they can "stop" the symptoms when the symptoms are no longer useful to them.[16]

In the Munchausen variation of Factitious Disorder (Factitious Disorder With Predominantly Physical Signs and Symptoms), "the individual's entire life may consist of trying to get admitted to, or stay in, hospitals. . . . All organ systems are potential targets, and the symptoms presented are limited only by the individual's medical knowledge, sophistication and imagination."[17]

Munchausen syndrome by proxy (MBP), an even rarer and more bizarre syndrome, was first described in the medical literature in the late 1970s. In this variation of Munchausen syndrome, the disturbed individuals create or feign physical illness not in themselves but in their children.[18] These Munchausen parents, almost invariably mothers, then present their "sick" children to medical professionals for treatment.

Typically, these MBP sufferers appear to be ideal parents who are especially caring and supportive toward their children and cooperative and closely involved with medical personnel. Rarely do they appear to be suffering from any psychosis or other major psychopathology.

Although MBP has been recognized for the past two decades or more, it has yet to fully earn recognition as a formal psychiatric diagnosis. In the *DSM-IV*, for example, MBP is referred to as a form of Factitious Disorder by Proxy but is listed not in the manual's text but in an appendix containing "proposals for new categories" for which there is currently "insufficient information to warrant inclusion . . . as official categories . . . in *DSM-IV*."[19]

The "essential feature" of Factitious Disorder by Proxy, says the *DSM-IV*, is "the deliberate production or feigning of physical or psychological signs or symptoms in another person who is under the individual's care."[20] Moreover, as the *DSM-IV* points out,

Typically, the victim is a young child and the perpetrator is the child's mother. The motivation for the perpetrator's behavior is presumed to be a psychological need to assume the sick role by proxy. . . . The perpetrator induces or simulates the illness or disease process in the victim and then presents the victim for medical care while disclaiming any knowledge about the actual etiology of the problem.[21]

Even though Munchausen syndrome by proxy may not yet be sufficiently researched to warrant its inclusion in the *DSM-IV*, a great deal of research and clinical experience with the disorder has led to the identification of at least seven common factors, all or some of which are generally found in cases of MBP:

- ❖ The child's prolonged illness, which presents confusing symptoms defying diagnosis and is unresponsive to medical treatment
- ❖ The child's recurring hospitalizations, surgery, and other invasive procedures
- ❖ The child's dramatic improvement after removal from the mother's access and care
- ❖ The mother's training as a nurse or in medically related fields
- ❖ The mother's unusual degree of attentiveness to the child's needs in hospital
- ❖ The mother's unusually supportive and cooperative attitude toward doctors and hospital staff
- ❖ The mother's symbiotic relationship to the child[22]

RECENT MUNCHAUSEN CASES

Several recent MBP cases have been reported in both the professional and the popular literature. Detailed accounts of two such cases are presented here.

❖ A White Plains, New York woman, Lori Z.—whose full name was withheld by the courts to protect the child's privacy—repeatedly took her daughter, Jessica, to physicians, complaining that the infant was vomiting and suffering from diarrhea. Eventually the baby was hospitalized and fed intravenously. She recovered quickly and was discharged but was readmitted shortly thereafter with the same symptoms. Surgery was done, and physicians were hopeful that the problem had been solved. But again the vomiting and diarrhea returned.

Reluctantly, surgeons performed another major operation on tiny Jessica, implanting a gastrointestinal tube and catheter. The vomiting stopped, but the diarrhea continued. Test after test was done, and "every conceivable diagnosis . . . from AIDS to cystic fibrosis, was considered and rejected."[23] After 55 days in the hospital, Jessica was sent home with artificial plumbing: two tubes and two pumps attached to her to regulate tubal feeding.

A week later, Jessica was back in the hospital—this time in shock and critically ill. While in an intensive care unit, where all her care was given by staff, she recovered quickly. But once she was placed in a private room, where her parents helped attend to her needs, the diarrhea resumed. Suspecting but not wanting to believe the possibility that Jessica was being poisoned, her attending physician had her stool tested and found evidence of phenophthalien—one of the chemicals commonly found in over-the-counter laxatives such as Ex-Lax.

The doctor confronted Lori and her husband. Both expressed surprise and denied any involvement in what appeared to be an intentional poisoning. The next day, however, Lori asked nurses on the pediatric ward to check the infant formulas, which were stored in an area to which she had access. When nurses did as Lori asked, they found a bar of Ex-Lax in the formula of another baby. Lori then told the nurses that this vindicated her. She also asked them not to tell Jessica's doctor that she had been the one to suggest checking the formula. Laboratory analyses revealed no trace of phenophthalien in the baby whose formula was contaminated, and no other infants on the ward were found to suffer from suspicious diarrhea.

Lori was charged with child abuse, and Jessica was removed from her parents' custody. In a 14-day trial, 21 witnesses, including Lori and her husband, testified. Jessica's doctor testified that he never even suspected that Jessica might be the victim of poisoning, much less poisoning at the hands of her own mother. He "never thought of it," he said, partly because the parents had been so trusting, helpful, and cooperative with Jessica's care.[24]

A psychologist and a psychiatrist testified that their examinations of Lori were consistent with MBP. Although Lori presented the testimony of a psychiatrist who disagreed, the Family Court judge found Jessica an abused child and accepted MBP as the explanation for her illnesses. Amazingly, however, the same judge ordered Jessica returned to her mother's custody. ❖

❖ In a similar but fatal California case, another Munchausen mother's acts of abuse went undetected until years after her adopted infant daughter died.

Priscilla Phillips, who held a master's degree in social work and worked as a volunteer for the local child abuse agency, had two young children when she and her husband adopted an infant who had been abandoned on the streets of Seoul, Korea. Tia, as the Phillips called her, arrived in California in November and was pronounced healthy by Dr. Aimy Taniguchi, a San Rafael pediatrician.

At the end of the following January, Priscilla brought Tia back to Dr. Taniguchi with a low-grade fever. Dr. Taniguchi diagnosed a urinary tract infection and prescribed an antibiotic. Although that treatment seemed effective, Priscilla brought Tia back to Dr. Taniguchi four more times within the next month. The first two visits were for an apparent ear infection. The third office call was for fever and violent vomiting. Finally, on March 2, Priscilla reported that Tia was not only vomiting but had developed a new symptom: brief staring spells.

Tia was hospitalized, seen by a neurologist and an ear, nose, and throat specialist, and subjected to dozens of tests as well as minor surgery to remove fluid from her eardrums. The neurological exam and all the tests were normal and the operation successful, so Dr. Taniguchi told Priscilla she would be discharging Tia within 2 days. The next day, however, Tia began vomiting and suffering diarrhea. These symptoms lasted 4 days and subsided only when feeding by mouth was discontinued and a regimen of intravenous feeding was started.

Each time mouth feeding was resumed, the vomiting and diarrhea started up again. And each time IV feeding was reinstituted, the symptoms stopped. Finally, a hyperalimentation catheter and nasogastric tube were implanted to allow direct feeding. On June 8, Tia was finally discharged, but by July 7, she was back in the hospital for an intestinal biopsy. When she developed acute diarrhea, projectile vomiting, and cramps, she was transferred to another hospital and scheduled for additional diagnostic surgery. That surgery was canceled when her condition suddenly improved after doctors accepted Priscilla's suggestion that they put Tia back on solid food. Tia responded so favorably to the solid food that she was discharged on July 28.

Tia's favorable response was short-lived. By August 6, she was back in the hospital, dehydrated and unresponsive to stimulation. Laboratory tests found an extremely high level of sodium and bicarbonate in her blood. Doctors had no explanation but discharged Tia when, after just 3 days, her condition was vastly improved.

Twice in September and October, the vomiting and diarrhea recurred, but Tia was not rehospitalized until November, when she finally had the diagnostic surgery. The surgeon found no abnormalities, and Tia was discharged November 26. Seven days later, she was examined and found to be healthy. Three days after that, Priscilla brought her to the hospital emergency room. Tia was in shock and vomiting convulsively. Again, mysteriously, her blood showed elevated levels of sodium and bicarbonate. Within five days, she was back on formula and was discharged.

Three hours after her discharge, Tia was back again, vomiting and suffering from diarrhea. No diagnosis was made, and 11 days later she was discharged.

The following February 2, Priscilla brought Tia to the hospital ER for what was to be the last time. Tia was having generalized seizures and had an extremely high level of sodium in her blood. Doctors struggled to save her, but she died the next day.

The story of Priscilla and Tia Phillips might have ended there since no efforts were ever made to investigate the baby's mysterious illness and death. But several months later, Mr. and Mrs. Phillips adopted another Korean infant—a girl they named Mindy.

On the following February 3, the anniversary of Tia's death, Priscilla brought Mindy to the hospital with the same symptoms that eventually killed Tia: vomiting, diarrhea, and an elevated sodium level. Mindy was hospitalized and then discharged when her symptoms quickly subsided. Discharged on February 10, she was readmitted 6 days later with exactly the same symptoms.

Fortunately for Mindy, Dr. Taniguchi noted the obvious similarities between the two cases. She presented the case to a pediatric staff conference on February 22, and her colleagues decided it was time to consider the possibility that Mindy was being poisoned.

Dr. Taniguchi ordered the usual series of tests but came up with nothing. The diarrhea continued and so did the abnormally high sodium levels. Ultimately, it was the simple hospital routine of monitoring a patient's input and output that led to accurate diagnosis and treatment.

On February 25, the pediatrician on call studied Mindy's input-output chart and noticed that her stool and urine were loaded with unaccountable sodium. She was excreting five times as much sodium as she was ingesting. The physician asked for a sample of Mindy's formula. After lab testing revealed that the formula contained 30 times the amount of sodium it should, Mindy was transferred to the intensive care unit, where Priscilla was forbidden to feed her or even visit except in the presence of hospital staff.

Once in the ICU, Mindy recovered rapidly. But by then, authorities realized that they might have a murder on their hands. Investigation revealed that throughout Tia's many hospital stays, the staff had been so impressed with Priscilla Phillips's intellect, devotion, constant presence, and willingness to help that they often let her assume routine nursing care for the baby. Such care, it was learned, even included administering formula through the nasogastric tube.

Then came the belated but apparently correct expert medical conclusions. The coroner said Tia died from sodium poisoning and that her sodium level was so high that she must have ingested large amounts of it through her gastrointestinal tract. And a pediatrician concluded that both girls had been poisoned with sodium bicarbonate, commonly known as baking soda. Just two or three teaspoons of baking soda dissolved in water, he said, would be enough to produce the symptoms displayed by both infants.

Priscilla Phillips denied having poisoned her adopted daughters but was charged with murdering Tia and willfully endangering the life of Mindy. At her trial, she took the stand and denied harming either child. Friends testified what a caring and truthful person and loving, devoted mother she was. Finally, psychiatrists testified for the defense that Priscilla was essentially a normal person and did not suffer from any significant mental illness.

Prosecutors presented a strong circumstantial case against Priscilla but no apparent motive. None, that is, until Dr. Martin Blinder, a forensic psychiatrist, took the witness stand and described Munchausen syndrome by proxy. Dr. Blinder told the jury how MBP mothers do not appear to be overtly mentally ill, appear to show great concern for their children, and, even when confronted with incontrovertible evidence that they have made their children sick, cannot accept responsibility.

Although Dr. Blinder conceded that without examining Priscilla he could not say to a reasonable degree of medical certainty that she was in fact suffering from MBP, the jurors were apparently satisfied with this explanation of Priscilla's motives. They convicted her of both murder and endangerment. ❖

More recently, two mothers were each caught red-handed, trying to suffocate their children as they lay in intensive care units being treated for mysterious breathing disorders. Amazingly, the actions of both women, who were later diagnosed as suffering from MBP, were captured on videotape.

On March 31, 1987, staff members at a San Diego hospital were shocked when the monitor for a video camera—set up to help them watch 15-month-old Amanda Walker—showed the child's mother holding a sheet of plastic over the baby's face. Amanda's 24-year-old mother, Pamela, was charged with attempted murder and felony child abuse.

Seven months later, in an almost identical case in Milwaukee, a hidden hospital camera caught a 28-year-old mother choking her 1-year-old son. She was charged with child abuse and endangerment.

Even more recently, two other apparent Munchausen mothers pleaded guilty to poisoning their children. In March 1989, Karen Sterchi of Illinois was placed on probation after the prosecutor acknowledged that she had been diagnosed as suffering from MBP. Karen admitted that, after her 5-year-old son was hospitalized for recurring infections, she injected bacteria from mold and feces into his intravenous tubes.

In January 1990, Tammie Lynn Smith of Reston, Virginia pleaded guilty to attempted poisoning after police charged her with putting mouse poison in her 2-year-old son Christopher's cereal and ice cream. Christopher was admitted to and released in one day from DeWitt Army Hospital after physicians were unable to pinpoint the cause of his sudden seizures. Next, he was admitted to Walter Reed Army Medical Center, suffering from internal bleeding.

When nurses at Walter Reed found a cup of the poison pellets in the boy's hospital room, they confronted Mrs. Smith, who claimed they were candy. Subsequently, she confessed to poisoning her son but told authorities she did it not to kill the boy but to make him sick enough that his father, a soldier stationed in Germany, would be sent home. Psychiatric examinations revealed that Mrs. Smith was competent to stand trial but was suffering from MBP.

DYNAMICS OF
MUNCHAUSEN BY PROXY KILLINGS

The true incidence of MBP is unknown, but there is little doubt that the cases that are detected represent just the tip of the iceberg. The disorder, although rare, is believed to be increasing. Approximately half of all documented MBP cases involve central nervous system illness, especially sleep- and breathing-related disorders of the sort found in almost all of the Woods and Tinning deaths. At the top of the list of MBP misdiagnoses is SIDS.

In most MBP cases, the child victim is presented to medical personnel with a sudden, often dramatic, and sometimes life-threatening illness for which there is no ready explanation. Generally, as in the Woods and Tinning cases, the acute symptoms of the illness occur when the parent is alone with the child. In most cases, also as in the Woods and Tinning deaths, neither physical examination nor laboratory testing reveals the true cause of the child's illness.

Research indicates that the perpetrators of MBP are generally women with psychological characteristics similar to those of Martha Woods and Marybeth Tinning—women who mask feelings of loneliness, inadequacy, incompetence, and low self-esteem by assuming the role of dedicated parent. Although their underlying motive is selfish—in most cases, gaining some form of attention or feeling of importance—Munchausen mothers often appear, as did Martha Woods, Marybeth Tinning, and Priscilla Phillips, to be model parents.

Finally, many such mothers are women who, like Marybeth Tinning, the ex-pediatric nurse's aide, have at least some degree of medical sophistication—at least enough to be able to fool the professionals.

Martha Woods, Marybeth Tinning, and Priscilla Phillips were never recognized as MBP sufferers over the years as they continually brought their children to hospital emergency rooms. Part of the inability of professionals to see these women as Munchausen mothers lies in the nature of the illness itself, but part of that failure has to be blamed on the ignorance of medical practitioners when it comes to this rare disorder.

Even now, years after these widely publicized cases, MBP is still not recognized by many professionals, even those who deal with children on a daily basis. For example, recent surveys of medical and social service personnel have found that the majority of professional caregivers are unfamiliar with the syndrome.[25]

The prognosis for Munchausen mothers and their children is often grim. Some child victims die, and others are maimed psychologically if not physically. Part of the problem in dealing with MBP is detecting it and doing something to stop it before the child is killed. Pediatricians, pediatric nurse practitioners, nurses, and other health care providers need to become more familiar with the disorder and alert for its signs and symptoms. These professionals also need to overcome their reluctance to confront apparently model parents suspected of harming their own children.

Significantly and sadly, given the outcomes in many MBP cases, experts agree that when a Munchausen mother is confronted by medical personnel, she usually stops abusing her child—if it is not already too late.

CHAPTER FIVE

Postpartum Homicides

❖ Michael Massip was born on St. Patrick's Day in 1987. He was an apparently healthy but colicky newborn who cried a lot—sometimes as much as 15 to 18 hours a day. Doctors told his mother that the crying was something Michael would grow out of. But he never did. He didn't live long enough.

On April 29, 1987, Michael's 24-year-old mother, Sheryl Lynn Massip of Anaheim, California, bundled up the 6-week-old infant and threw him in front of a moving car. When the driver swerved and missed the baby, Sheryl picked Michael up, placed him under a tire of the family Volvo, and backed over him. She then threw his body in a nearby trash can. Later that day, Sheryl told her husband that Michael was kidnapped, but she readily confessed to the killing once the couple got to the police station to make a report.

Sheryl Massip was charged with murder and pleaded not guilty by reason of insanity. At her trial, jurors learned that, before giving birth, Sheryl had been a happy and healthy woman, looking forward to motherhood. But when Michael was born and cried so much, the young mother could neither eat nor sleep. She became confused, started feeling worthless, and began to hear voices telling her that Michael was in pain. These voices, Sheryl said, eventually told her to kill Michael to put him out of his misery.

The jury rejected Sheryl's claim of insanity and unanimously convicted her of second-degree murder. Her lawyers immediately made a series of posttrial motions. Hoping at best for a new trial, they were overjoyed when the judge, Robert Fitzgerald, responded by reducing the jury's verdict to voluntary manslaughter, a much less serious crime. But, to their surprise, Judge Fitzgerald didn't stop there.

The Orange County Superior Court judge stunned everyone in the courtroom by announcing that he was going to do something that judges almost never do. He rejected the jury's verdict altogether and found Sheryl not guilty by reason of insanity. The evidence, Judge Fitzgerald said, clearly showed that Sheryl Massip was seriously disturbed when she ran over and killed her baby. Thus, he announced that he had no alternative but to find the young mother legally insane.

That ruling, although certainly welcomed by Sheryl, was not the end of her worries. Instead of facing prison time, she now faced an indefinite period of confinement to a state hospital for the criminally insane. California law requires that a criminal defendant found not guilty by reason of insanity be committed to a state mental hospital for at least 180 days.

That was the minimum. In Sheryl's case, mental health examiners and the prosecutor urged a much longer confinement: no less than 6 months. Even then, there would be no guarantee of quick release.

Thus, when Sheryl Massip returned to court to learn her fate, she fully expected to be locked up for a long time to come. But Judge Fitzgerald had yet another surprise for Sheryl and everyone else in court that day. He completely rejected the requested period of commitment and ordered Sheryl to undergo a year of outpatient counseling in the community.

A little more than a year later, after Sheryl had completed the required course of therapy, an appellate court accepted part of the prosecution's argument and ruled that Judge Fitzgerald had exceeded the bounds of his authority when he replaced the jury's guilty verdict with his own verdict of not guilty by reason of insanity.

Although the appeals court found that Judge Fitzgerald had the power only to order a new trial on the sanity issue, the three-judge appellate panel affirmed the acquittal, concluding that prosecutors had waited an unreasonable length of time before bringing the appeal. Requiring a new trial now, the appellate judges agreed, would "have a disruptive effect on

[Sheryl's] progress and may result in setbacks."[1] Finally, the appeals court refused to overturn Judge Fitzgerald's decision to ignore the 180-day commitment requirement. ❖

❖ Laura Bartek's life was even shorter than that of Michael Massip. Laura was just 23 days old when her mother killed her.

On May 26, 1986, Beverly Bartek, a 33-year-old Nebraska woman on maternity leave from her job as deputy superintendent of a nearby nature center, dialed 911 and asked for emergency medical assistance. Firefighters who responded to the mother's desperate call found the 3-week-old infant in the kitchen sink, wrapped in a diaper, a nightshirt, and a wet towel. They tried to revive the drowned baby but failed, and Laura was pronounced dead at the scene.

Charged with first-degree murder, Beverly Bartek spent a month or so in a psychiatric hospital and then was allowed to await trial at home, where she was ordered confined under the supervision of her husband and mother except for court appearances and medical appointments.

When she finally went to trial, Beverly waived a jury and opted for a bench trial before Judge Jeffrey Cheuvront. During the 2-day trial, three expert witnesses, all psychiatrists, testified that Bartek was psychotic when she drowned her baby, drained the sink, and then waited 40 minutes to call 911.

According to the psychiatrists, Beverly Bartek had conceived through artificial insemination because her husband was sterile. After the baby was born, she became obsessed with the mode of conception—worrying about the identity of the man whose sperm was used to impregnate her, fretting over the moral implications of the entire process, and fearing that her husband might leave her because the baby was not his child. As the days went by, she became virtually unable to sleep and started losing weight rapidly. What little sleep she did get was punctuated repeatedly by nightmares.

According to Dr. Y. Scott Moore, one of the experts who testified on Bartek's behalf, although the artificial insemination was apparently incorporated into her psychosis, it was not the psychological basis for it. Another witness, Dr. Leonard Woytassek, testified that Bartek heard a male voice tell her that she and the baby were evil and that the baby must die.

After hearing these witnesses, Judge Cheuvront found Beverly Bartek not guilty by reason of insanity and continued her supervised release pending a decision as to whether she was mentally ill, dangerous, and thus to be committed to a state psychiatric hospital. Although the prosecutor demanded that Bartek be committed, the judge ultimately concluded that she was not a danger to herself or others and that confining her would be counterproductive. ❖

❖ Ann Green, a New York City pediatric nurse, gave birth to three children within a period of 5 years. Patty was born in 1980, Jamie in 1982, and Larry, Jr. in 1985.

Patty Green died when she was 5 days old, just a day after her mother brought her home from the maternity ward at New York Hospital. The New York City Medical Examiner's Office investigated but could not explain Patty's death. Ultimately, an unexplained heart defect was listed as the tentative cause of death.

Two years later, in November 1982, Jamie Green also died at the age of 5 days. His death, also never fully understood, was chalked up to SIDS. Officials were suspicious of both children's early and inexplicable deaths, but no action was taken until almost 3 years after Jamie died.

Ann Green's third baby, Larry, Jr., was born in July 1985. Medical personnel, by now quite familiar with the Green family history, took no chances with little Larry. They kept the baby boy hospitalized for 3 weeks before sending him home to his parents.

On August 6, 1985, just a day after Larry was discharged from the hospital with a clean bill of health, Ann Green rushed him, clinically dead, to the home of a neighbor, who was also a pediatric nurse. The neighbor revived Larry and then returned him to the hospital. Suspecting the worst, hospital officials contacted the New York City Office of Special Services for Children (OSSC).

After conducting its own investigation, the OSSC referred the case to the District Attorney's Office. On March 4, 1986, after several months of additional investigation, Manhattan DA Robert Morgenthau announced that a grand jury had charged Ann Green with murdering Patty and Jamie and attempting to murder Larry, Jr.

Freed on $125,000 bail, Ann Green spent the next 2 years awaiting trial. When her trial finally began in September 1988, she pleaded not guilty by reason of insanity. In his opening statement, Green's attorney told the jury that his client's homicidal acts were the result of a chronic and severe mental illness.

Testifying in her own defense, Ann Green told jurors she knew she killed her babies, but, that at the time, it had felt like someone else was doing it. Under cross-examination, Green said she could not remember either killing until a month or so later.

Dr. Stuart Asch, a New York City psychiatrist who had examined Green prior to trial, told jurors that the mother's homicidal actions were beyond her conscious control. Her mental illness, he testified, left her without a choice.

After deliberating for 10 hours, the jury of five women and seven men acquitted Ann Green of all charges, finding her not guilty by reason of insanity. Explaining the verdicts, the jury foreman said the jurors relied heavily on the expert testimony. He added that the jurors felt the state had failed to meet the burden of proving Green sane.

Interestingly, and perhaps significantly, the prosecution bore no such burden. Four years before Ann Green was tried, the New York State legislature responded to John Hinckley's controversial insanity acquittal by amending New York's insanity law. Since 1984, New York prosecutors have no longer borne the burden of proving sane a defendant who claims insanity. Instead, the law has required defendants to prove their insanity by a preponderance of the evidence.[2]

Following her insanity acquittal, Ann Green was evaluated at a state forensic mental hospital for 37 days before being freed by a judge who concluded that she was not then dangerous to herself or others. ❖

❖   While Sheryl Massip, Beverly Bartek, and Ann Green were all tried and acquitted by reason of insanity, Michelle Remington killed her 6-week-old baby and was never even tried.

On Saturday, April 5, 1987 at about 6:10 p.m., police in Bennington, Vermont responded to a report that two persons had been shot in Remington's apartment. When they arrived at the scene, officers found the 29-year-old mother and her 6-week-old son, Joshua, both seriously wounded. Joshua was dead on arrival at the local hospital; his mother was in serious condition, suffering from a single gunshot wound. Even before interviewing Michelle, police ruled Joshua's death a homicide and were convinced that his mother had killed him.

Over the next 9 months, Michelle Remington recovered from her self-inflicted wound and underwent extensive psychological and psychiatric evaluation and treatment.

In January 1988, she appeared in court to answer first-degree murder charges. Her lawyer told Judge Theodore Mandeville that Remington had been psychotic, depressed, out of touch with reality, and legally insane when she shot and killed baby Joshua. Five psychiatrists could vouch for that, the defense attorney told the judge.

Agreeing that the evidence was clear and that if tried Remington would be found not guilty by reason of insanity, the prosecutor said it would be a waste of tax dollars to try the young mother. In response, Judge Mandeville canceled the trial and agreed that Michelle Remington should undergo counseling in the community rather than be committed to a state mental institution. ❖

THE INSANITY DEFENSE

The insanity defense—invoked by Sheryl Massip, Beverly Bartek, Ann Green, and Michelle Remington—is used in fewer than 1 percent of all criminal cases that go to trial.[3] Even in those few cases, the defense is rarely successful. In short, most criminal defendants who plead insanity are convicted. And those few who are acquitted by reason of insanity are almost always locked up in state mental hospitals for considerable periods of time, often longer than they would have been incarcerated had they been found guilty.

How then did all four of these women beat the odds, not once but twice? How did they not only succeed with the insanity defense but avoid being committed to mental institutions?

As it turns out, one of the few crimes for which the insanity defense is predictably (though not always) successful is infanticide committed by a mother suffering from postpartum depression. Every one of these mothers—Sheryl Massip, Beverly Bartek, Ann Green, and Michelle Remington—was diagnosed as suffering from this temporary but often overwhelming mental disorder at the time she killed her baby.

BABY BLUES?
OR POSTPARTUM DEPRESSION?

Often referred to as simply the "baby blues," postpartum depression is not uncommon or new. Symptoms ranging from sadness to major depression to psychosis frequently occur during the first year after giving birth and are almost always short-lived. Fifty percent to 80 percent of all women experience some degree of depressed mood after giving birth.[4] Among those who do, roughly one-sixth will experience serious depressive symptoms such as major mood swings, insomnia, anorexia, and suicidal ideation.[5] At most, only 2 women in 1,000 actually become psychotic—lose touch with reality—as a result of postpartum depression.[6]

Although widely recognized as a legitimate mental disorder since first being noted by the physician Hippocrates in the fourth century, postpartum depression is not well understood. Mental health professionals debate whether it is, in fact, a separate and discrete diagnostic entity, and it has only recently become recognized in the *DSM-IV*, which uses the term *postpartum onset* as a so-called specifier for various diagnoses, including Major Depressive Disorder and Brief Psychotic Disorder "if the onset is within 4 weeks of delivery of a child."[7]

The *DSM-IV* further acknowledges the relationship between infanticide and symptoms of mental disorders with postpartum onset:

> When delusions are present, they often concern the newborn infant (e.g., the newborn is possessed by the devil, has special powers, or is destined for a terrible fate). In both the psychotic and non-psychotic presentations, there may be suicidal ideation, obsessional thoughts regarding violence to the child, lack of concentration, and psychomotor agitation. . . . Infanticide is most often associated with postpartum psychotic episodes that are characterized by command hallucinations to kill the infant or delusions that the infant is possessed, but it can also occur in severe postpartum mood episodes without such specific delusions or hallucinations.[8]

Significantly, the *DSM-IV* also notes that the risk of postpartum episodes of psychosis is greatly increased for women who have previously had such episodes: "Once a woman has had a postpartum episode with psychotic features, the risk of recurrence with each subsequent delivery is between 30% and 50%."[9] Other psychological authorities estimate that the odds that a postpartum depression (with or without psychotic features) will recur are somewhere between 30 and 84 chances in 100.[10]

Even though postpartum depression has now gained at least some form of "official" recognition among psychiatric and other mental health professionals, the cause of the disorder remains uncertain. Some researchers and clinicians link the disorder directly to biology, pointing out that levels of hormones such as estrogen and progesterone increase tremendously during pregnancy and then suddenly drop back to normal after a woman gives birth.[11]

Others suggest that postpartum depression is more a product of environment—the major physical and emotional demands of parenting a newborn, demands that tax even the most well-prepared and psychologically healthy mothers.

Still other mental health professionals see an interaction between hormonal changes and environmental stress as being at the root of postpartum depression.

The relationship between postpartum depression and infanticide, although now "officially" recognized, is also far from clear. Many women who become psychotic as a result of postpartum depression report experiencing the impulse to kill their newborns. The vast majority of these women, however, manage to control these drives, and only a tiny percentage succumb to the impulse and actually commit infanticide.

The experiences of Angela Thompson, a California mother whose postpartum psychosis drove her to drown her 9-month-old son in 1983, are typical and help explain how postpartum depression sometimes leads to infanticide:

Angela Thompson's postpartum problems began after the birth of her first child, daughter Allyson, in 1980. When Allyson was just a few months old, the new mother began having trouble sleeping. Before long, she started to believe that she didn't need sleep. Then, sleeplessness gave way to confusion and hallucinations. She responded to the hallucinations at first by turning on all the lights, running water from every faucet, and singing familiar hymns.

Neither Angela nor her husband, Jeff, suspected that her mental problems were somehow related to childbearing. Indeed, because Angela's hallucinations dealt with darkness, evil, and religion, she and Jeff first sought not medical, psychiatric, or psychological assistance but religious help. Their pastor prescribed prayer and what appeared to Jeff Thompson to be an exorcism. Only when those rites failed and Angela grew increasingly psychotic did they turn to the mental health professions.

Angela was hospitalized for 3 days on a psychiatric unit. She seemed to recover quickly and was discharged from the hospital, but shortly thereafter she threw herself off a bridge into the river below.

Hospitalized again, Angela stabilized rapidly and was discharged to outpatient care. Before long, she was back to normal, and the couple agreed to forget about the whole episode.

And they did pretty much that—at least until Angela became pregnant again 2 years later. Angela told a nurse-midwife she feared that the strange illness might reoccur, but the midwife told her she need not worry about it. Angela's physician, perhaps unaware of the statistical likelihood of recurrence, was similarly reassuring.

Angela Thompson's second child, Michael, was born in December 1982. Things went well for a time, until Angela stopped nursing the baby. That seemed to be a turning point, as it is for many women who suffer from postpartum depression. Before long, Angela was again psychotic: experiencing delusions, hallucinations, and a continuing obsession with the Devil. Preoccupied and entirely self-absorbed, at times she barely spoke to her husband or their 3-year-old daughter.

On September 1, 1983, Angela broke her silence. At 6:45 p.m. she greeted her husband at the door as he returned from work. She had a peculiar far-away expression on her face. Her pupils were dilated and her eyes glassy. She told her husband that their son was dead.

Fearing the worst but unable to really believe what he had just heard, Jeff Thompson ran through the house searching for his son. When the baby was nowhere to be found, Jeff looked outside. There, in the yard, he found Michael covered with a towel in a box, dead.

Angela was hospitalized again and treated with antipsychotic medications. Only weeks later did she realize what she had done. She had drowned the baby in a bathtub, she said, in response to the voice of God. God's voice said Michael was the Devil, that if Angela killed the baby her husband would raise him from the dead 3 days later, and that the world would thereafter recognize her son as Jesus Christ.

Charged with murder, Angela Thompson was committed to two psychiatric hospitals before trial. Ultimately, the charges were reduced to manslaughter and felony child abuse, and Angela pleaded not guilty by reason of insanity. After four psychiatrists found that she suffered from postpartum psychosis when she killed her baby, Angela was found insane and acquitted on that basis. Following her acquittal, she was ordered to spend 90 days at a psychiatric halfway house and then undergo years of outpatient psychiatric counseling.

Angela, a registered nurse, later returned to school to study nursing education, hoping to teach medical personnel about the disorder that caused her to kill. In spring 1987, she gave birth to another child. Even though she did suffer from some relatively minor symptoms of postpartum depression after that birth, she was well prepared to handle them. Professionals, family, and friends pitched in to provide her with 24-hour-a-day monitoring during the first few months of her new baby's life.

With help over a few rough spots, Angela and her baby both survived. Since then, Angela Thompson and her husband have established a state-wide program to help law enforcement authorities identify and deal with mothers who suffer postpartum depression. ❖

THE LAW'S RESPONSE:
PUNISHMENT? OR TREATMENT?

Although understandable, the law's response to Sheryl Massip, Beverly Bartek, Ann Green, Michelle Remington, and Angela Thompson—essentially excusing the homicides committed by these young mothers—is not without controversy.

The major arguments against punishing women who murder their babies while in the throes of postpartum depression seem to be that (1) these women's homicidal acts were caused by an illness beyond their control; (2) they have already suffered enough, having lost their babies and now having to live with the guilt of infanticide; and (3) they pose no danger to others as long as they do not have any more children.

These arguments were, for example, all used forcefully and effectively on behalf of Ann Green, who killed two of her children and tried to kill the third while suffering from postpartum depression. The psychiatrist who examined her and testified on her behalf told the jury that her illness left her no choice but to kill her baby. Another of her defenders pointed out that the grieving mother and former pediatric nurse had lost not only her baby but her career to this illness. And her lawyer, successfully arguing against confining Ann to a state mental hospital, told the judge that his client was no longer a threat to others because by being sterilized she had prevented any recurrence of the psychosis that caused her to kill.

In Ann Green's case and most others like it, there is a good deal of force to these arguments, and judges and juries frequently accept them. But not always. Dr. Daniel Katkin, a criminologist and professor of criminal justice at Pennsylvania State University, has studied the legal outcomes in 18 cases in which mothers killed their babies and then claimed insanity, based on a diagnosis of postpartum depression. In half these cases, the insanity pleas were successful.[12]

That is an extremely high rate of success for the insanity defense generally, but it still means that half of these women failed to convince a judge or jury that they were insane when they killed their infants. And these women have not gone unpunished; their sentences ranged from probation to an 8- to 20-year prison term.[13]

Dr. Katkin and others think that the dispositions in postpartum infanticide cases probably depend largely on who sits in judgment of these women.[14] A woman who confronts a sympathetic judge or jury is acquitted, whereas one who faces a less sympathetic trier of fact is convicted. The verdict lies in the luck of the draw.

Sheryl Massip's case perhaps makes the point most clearly. The jury rejected her insanity plea and convicted her of murder, but the judge, who sat through the very same trial and heard all the same evidence, said the killing was manslaughter at most and that he thought Massip was insane when she killed her infant son. A higher court decided that the judge had no business substituting his verdict for the jury's but nevertheless—perhaps reacting to its own sympathy for the young mother—used a technicality to affirm Massip's insanity acquittal.

Some experts seem to feel that a claim of postpartum psychosis should provide a virtually automatic legal excuse for a mother who kills her baby, but others are more cautious when it comes to linking the diagnosis to any absolute legal defense.

Dr. Susan Hickman, a California psychologist who is an advocate for women with postpartum depression and frequent expert witness on their behalf, testified for Sheryl Lynn Massip. Hickman says that mothers who kill their infants are obviously disturbed. Pointing to England—where under the Infanticide Act of 1938, a mother who kills her infant during its first year of life cannot be convicted of murder, only manslaughter—Hickman argues for a more sympathetic and enlightened legal approach to postpartum infanticide in the United States.[15]

A San Francisco psychiatrist and leading authority on postpartum depression, Dr. James Hamilton, takes a more cautious approach when it comes to legally excusing depressed mothers who kill their babies. Hamilton notes the need to distinguish postpartum homicides from ordinary child abuse killings and says that there ought to be evidence of actual psychosis before such a defense is considered legally viable.[16]

Hamilton also cautions against sanguine predictions that mothers who kill their babies and are acquitted by reason of insanity are no longer dangerous. The prognosis for future harm, he observes, depends a great deal on what kind of treatment the woman receives.[17] Those who receive proper care can lead normal lives, but those who do not may continue to pose a significant danger to themselves and any other children to whom they give birth.

CHAPTER SIX

Disappearing, Disposable Babies

❖ The day Loralei Sims was born, her mother called a friend to say that the Lord had blessed her with a baby girl. Hours earlier, Loralei's aunt, a professional photographer, had taken photos of the baby and her proud parents, Paula and Robert Sims.

The joy surrounding Loralei's birth was short-lived. On June 17, 1986, just 12 days after her birth, Loralei turned up missing and was never again seen alive.

On Tuesday, June 17, 34-year-old Robert Sims left his 27-year-old wife and newborn daughter in their home in rural Illinois, roughly 25 miles north of St. Louis, Missouri. According to Robert, he left the home for his job, unloading coal cars, at about 8:30 p.m. He was not scheduled to start work until 11 that night, and his job was just 12 miles away, but he had errands to run, so he left the house early. Robert got to work at about 10:15. Fifteen minutes later, Paula called to tell him Loralei was gone.

What Paula told her husband, and what she would later tell the police, was that Loralei had been kidnapped. Paula said she was watching the evening news on television when, just before 10:30, an intruder appeared out of nowhere. The man, wearing a nylon stocking over his head, pointed a gun at Paula, ordered her to the floor, and threatened to kill her if she did not stay put for 10 minutes. Paula did as she was told. But after hearing the screen door slam, she got up, found the baby missing from her bassinet, and then ran out the door and down the long driveway in pursuit of the masked man, who got away on foot.

Hearing Paula's account of what happened, Robert left work and raced home. Local, state, and federal law enforcers were not far behind. Almost immediately, authorities began an intensive search and investigation.

Roadblocks were set up near the Sims's home, and drivers were stopped and questioned. Scuba divers probed the depths of a 2-acre pond adjacent to the Sims's property while police in a boat used sonar to search for any trace of Loralei in the heavy vegetation beneath the muddy water. Police dogs and even a search plane equipped with infrared sensors were called in to scour the woods surrounding the Sims's home.

After 2 days of investigating and searching, police admitted they were stymied. No ransom note had been sent, and authorities had no leads. As hope of ever finding the baby began to fade, community groups and private companies offered thousands of dollars in reward for any information that would lead them to Loralei—first $2,000, then $6,000, and finally $14,000.

Thousands of posters with Loralei's picture were printed and distributed around the state. Robert and Paula Sims publicly pleaded for their daughter's safe return. They appeared on television wearing pink ribbons they said they planned to wear until Loralei was found. A despondent but still hopeful Robert Sims told reporters of his faith that God would return his daughter.

Other members of the Sims' family joined Robert and Paula in their public pleas for Loralei's safe return. They also deflected any hint that the kidnapping might not be what it appeared to be. Paula's father told the press that the culprit was either a baby seller or someone who had lost a baby of his own. And lest there be any doubt about Robert and Paula, Robert's brother-in-law announced to the media that both parents had taken and passed polygraph tests, thereby clearing themselves of any suspicion that they had been involved in Loralei's disappearance.

That was Friday, 3 days after Loralei disappeared. The following Tuesday, a week after the kidnapping was first reported, searchers still had not given up. The wind had shifted in direction, and Sheriff Frank Yocom thought it was worth giving the ground around the Sims's home one more look. Before long, a police dog named Judd seemed to be onto something.

The canine led his handlers to a site in a ravine about 50 yards from the house. Searchers had pondered the same site almost a week before but had been warned away from it by Robert Sims, who said it was full of poison ivy. Pulling back the heavy underbrush, police found the badly decomposed body of a tiny infant.

Although the body was so decomposed that a cause of death could not be ascertained, a forensic odontologist examined the jaw and was able to determine that the body was that of an infant in its first weeks of life. Subsequent genetic tests of bone marrow and blood samples indicated less than a 3 percent chance that the baby was not the child of Robert and Paula Sims. That was good enough for the police, but Robert and Paula refused to accept the skeletal remains for burial. Their attorney told reporters they were not satisfied that the dead baby was Loralei.

In the days and weeks that followed, authorities revealed that, contrary to earlier assertions, Robert and Paula Sims had not passed polygraph tests. A grand jury was convened to investigate the baby's death. Robert and Paula were called to testify but asserted their Fifth Amendment rights and refused to answer questions. Left with strong suspicions but no solid evidence, prosecutors dissolved the grand jury before any vote was taken. The investigation was shelved, but the case remained officially open.

Asked about the status of the case at that point, Sheriff Yocom said it was far from over. He was right.

Over the next 3 years, the Sims moved to another town, not far away, and got on with their lives. Paula gave birth to two children, Randy and Heather. When Heather was born in March 1989, Randy was already a toddler. With two healthy and beautiful children, Robert and Paula seemed to be putting Loralei's death behind them.

Then, on April 29, 1989, not quite 3 years from the day Loralei Sims disappeared, tragedy struck the family again. Robert Sims arrived home from work at about 11:30 p.m. and found his wife apparently unconscious. Fifteen-month-old Randy was asleep in his crib, but 6-week-old Heather was nowhere to be found.

It took Robert maybe 10 minutes to revive Paula. Once she regained consciousness, she told Robert a familiar story: At about 10:30 that night, she had been taking out the trash. Suddenly, a masked man with a pistol in his hand confronted her, forced her into the house, and beat her into unconsciousness. Then, Paula reasoned, he must have taken the baby.

Robert and Paula related this same story to the police. Understandably, the authorities greeted Paula's claim with a feeling of déjà vu mixed with deep skepticism. This time there would be no rewards, no parental appeals, no television appearances, no pink ribbons. Authorities investigated and appealed to the public for leads but with no expectation that Heather would ever be found alive.

Four days later, at 7:30 on Wednesday evening, a fisherman on the nearby Mississippi River saw a stranger who appeared to be doing something to a large oil drum that was used as a trash barrel. The fisherman did not get a good look at the stranger but became suspicious and approached the oil drum when the person left. In the drum, he found a plastic garbage bag. In the bag was the nude, intact body of a baby girl.

An autopsy was performed the next day, and the medical examiner positively identified the dead baby as Heather Sims. The autopsy further revealed that death was caused by intentional suffocation and that the baby's body had been frozen for some time before being dumped in the trash barrel.

That night, a judge issued search warrants for the Sims's home as well as for the nearby home of Paula's parents. The next day, the state's attorney ordered the Department of Social Services to take custody of Randy Sims pending a judicial hearing to determine whether he was an endangered child.

In response to these actions, the Sims's attorney went public, telling media sources that Paula and Robert denied any wrongdoing. He added that they hoped police would keep open minds and that the perpetrator would be apprehended. The defense attorney also told police that, on his advice, the Sims were refusing to take polygraph examinations.

The police obviously did not believe the Sims's denials. Less than a week after they reported their baby missing, Robert and Paula were told to expect to be charged with murder. Over the next week or so, police slowly made public the case against Paula Sims.

FBI tests showed that the plastic garbage bag used to wrap the baby probably came from a roll of bags found in the Sims's home.

Police found pieces of human hair in a deep freezer at the home of Paula's parents.

The woman who shared a hospital maternity room with Paula Sims when Loralei was born came forward; she said Paula had been upset that Loralei wasn't a boy.

The woman who was Paula's hospital roommate later when Heather was born was also interviewed; she told police that Paula had described for her the circumstances surrounding the kidnapping of her first child. But the story Paula told this woman included the details not of the first but of the second alleged kidnapping—that of Heather— which had yet to occur.

Finally, the police announced that even Robert Sims had confessed to having doubts about his wife's story.

On Friday, May 12, 1989, Paula Sims was finally charged—not with the murder of Heather but with obstructing justice and concealing a homicide, the death of her first child, Loralei.

Paula was released on bail, but her freedom was short-lived. On the first day of July, she was arrested at her parents' home. Again, the charges were obstructing justice and concealing a homicide, but this time the charges stemmed from the death of Heather.

Ten days later, authorities had more bad news for Paula: A grand jury had just accused her of murdering Heather. The grand jury handed down the indictment only after hearing the testimony of Paula's mother and father, who initially refused to testify but were then granted immunity and compelled to cooperate. This time there would be no bail for Paula Sims.

After months of pretrial maneuvers by attorneys for both sides, Paula's lawyer won a change of venue. As a result of the extensive local pretrial publicity, the case was moved halfway across the state to Peoria, Illinois. Trial opened there on January 8, 1990, slightly more than 8 months from the day Heather Sims was killed.

In his opening statement, the prosecutor denounced Paula as a ruthless and cold-blooded killer who murdered her children and then placed the blame on an imaginary culprit. The motive for the murders, he added, was simple: Paula and her husband disliked little girls.

Paula Sims sat largely motionless and expressionless as the jury of eight men and four women listened for 5 days to the circumstantial but compelling evidence against her. Then came the case for the defense. Friends and family members testified that Paula and Robert were overjoyed when their daughters were born and devastated when they disappeared.

Robert Sims took the stand for 4 hours and said he had been fooled by the FBI into thinking that his wife might be guilty. He testified that he now believed her story and told the jury that Paula had been both a good wife and mother. Finally, he denied that he had any involvement in either of his daughters' deaths.

Paula Sims was the last witness for the defense. On the stand for 5 hours, she was obviously nervous but kept a stiff upper lip. Paula rejected the accusations against her and stuck to her earlier stories. She cried only once, when asked what plans she might have had for her daughters. Under intense, often withering cross-examination by the DA, she frequently claimed to be unable to remember.

The trial of Paula Sims ended with a witness called by the prosecutor. Robert and Paula had both testified that neither Heather nor Paula had ever left the Sims's home from the time the baby was born until the time she disappeared. The rebuttal witness, a local storekeeper, testified that just a few days before the alleged kidnapping, Robert and Paula had come into her store with Heather. The baby, the storekeeper-witness said, never moved or made a sound.

Outside the presence of the jury, the DA told the judge that this testimony not only proved Paula and Robert lied but also supported his theory that the baby was already dead and that the visit to the store was an effort to create an alibi.

In their closing arguments to the jury, both attorneys used visual aids. The prosecutor used a lima bean and nutshells to illustrate his contention that Paula killed her baby, hid the baby's body in her parents' freezer, and then moved it back to her own freezer before discarding it. Paula's attorney responded with photos showing Paula and Robert smiling after the births of their daughters.

After 10 hours of deliberations, the jury convicted Paula Sims of murder, obstructing justice, and concealing a homicide. A day later, the prosecutor asked the same jury to impose the death penalty.

Meanwhile, as a local television station conducted a public opinion poll, asking viewers whether Paula Sims should be executed, Paula herself told her attorney she wanted a death sentence.

In the one poll that really counted, after 2 hours of deliberation, the jury rejected the DA's request for the death penalty and sentenced Paula to life in prison without hope of parole.

On April 30, 1990, a year and a day after Heather Sims was reported missing, Paula's initial appeal of her conviction was rejected. The next day she pleaded guilty to obstructing justice and concealing a homicide in the death of her first daughter, Loralei. Although a grand jury was convened to consider evidence of Robert Sims's role in Heather's death, proceedings were adjourned indefinitely. ❖

❖ Daniel and Kathleen Householder, a young West Virginia couple, must have sighed with relief when 1985 ended and 1986 began, for 1985 had been a trying year for them. First, Daniel lost his driver's license because he had accumulated so many speeding tickets while commuting to his job as a carpenter in Washington, D.C. Then, in March, Daniel was involved in a fatal car crash. Police said he was not only unlicensed but drunk, speeding, and driving on the wrong side of the road when his car collided with another. Within a month, Daniel was indicted on criminal charges.

In November, a flood virtually destroyed the first floor of the Householders' home. The couple not only lost most of their belongings but were forced to move out while the structure was repaired. A month later, on December 17, 1985, Kathleen gave birth to the couple's second child. Although the baby's birth brought a ray of hope to what had otherwise been a rather hopeless year, even that bit of sunshine did not last for long.

On January 3, 1986, Kathleen Householder and her 2-year-old son, Dustin, walked into a small supermarket in rural West Virginia. Kathleen bought a pack of cigarettes, cashed her paycheck, and left. Within minutes she returned to the store, told the cashier her baby was gone, and asked him to call the police.

The 21-year-old mother explained to police officers that she had left her 2-week-old daughter, Lindsay, asleep in the family pickup truck while she and Dustin went into the store. When mother and son returned to the truck, the baby was gone.

Kathleen Householder's report of a missing child triggered a major search for the baby, said to be dressed in pink shorts, white booties, and a pink and white shirt with "baby" printed on the front. Police looked all around the small town but found no physical evidence. Investigators questioned everyone nearby to no avail. Specially trained police dogs sniffed in vain to pick up any scent of the missing baby.

When the search hit a dead end, Kathleen Householder met with agents from the FBI and the National Center for Missing and Exploited Children. They agreed to lend a hand in the search for little Lindsay. Kathleen got the Maryland-based National Missing Child Search Society to put up a reward of $15,000. Meanwhile, Kathleen appeared on numerous television broadcasts, pleading for her baby. In one especially touching broadcast appeal, a sobbing Kathleen begged for her daughter's safe return.

In response to Kathleen's pleas and other publicity, reports came in from all over—even Florida and Louisiana—but not a single lead panned out. Finally, as the search for Lindsay Householder approached 3 weeks' duration, officials from the National Center for Missing and Exploited Children made what turned out to be their major contribution to the investigation: They encouraged police to polygraph the Householders.

Daniel Householder said he believed his wife's story; the polygraph said he was telling the truth. But when Kathleen responded to questions about her baby's disappearance, polygraph experts were skeptical.

Under pointed questioning by a state police investigator who administered the polygraph, Kathleen Householder gradually changed her story, admitting that Lindsay was dead. First she said the baby had fallen from her bassinet and hit her head on the floor. Then she said the baby had fallen from her arms as she was carrying her down a flight of stairs.

Finally, after the polygrapher told Kathleen that the autopsy would show how the baby died, she admitted striking the baby in the head with a rock the size of a baseball. After that, Kathleen told police, Lindsay began to convulse, so she placed the baby in a plastic garbage bag and threw the bag into the Shenandoah River.

Not long after her confession, Kathleen helped police find her daughter. Lindsay's body was found about 10 miles from the Householders' home, roughly 200 yards downriver from where Kathleen said it would be. A local game warden found the body of the 8½-pound baby, sealed in a garbage bag and lying in a foot-and-a-half of water near the Shenandoah shoreline.

Lindsay was dressed exactly as her mother said she would be—in the pink and white "baby" outfit. An autopsy revealed that she died from a blow to her head but also suffered asphyxiation. The medical examiner could not say whether Lindsay was dead or alive when her mother stuffed her into the plastic bag and threw her into the river.

Kathleen Householder was immediately charged with first-degree murder and ordered jailed pending trial after failing to post $40,000 in bail. In a series of pretrial maneuvers, Kathleen's attorney asked the court to assist her defense in several ways. He asked for money to conduct a survey to see whether members of the community, from which a jury would ultimately be drawn, were biased against her. He also asked for public funds to pay for psychological examinations to support a possible defense based on a claim of mental illness.

Before the case was tried, however, Kathleen Householder dropped plans to offer any defense—psychological or otherwise. Exactly 1 year after her arrest, she pleaded guilty to involuntary manslaughter in a deal that saw murder charges dropped and made her immediately eligible for parole. Although sentenced to serve 1 to 5 years in prison, Kathleen had already been jailed for a year awaiting trial. She and her attorney anticipated that she would be released quickly after she pleaded guilty and was sentenced. After all, they reasoned, she had been a model inmate.

Kathleen probably would have been paroled, except that shortly after her guilty plea, jailers found that she was pregnant. Because she had been in jail for more than a year, it was clear that she had conceived there. Kathleen's pregnancy led to an investigation of the jail, which concluded that because she was such a model prisoner she may have been allowed an unlawful conjugal visit with her husband in the jail's kitchen.

Shortly thereafter, instead of being paroled, Kathleen was sent to state prison. At about the same time, Daniel Householder was sentenced to serve a year in jail for causing a fatal accident while driving drunk.

On September 17, 1987, Kathleen gave birth to a baby girl. The child was born in an ambulance that was transporting Kathleen from prison to a hospital. The baby, whose parents were both still jailed, was turned over to family members. Three and a half months later, after serving just under 2 years behind bars for killing her baby daughter, Kathleen Householder was released from custody. ❖

❖ The police believed the young mother's story was true but could find no independent witnesses to corroborate it. That is what Capt. Thomas Seamon of the Philadelphia Police Department told the press the day Tanya Dacri reported that her son Zachary had been kidnapped. On January 11, 1989, Tanya Dacri, a 20-year-old White woman, told police she was taking 2-month-old Zachary to the doctor when two Black men snatched the baby from her arms in the busy parking lot of a large shopping mall in northeast Philadelphia. After grabbing Zachary, she said, the men fled in a waiting car; the car was driven by a third man and had no license plates. Tanya also told police she suspected that her father had hired the kidnappers to retaliate for sexual abuse charges she had recently filed against him.

No witnesses, no motive, no car, and no men were ever found. Despite Capt. Seamon's statement to the press, the police turned almost immediately to Tanya and her 22-year-old husband, Phillip, for answers. After interrogating the couple at length, police officers knew right where to look for Zachary. The day after the reported kidnapping, it took police very little time to find the baby boy—at least part of him.

On January 12, 1990, after dragging a suburban Philadelphia creek for about 4 hours, police divers found five packages—each containing parts of

Zachary Dacri—his head, arms, and legs. The baby's torso washed ashore by itself 2 days later.

Initially, police refused to say what led them to Zachary's remains, but eventually they acknowledged that Tanya and Phillip Dacri had both made incriminating statements. Phillip told police he learned of Zachary's death on January 7 when he called his wife from work. Tanya told him she couldn't take any more of the baby's crying, that she had done something to put an end to it, and that Phillip would find out what she meant when he got home.

When Phillip got home he found Zachary dead and wrapped in a plastic trash bag. The next day, when he returned from work, he found that Tanya had dismembered the body.

In her confession, Tanya told police that the baby had been crying for what seemed like hours. When she could no longer tolerate the crying, she put him in a bathtub full of water and let him drown. Tanya then described in detail how she cut up the body with a kitchen knife, packed the torso, head, and limbs in brown paper bags, sealed them with strips of cloth, and then weighted them with her husband's barbells. Finally, she told police how she and Phillip drove to two spots and dumped the bags into the river.

Following their statements to the police, Tanya and Phillip Dacri were arrested and charged with a host of crimes. Tanya was charged with murder, conspiracy, possession of a weapon, and abuse of a corpse. Phillip was charged with conspiracy and abuse of a corpse. Police said they did not believe that he was involved in killing or cutting up the baby but had simply assisted his wife in disposing of the body.

Initially, it appeared that Tanya Dacri would plead insanity, but after several psychological and psychiatric examinations, acting against her attorney's advice, she pleaded guilty to an open charge of murder, leaving it to the judge to decide whether she was guilty of first- or third-degree murder—essentially whether or not she had intended to kill Zachary.

Although he disagreed with her plea, Tanya's attorney said there was little chance the judge would settle on first-degree murder. He expected a finding of third-degree murder, the least serious murder conviction possible.

Two psychologists testified at the bench trial. One said that Tanya was undergoing a brief psychotic episode when she drowned and dismembered her infant. The other doctor told the judge that Tanya suffered from a borderline personality disorder—a mental illness characterized by occasional lapses into psychosis—and that she did not have the mental capacity to form the kind of intent required for first-degree murder.

The prosecution, however, presented the testimony of the pathologist who did the autopsy on baby Zachary. He testified that even though Zachary was only 2 months old at the time of his death, his body bore numerous signs of prior abuse, new and old: that 3 to 4 weeks before his death Zachary had suffered two broken collarbones and five broken ribs and that within 24 hours of his death he had suffered bruises and a hairline skull fracture.

Finally, the judge also learned that the Dacris were being monitored by child welfare authorities at the time of Zachary's death. Just a year before his death, the couple's other child, then 6 weeks old, had almost drowned in a bathtub. Doctors who treated the baby girl found her bruised and undernourished. They reported the case to the authorities, and the baby was briefly placed in foster care but eventually returned to the Dacris. Child welfare workers who monitored the Dacris thereafter said they saw no evidence of abuse to either child and were about to terminate their monitoring when Zachary was killed.

After hearing all the evidence, the judge found Tanya Dacri guilty of first-degree murder and sentenced her to life in prison without hope of parole. Phillip Dacri pleaded guilty to helping Tanya dispose of Zachary's body. At sentencing, his lawyer pleaded for leniency, telling the judge that Phillip had played only a minor and understandable role in the crime. The judge rejected the notion that Phillip was a mere pawn in the events following Zachary's death and sentenced him to serve from 9 to 23 months in county jail. ❖

MENTALLY ILL? OR ANTISOCIAL?

Mothers who kill their infants and then concoct elaborate stories of kidnapping to cover their crimes are undoubtedly disturbed women. But how disturbed are they, and should their mental disorders excuse their homicidal behavior?

At one end of the continuum are cases like those of Paula Sims, Kathleen Householder, and Tanya Dacri—apparently immature but cunning women who, unable to cope with the demands of parenting, kill their babies in fits of anger and frustration and then try not only to deceive the authorities but also to portray themselves as victims. Not surprisingly, these women generate little if any sympathy from the public or the courts once their cruel deceptions are revealed.

But there is also the other end of the continuum —another group of mothers who kill their babies and try to cover up their deadly deeds. These mothers are more deserving of, but do not always get, sympathy from the public and leniency from the courts. Consider, for example, Lucrezia Gentile and Sharon Comitz.

❖ When her first child was 3 years old, Lucrezia Gentile and her husband decided it was time to have another child. After having difficulty becoming pregnant, Lucrezia sought medical help. Unfortunately, the "help" she got made the problem worse. Injected with an experimental diagnostic dye, she became sterile. Only after spending $20,000 on additional treatment and undergoing surgery did she become pregnant.

After a difficult pregnancy, Stephen Gentile was born via cesarean section in February 1988. Two months later, on April 20, 1990, he disappeared. Lucrezia told New York City police that she had been lured out of her house by a phony telephone report that her 6-year-old son was sick at school. Pushing Stephen in a stroller toward the school, the 36-year-old mother said, she was accosted by two men who snatched Stephen and then drove away in a black sedan.

Police doubted Lucrezia's story. There were no witnesses, no ransom demands, and no motive. Still, officers conducted a massive search for the baby, stopping dark sedans and questioning drivers. Although it lasted barely 2 days, the police investigation triggered rumors of men roving the neighborhood, trying to lure children into their blue van. Terrified parents walked their children to and from school, and school administrators fanned the flames of fear by sending home warning notices.

The day after she reported her son missing, Lucrezia Gentile broke down and told police officers what really happened. Unable to stop Stephen from crying, she drowned him in a bathtub. Then, after dressing the body in a hat and snowsuit and wrapping it in a plastic bag, she used a baby stroller to wheel it to a neighbor's garbage can, where she dumped it.

Lucrezia was charged with murder. As she was led handcuffed out of the police station, people in the waiting crowd denounced her as a murderer who should be burned.

Although Lucrezia Gentile was a murderer in the eyes of some, others who knew her well or got to know her thought otherwise. Her family and members of her church rallied behind her. Four psychiatrists and psychologists—including one doctor hired by the prosecution—examined her, and all four concluded that she was suffering from postpartum depression when she killed her 2-month-old son.

Even the prosecutor agreed that Lucrezia was in the throes of severe postpartum depression at the time of the killing. He joined the defense attorney in asking the judge to accept Lucrezia Gentile's plea of insanity.

After an hour-long hearing, the judge agreed that Lucrezia was suffering from postpartum depression and, as a result, not responsible by reason of mental disease or defect. ❖

❖ Sharon Comitz was not so fortunate. Sharon, a 27-year-old Pennsylvania mother of two, also suffered from postpartum depression. Like Lucrezia Gentile, she killed her infant son and then concocted a tale of kidnapping to cover her tracks. Also like Lucrezia, she entered a plea based on her mental illness, and that plea was accepted. But unlike Mrs. Gentile, who was simply ordered to receive treatment, Sharon Comitz was sentenced to serve from 8 to 20 years in prison.

Sharon Comitz's tragedy began well before the day she killed her son. Four years earlier, when her first child, Nicole, was born, Sharon had suffered from severe postpartum depression. She avoided being left alone with Nicole, fearing she would kill the newborn. When Nicole was just 17 days old, Sharon took her to the hospital, complaining that the baby was having difficulty breathing.

According to medical records, Sharon was extremely depressed and told doctors that she'd tried to suffocate her baby because she wanted a life alone with her husband. Both child and mother were hospitalized—Nicole for observation and Sharon for psychiatric treatment.

Eventually Sharon's depression cleared. No one told her or her husband, Glenn, about the chance, if not the likelihood, that it would recur. A few years later, the Comitzs decided to have another child.

Garrett Comitz was born on December 3, 1984. Although at times Sharon seemed unable to cope, her husband did his best to support her and reassure her that her problems would not last. But they did.

On January 3, 1985, exactly one month after his birth, Garrett Comitz was reported missing. Sharon told police she had been shopping at the Ames Plaza Shopping Center when someone took Garrett from her car. According to Sharon's account, she had returned to the car with Garrett and found her keys missing. Leaving Garrett alone in the car, she had gone to search for her keys. When she returned 2 minutes later, Garrett was gone.

Terming the disappearance a kidnapping, local police searched the surrounding hills and woods to no avail. The next day, Garrett's body, clad in a yellow infant sleeper, was found floating in a nearby creek. Although now a suspect, Sharon denied any wrongdoing, stuck to her story of kidnapping, and even passed two polygraph tests.

Three weeks later, Pennsylvania State Police called a press conference and announced that their investigation of Garrett's death was complete and that they had concluded that he was not kidnapped.

Lt. Jerry Clemens told reporters that the investigation had led to evidence indicating that Sharon was responsible for Garrett's death.

Later that day, Sharon was arrested and charged with first- and third-degree murder.

Initially, Sharon pleaded not guilty. Six months later she pleaded guilty but mentally ill to the charge of third-degree murder—willful but unpremeditated homicide. The plea, an admission of guilt tantamount to a conviction, carried a possible maximum sentence of 10 to 20 years in prison but left open the possibility that psychiatric treatment could be imposed instead.

At a sentencing hearing, Dr. Robert Sadoff, a nationally known forensic psychiatrist, testified that Sharon had been unable to acknowledge the killing until he hypnotized her. The hypnosis, Sadoff testified, unearthed memories that Sharon had repressed, enabled her to acknowledge having killed Garrett, and confirmed that she had been in a pathological dissociative state at the time of the killing. Explaining that dissociative states range from everyday distractions to sleepwalking to multiple personalities, the forensic psychiatrist told the judge that Sharon's dissociation was abnormal and close to that found among individuals with multiple personalities.

Even the prosecution's psychiatrist, Dr. Stephen Ragusea, conceded that Sharon was mentally ill when she killed Garrett. According to Dr. Ragusea, however, Sharon was not psychotic, suffering from a multiple personality disorder, or dissociating at the time of the killing. Both experts agreed, however, that Sharon needed and would benefit from psychological treatment.

After hearing the psychiatric evidence, the judge sentenced Sharon Comitz to 8 to 20 years in prison—just 2 years short of the maximum term allowed by law. In 1987, the Superior Court of Pennsylvania affirmed the sentence. ❖

Why was Sharon Comitz dealt with so harshly when there was no question that she suffered from severe postpartum depression and was mentally ill when she killed her month-old son? The answer seems to lie in people's reaction to mothers who not only kill their own children but then create elaborate fabrications that cast suspicion away from themselves.

The prosecutor in the Comitz case, who still feels Sharon received a fair sentence, argued that her fabrication of the kidnapping scenario was proof that she acted rationally when she murdered her baby.

District Attorney Ray Gricar acknowledged that Sharon was depressed and lost control, but he argued that she had known what she was doing when she killed her son and then concocted a story to cover her crime.

An alternative explanation may be that Sharon Comitz was not treated all that harshly after all. Some might say that she got what she deserved, even taking her postpartum depression into account. Eight to 20 years in prison is, by any light, much less severe than the sentence of life without parole meted out to both Paula Sims and Tanya Dacri.

But then consider that Paula Sims probably killed two of her children and that Tanya Dacri not only killed her son but chopped his body to pieces. Furthermore, compare Sharon's sentence with the "no jail time" sentence imposed on Lucrezia Gentile—whose case is virtually identical to Sharon's. Finally, contrast Sharon Comitz's sentence and the 22 months served by Kathleen Householder, who, in a fit of anger, killed her 2-year-old son and then led police and the public on a 3-week-long, tear-jerking, gut-wrenching, wild goose chase before she confessed.

DISPOSABLE BABIES, DESPERATE MOTHERS

On April 29, 1991 at about 9:30 p.m., a New York City police cruiser pulled to the curb in front of a three-story brownstone in Brooklyn. Two police officers, responding to an anonymous tip, opened a plastic bag lying next to a garbage can. In the bag they found the tiny, powdered, diapered, and pajama-clad body of a newborn girl named April Olivia.

Also in the bag was a hand-printed note, stating the baby's name, the time and date she was born, and the time she had 3 three days later. The note added that the baby's mother loved her and hoped the finder would take good care of her.

In 1990, at least nine newborns were dumped into trash bins or other garbage containers in New York City alone.[1] And in 1991, by the month of August, April Olivia was just one of at least seven newborns known to have been dumped into the trash in the nation's largest city.[2]

For example, on March 26, 1991, in the East New York section of Brooklyn, police found the corpse of a newborn boy, with the umbilical cord still attached, stuffed into a curbside trash bag. The baby's mother—who had checked into a local hospital hours earlier, suffering from birth-related complications—was charged with murder after the medical examiner ruled that the newborn had been strangled.

Two days later, on March 28, again in Brooklyn, maintenance workers were about to start a garbage compactor in the basement of a six-story tenement when they heard what sounded like the cries of a baby coming from inside the machine. The workers called the police, and minutes later an NYPD sergeant crawled into the compactor, shined his flashlight into a pile of garbage that was about to be crushed, and found a living, 6 pound–10 ounce newborn boy.

After a brief investigation, a 12-year-old girl, who lived on the fourth floor of the building, told police she had given birth earlier that morning and had tossed the baby down a garbage chute outside her apartment. Somehow the newborn had managed to survive a fall of four flights as well as several hours in the garbage.

In June 1991, in two separate incidents on the same day, two newborn girls were found in New York City trash cans. Coincidentally, and ironically, each baby was wrapped in a plastic "I Love New York" shopping bag—the kind used to tout New York City's appeal as a tourist attraction.

At 4:10 on the afternoon of June 19, a man rummaging through a trash bin in search of returnable bottles came across a plastic shopping bag. Ripping the bag open, he found a live baby girl, just a few hours old, her umbilical cord tied with a piece of string. Police rushed the baby to a nearby hospital where—weighing in at 5 pounds–13 ounces—she was pronounced likely to survive.

Two hours later, another man, digging for a newspaper in a trash barrel on a Manhattan subway platform, discovered a tote bag. Inside the bag, wrapped in another plastic "I Love New York" bag, he found the bloody body of a newborn girl attached to a placenta and umbilical cord. Police rushed the full-term baby to a nearby hospital, but she was dead on arrival. Doctors who examined her said she was no more than an hour old, leading police to speculate that she had been born somewhere in the subway station.

On August 12, 1991, in the fifth such reported incident in New York City in less than 5 months, yet another newborn was thrown into a garbage chute and landed in a trash compactor 10 flights below. An autopsy revealed that the baby, who had been born just hours earlier in a stairwell of the Coney Island housing project, was alive when dropped into the chute and died as a result of the fall. The child's mother, a 19 year old who lived on the 10th floor of the building, went to a nearby hospital following the birth and told a social worker there what she had done. Authorities charged the teenaged mother with second-degree murder.

No one knows exactly how many newborns end up in the trash each year, deposited there by mothers who cannot or will not care for them. The American Humane Association (AHA), a national child abuse and neglect watchdog agency, estimates that more than 17,000 youngsters of all ages are abandoned each year by their parents.[3] But the AHA acknowledges that this is probably an underestimate of the problem, the magnitude of which is growing annually.

Others estimate that each year some 600 or more of these abandoned children are simply thrown away—literally tossed into the trash.[4] Only those who are found—those who manage to escape garbage compactors, incineration, solid waste disposal, and other methods by which Americans dispose of their refuse—are known and counted, and there are no national or even good local data on their numbers. Still, there is every reason to believe that an estimate of 600 American babies tossed into the trash annually is probably no exaggeration.

For example, in 1989, the *Los Angeles Times* reported having tracked 16 cases of parental abandonment over the preceding year.[5] Five of these children were babies abandoned in trash cans. More recently, in a single month, California authorities reported finding the abandoned bodies of four newborns—two in trash bins, another in a dumpster behind a motel, and a fourth in a portable outdoor toilet used by migrant farm workers.[6]

In the much smaller but still relatively large metropolitan area of Tampa, Florida, 12 children were reportedly abandoned between 1988 and 1990 on doorsteps and in trash cans and dumpsters.[7] Nine of the 12 were newborns.

And on New York's Long Island—a large and diverse but generally upscale and affluent geographic area ranging from the suburbs of New York

City to remote rural areas many miles from the city—six young women have been charged with killing their newborn babies and disposing of their bodies over a 7-year period.[8] Authorities on Long Island are still investigating numerous other unsolved cases in which abandoned infants have been found dead on doorsteps, in trash cans, and at garbage dumps.

Not all newborns thrown into the trash die. But there can be little doubt that these tiny victims are left to die, or when they do survive, that their survival is anything more than mere fortuity.

Although mothers dump their newborns for a variety of reasons, there is generally little if any question of what they intend when they toss their babies into trash cans, dumpsters, or garbage chutes.

In a surprisingly large number of cases, especially hearty full-term newborns (like the first "I Love New York" baby described above) do somehow survive being thrown away, but only when they are lucky enough to be found before they die from exposure, malnutrition, dehydration, and/or anoxia. Clearly, the length of time a newborn survives such abandonment depends on a variety of factors such as temperature, clothing, and developmental level of the child.

WHO ARE THESE MOTHERS?

Who are these mothers who throw their newborns away, why do they do it, and what becomes of them once their crimes are uncovered?

Not surprisingly, most mothers who trash their babies seem to be unmarried, uneducated, young, and poor. Dr. Robert Sadoff, the forensic psychiatrist who examined Sharon Comitz, has treated 25 such mothers over a 15-year period. Sadoff says the majority of mothers who dump their newborns are young, White, poor and not well educated.[9] Criminologist Ronald Holmes, who has interviewed many of these women in prison, concurs. He says they "typically become pregnant very young, are single, have few financial or family resources, and are often depressed or suffer from great feelings of anomie."[10]

Many of these young mothers are themselves victims of abuse and neglect, and a growing number are also drug abusers. In many cases, friends and even family members are not aware of their pregnancies.

The plight of two of these young mothers appears sadly typical:

❖   Twelve-year-old Tina's parents died in a fire when she was 4 years old, and she was raised thereafter by an emotionally unstable aunt in a run-down, drug-infested, Brooklyn housing project overrun by crack dealers and gun-toting juvenile gangsters. So dangerous was the environment around her that Tina left the apartment—which she shared with the aunt, the aunt's son, and two other men—only to attend school, where she was classified as a slow learner.

Cooped up in the apartment for long periods with little to do and not much parenting, Tina was exposed to drugs, alcohol, and sex from an early age. Indeed, following the birth and dumping of her baby down the garbage chute, police discovered that the baby's father was Tina's 21-year-old cousin, who had been sexually abusing her while her aunt was out of the apartment. Police also learned that Tina had somehow managed to hide her pregnancy from everyone around her, including her aunt and cousin.

To spare Tina from having to testify against her cousin, who was charged with rape, prosecutors allowed him to plead guilty to reduced charges and be sentenced to only 6 months in jail. ❖

❖   Kendra Nowak, whose newborn baby was discovered in a garbage bag in her Michigan home, was a physically and emotionally abused teenager. She was 19 and single when she gave birth in the home she shared with her mother. No one had even known she was pregnant. Indeed, the child was born just hours after Kendra was examined at a local hospital emergency room, where she had gone complaining of back pain. Amazingly, medical personnel had examined Kendra that day and discharged her without discovering that she was pregnant.

Following the baby's birth, Kendra again sought medical care. This time, however, it was obvious that she had been pregnant and given birth. When she was unable to produce her baby, the examining physician became suspicious and alerted the police.

Suspecting that Kendra had given birth and then dumped the baby in the trash, police spent a week combing a local landfill. Finally, they turned their attention to Kendra's home and found the baby's remains in a closet. Authorities said the baby had lived for two days but had been dead for a week when it was found.

Although Kendra was charged with manslaughter, she was allowed to plead guilty to misdemeanor child abuse and placed on 2 years' probation by a judge who cited the physical abuse she had suffered at the hands of her father and the emotional harm inflicted upon her by her neglectful mother. Judge James Batzer said that if it had been within his power he would have sentenced Kendra's parents to jail for neglecting and abusing her. ❖

WHY DO THEY
DUMP THEIR BABIES?

What motivates a mother not only to abandon her newborn baby but to do so in a way that both equates the infant with garbage and leaves its chance for survival completely in the hands of fate? Why do some mothers throw their babies in the garbage, when they could place them for adoption or even simply leave them on someone's doorstep?

There are undoubtedly many reasons why some mothers feel the need to literally throw their newborns away, but the two most common motives are likely shame and hopelessness.

In many if not most cases, mothers who throw their newborn babies away are clearly motivated, at least in part, by a desire to keep the pregnancy and birth a secret, to avoid the stigma and disgrace still associated in some quarters, even in this enlightened era, with out-of-wedlock birth.

Consider, for example, the case of 15-year-old Dawn Chapman, a small-town 10th grader who gave birth, put her newborn baby in a plastic bag, and threw the bag down an embankment behind her upstate New York home. Dawn, who managed to hide her pregnancy and the birth from her whole family, told police she gave birth alone at home, cleaned the baby, tied off his umbilical cord, wrapped him in a towel, placed him in the bag, and then tossed the bag down the embankment because she feared that otherwise her mother would find out that she had been pregnant and given birth.

Dawn's aunt described the teenager as simply confused. Prosecutors and the police saw it differently; they charged Dawn with second-degree murder.

Typically, the mother who throws her baby away to avoid the stigma of pregnancy and childbirth is an unmarried teenager, who becomes pregnant and tries to deny the pregnancy, even to herself. As a result, she misses whatever opportunity might exist for abortion. As the pregnancy progresses and she begins to "show," she covers herself—literally and figuratively—with heavy, baggy clothing and lies about unexpected and inexplicable weight gain. In rare cases, pregnant teens actually succeed in convincing themselves that they are not pregnant, despite every physical indicator to the contrary. As Pitt and Bale have explained,

> Women who commit neonaticide generally have made no plans for the birth or care of their child. They often conceal the pregnancy from both family and friends. Massive denial of the gravid state is a prominent feature. . . . The denial can be so powerful that it affects not only the mother's own perception but those of her family, friends, teachers, employers and even physicians.[11]

In these cases, the birth, like the pregnancy, is generally also hidden. Young mothers who throw away their newborns typically give birth alone—sometimes in their bedrooms and bathrooms but also in closets, public rest rooms, and even subway stations. Having thus far succeeded in fooling others, all that remains is the hardest part—getting rid of the ultimate product, the newborn child.

It is at this point in the process that the young mother must overcome her maternal instincts and find a way to rid herself of the child she has just brought into the world. Perhaps it is no coincidence that so many newborns who are abandoned by their mothers end up in the trash or garbage. First of all, it appears that very few of these mothers actually kill their babies in any active sense—although there are clear exceptions. Most of these young mothers cannot bring themselves to stab, strangle, beat, or drown their helpless newborns. Instead, they simply dump them and leave the rest to chance or fate.

Moreover, the choice of dumping medium and place is logical. Plastic garbage bags are a readily available, even though not perfect, medium for cleaning up and disposing of the mess associated with childbirth—newborn, placenta, and afterbirth. Not only is a trash bin, compactor, garbage can, or dumpster the logical place to throw a garbage bag, whatever its contents, but such containers are places unlikely to be searched or to have their contents scrutinized by others. Thus, if the mother's goal is to forever break any link between herself and the newborn, a refuse container is an excellent choice, both practically and symbolically.

No one knows how many young mothers actually succeed in their efforts to avoid the shame and stigma of out-of-wedlock pregnancy by hiding their pregnancies, giving birth secretly, and then throwing their newborns in the trash or garbage, but the number is probably greater than many would expect. In most cases, the mothers of newborns found dead or alive in the trash are never located. Indeed, where the mother of such a "throwaway" is found, it is generally because—like Tina, who tossed her newborn down the garbage chute in her own apartment building, or Dawn Chapman, who disposed of her infant in her own backyard—she has made the mistake of depositing the baby in a refuse container or some other hiding place in or near her own dwelling.

Hopelessness, an emotional response so tragically common among inner-city youths today, is implicated in a host of evils that plague America's decaying urban neighborhoods. Teens growing up in these blighted, impoverished, and crime-ridden ghettos, where life is cheap, correctly sense that they have been largely written off by the greater society around them. Faced with substandard housing and schools, dwindling social welfare programs, extremely limited or nonexistent economic opportunities, and little if any hope for anything better, these youngsters often turn to drugs, violence, and crime.

In many cases, this same hopelessness seems to play a major motivating role in the thinking of young mothers who throw their babies away. Faced with crushing poverty and no real prospects for a better life for themselves or their babies, some unwed teenage mothers throw their newborns away in what can only be described as an act born of hopelessness and despair. Perhaps the classic example is the case of Juana Lopez:

❖ By the age of 14, Juana, a Mexican immigrant, had dropped out of junior high school to give birth to and care for one baby. Although she and her family had immigrated to Southern California and she had attended junior high school briefly, Juana spoke almost no English. Her impoverished parents did the best they could to support Juana and her baby but told her that if she ever got pregnant again she would have to leave home because they simply could not afford to support another child.

At age 15, Juana became pregnant a second time. Again, as with her first pregnancy, Juana hid the fact that she was expecting. Even her parents never suspected. Ultimately, Juana gave birth alone at home. She then wrapped the newborn in a plastic bag and tossed the bag into a dumpster, where the baby was later found dead from suffocation.

After the baby was found and traced to Juana, the teenage mother pleaded guilty to a charge of second-degree murder. Arguing for leniency, Juana's attorney succinctly summed up her young client and her motives. Public defender Laureen Gray told the judge that Juana was a young, unsophisticated girl who saw no other way out.

Although the prosecutor asked for a prison sentence of 7 years or more, Judge Robert Jameson instead remanded Juana to Los Angeles Juvenile Hall for 1 year of counseling and participation in other rehabilitation programs. ❖

CHAPTER SEVEN

Child Abuse Fatalities

✦ When Elisa Izquierdo was born on February 11, 1989, her mother was living in a New York City shelter for the homeless. Awilda Lopez had two other children who were placed in foster care a month before Elisa's birth. Authorities concluded that she had left the children (ages 1½ and 2½) without supervision or food for extended periods of time, during which she was apparently on crack cocaine.

At birth, Elisa tested positive for drugs and was immediately placed in foster care. When she was 5 months old, Elisa was sent to live with her biological father. Gustavo Izquierdo took parenting classes and vowed to become a good father. He enrolled Elisa in a Montessori preschool, where she became a popular student. When Izquierdo could no longer afford Elisa's tuition, a benefactor stepped forward and agreed to pay it. Indeed, Prince Michael of Greece was so taken with Elisa that he offered to pay for her private schooling through high school.

Meanwhile, however, Awilda Lopez had married and managed to regain custody of her two older children. She then convinced social welfare authorities and the courts to give her unsupervised visits with Elisa. During these visits, Lopez began abusing the child. Concerned about his daughter,

Gustavo Izquierdo complained to child welfare authorities, but no action was ever taken.

In May 1994, Gustavo Izquierdo died of cancer before he could carry out his plan to move Elisa to Cuba and leave her with relatives there. When Izquierdo died, a cousin filed for custody of Elisa. Awilda Lopez went to court, branded the cousin a "witch," and was granted custody of the child despite her history of child neglect and substance abuse and allegations that she had abused Elisa.

Once Awilda Lopez gained custody of Elisa, she took the child from the Montessori school, then removed her from school altogether, virtually confining her to one room in the family's apartment. Neighbors reported hearing frequent screams coming from the apartment where Elisa was kept. Over the next year and a half, dozens of teachers, neighbors, and relatives complained that Elisa was being abused, but nothing was done to stop it.

Although they suspected Elisa was being seriously abused, those who made these complaints could not have known just how badly Lopez was treating the first grader. Behind closed doors, Lopez was beating the child regularly and torturing her anally with a hairbrush. When Elisa lost control of her bladder and bowels, her mother smeared her face with feces, forced her to eat her own excrement, and mopped the floor with her hair.

The brutal abuse of Elisa Izquierdo came to an end in late November 1995 when paramedics were summoned to the Lopez apartment. Nearly 2 days earlier, Elisa had defecated in the apartment, and Awilda Lopez had responded by knocking the 6-year-old's head into a concrete wall. The blow left the child unconscious, with brain fluid oozing from her mouth, nose, and ears.

When paramedics arrived, they found the child's face and body covered with sores, cuts, and what appeared to be cigarette burns. One of the emergency response personnel said that in 22 years on the job he had never seen a worse case of child abuse.

Awilda Lopez was charged with murder and in 1996, after months of protesting her innocence, pleaded guilty. In a plea bargain, struck to avoid having her two older children testify against her, she was given the minimum sentence: 15 years to life in prison. ❖

❖ Like Elisa Izquierdo, Emily Hernandez was born to a drug-abusing mother. Like Elisa, Emily also had several siblings who had repeatedly been placed in foster care. Like Elisa, Emily lived in squalor and deprivation:

The house had no heat, there was no food in the cupboards, and the beds were littered with animal excrement.

Unlike Elisa, however, Emily did not live long enough even to see her first birthday. On March 13, 1995, the 9-month-old Connecticut infant was left in the care of her mother's boyfriend, a drug abuser with a lengthy criminal record. While bathing Emily, the boyfriend raped the baby, and she died 3 days later from injuries sustained in the sexual attack.

Subsequent investigation revealed that Emily had been the subject of three substantiated child abuse reports. Just 3 weeks before she was killed, Emily suffered a broken leg, which was reported to authorities, who accepted her mother's claim that the fracture was the result of an accident. ❖

❖ In August 1984, Anthony and Gwendolyn Mikell were investigated for allegedly abusing their first child, who was then 2 weeks old. That child and two others all tested positive for cocaine when they born. Despite a decade or more of child abuse complaints against them, the Mikells managed to get their children back from foster care.

Kevin, next to the youngest of the four children, was placed in foster care at the age of 10 days in an effort to separate him from his drug-addicted mother. His father, also an addict, completed a drug rehabilitation program and then successfully petitioned the court for custody of Kevin, who was then 10 months old. In granting custody of the infant to Mr. Mikell, the Family Court judge noted that he had already been caring for his two older daughters without evidence of abuse or maltreatment and that the Child Welfare Administration had expressed confidence that Kevin would receive similar care. Kevin's younger brother, Kenneth, then less than a year old, remained in the custody of his mother, who was living in a New York City homeless shelter.

That was in summer 1994. Thereafter, neighbors said they regularly heard sounds of beatings coming from the apartment Kevin shared with his father and two older sisters, 6-year-old Kelly and 11-year-old Antoinette. On February 20, 1996, the abuse ended—at least for Kevin. On that day, his father forced the 2-year-old to sit on a toilet for more than 12 hours in a futile effort to toilet train the boy.

While the boy sat on the "potty," his father alternately struck him and fed him. When the ordeal was done, Kevin Mikell was found in the apartment by paramedics summoned by a neighbor. Kevin was unresponsive and bruised; his arm was dislocated and there were cigarette burns on his body. He appeared to have been dead about 4 hours. An autopsy revealed that the toddler died from blows so hard that they caused a brain hemorrhage and tore the boy's intestines. ❖

❖ Rufus Chisholm thought that by using physical force to reprimand his children he could keep them from becoming criminals and drug abusers. At least that is how he explained his treatment of his 5-year-old son, Adam Mann, who was pronounced dead on arrival at a New York hospital on March 5, 1990.

For years, Chisholm had brutally abused Adam. In the weeks leading up to the boy's death, Chisholm repeatedly beat the youngster for eating cake in the middle of the night. Chisholm, who estimated his weight at 275 pounds, admits that on March 5 he caused the boy's death. But his story differs greatly from that of his other sons, who saw what he did to Adam that day.

Chisholm says he awoke to find that Adam had gotten into the cake again. He says that when he found Adam asleep, he put his knee into the boy's back. According to his account, Adam began to cry, and Chisholm thought he was choking on food. He soon realized that the boy was dying.

Apparently unknown to Chisholm, Adam's three brothers witnessed Chisholm hang Adam from a coat rack and punch him as he begged for mercy. Autopsy results supported the boys' account: Adam's body was riddled with welts, cuts, and bruises. He had been beaten so severely that his liver was nearly torn apart.

Rufus Chisholm pleaded guilty to manslaughter and was sentenced to serve from 7 to 14 years in prison. In 1996, as Chisholm approached his first eligibility for parole, he indicated that when released he would seek to resume custody of his surviving children.

Amazingly, his pursuit of custody was briefly supported by a report from the social services department recommending that the boys be returned to their parent rather than freed for adoption. Chisholm's hopes were dashed, however, when the chairman of the New York State Parole Board promised that if Chisholm were ever paroled, it would only be granted on the condition that he could not live with his children. ❖

❖ On Super Bowl Sunday in January 1996, Teresa Sulsona left her New Jersey home to buy snacks for a game-time gathering. When she went shopping, Mrs. Sulsona left her 2-month-old son, Michael, in the care of the boy's father, also named Michael Sulsona.

When Mrs. Sulsona returned, she was unable to arouse the infant. She called the family pediatrician, who advised allowing the boy to sleep awhile longer. When it became obvious that something was seriously wrong with the child, the Sulsonas called an ambulance. The baby was taken to a local hospital where he died two days later. Police investigators said the boy died from Shaken Baby syndrome—internal injuries resulting when a very young infant is shaken vigorously.

Pressed by police investigators, Michael Sulsona admitted that he had shaken the child. According to authorities, Michael Sulsona was watching a pregame show on television when the baby started crying. They said that Sulsona then shook the infant about 10 times.

Later, while Sulsona awaited trial on criminal charges, his attorney emphasized that the injuries were the result of an accident, that Sulsona loved his son, and that the young father had never meant to hurt the boy. ❖

❖ Separated for 4 years, Maggie Davila obtained a restraining order against her estranged husband, José. Although the Massachusetts court's mandate kept José Davila away from her, it did not deny him continued access to the couple's two children. Exercising his weekend visitation rights, Davila picked up his sons, 8-year-old Alberto and 4-year-old Joshua, on Friday, August 28, 1992. The next morning, he returned the boys to their mother but picked them up again around noon.

At 7:00 that evening, Davila called his wife and told her that if she did not resume their relationship she would never see her sons again. Maggie Davila called the police, who failed to find Davila and the boys.

José Davila was not located until the next day when, at about 1:45 p.m., New Hampshire police found him on a highway overpass, threatening to throw himself off. Once officers talked Davila down, he told them where to find his sons. When Massachusetts police entered the motel room specified by Davila, they found the bodies of both boys. Alberto had been stabbed repeatedly and Joshua strangled.

After the killings, neighbors said they suspected that Davila had abused the boys. One neighbor recalled how Davila yelled at his sons. Another said he often saw Joshua with a black eye.

José Davila was charged with two counts of first-degree murder. A jury rejected his psychiatric defense and convicted him on both counts. In September 1994, he was sentenced to two consecutive life terms without hope of parole. ❖

INCIDENCE AND PREVALENCE
OF FATAL MALTREATMENT

Elisa Izquierdo, Emily Hernandez, Kevin Mikell, Adam Mann, baby Michael Sulsona, and the Davila brothers are just a few of the children killed each year by child abuse. In 1995, there were 1,215 documented cases in which children in the United States died from abuse and/or neglect.[1] Although 1,215 represents a slight decrease from 1994, it still represents a 40 percent increase in abuse/neglect fatalities since 1985.[2] Perhaps even more significant is the finding that among these 1,215 children, 46 percent had previously been (or were at the time of their deaths) under investigation by child protective agencies.[3]

Since not all deaths of young children are fully investigated, many believe that these documented fatalities seriously underestimate the number of actual cases in which children die as a result of abuse and/or neglect. For example, in 1993, Dr. Phillip McClain and his colleagues published a report integrating data from death certificates with data from the FBI's Uniform Crime Reports. These researchers concluded that in the decade from 1979 to 1988, the annual number of abuse/neglect fatalities ranged from 861 to 1,814.[4]

WHO ARE THE VICTIMS
AND THE PERPETRATORS?

A variety of studies have examined the details of these abuse/neglect fatalities and shed light on who the victims and perpetrators are and why these deaths occur.

As might be expected, the perpetrators in these cases are nearly always the child's caretakers. As Dr. Murray Levine and his colleagues summarized after reviewing the relevant studies, "Perpetrators of maltreatment fatalities were most often the child's natural parents. This is followed by caretaker paramour, where most perpetrators were male. Seldom did a fatality involve a father's girlfriend."[5]

According to Levine et al., not only are males "predominantly the perpetrators in abuse-related fatalities" but "the presence of a male in the household increases the risk of maltreatment-related fatalities, especially from physical abuse."[6] Indeed, they cite one Colorado study of child maltreatment fatalities in which "80 percent of deaths from head and body trauma were attributed to male perpetrators."[7]

There have been few systematic efforts to characterize men who kill their children, but Dr. J. F. Campion and colleagues described 12 such men who were examined in a forensic unit between 1970 and 1982.[8] Although the sample may have been skewed by its nature (i.e., homicidal fathers who were referred for forensic psychiatric evaluations) the description provided by these researchers does shed at least some light on men who kill their children. For the most part, the men in the Campion et al. sample had been raised in situations of great stress, including parental violence, abuse, separation, and/or death. Three-quarters of these men had neurological or psychiatric disorders as children, several had been physically or sexually abused, and a number of them had been placed outside their homes due to their own aggressive behavior and/or their parents' incompetence.

Although the popular image of the parent who kills his or her child seems to be that of the teenage offender, in fact few perpetrators of fatal child abuse are in their teens. Two recent studies found that between 40 percent and 50 percent of these perpetrators were in their 20s, while 6 percent or fewer were under the age of 18.[9]

Researchers have also identified two age groups of children most at risk to die as a result of homicide: adolescents and children under the age of 4. According to a review of the literature by Levine and his colleagues, "75 percent or more of maltreatment-related fatalities occur in children under the age of four."[10] As Levine et al. note, although deaths of adolescents generally "can be described as extrafamilial and the perpetrator is rarely a . . . caretaker, deaths of younger children are more often 'intrafamilial' " and "can be attributed most often to fatal child abuse and neglect."[11]

CLASSIFYING FILICIDE: WHY DO PARENTS KILL?

Several researchers have attempted to classify cases of filicide (parents killing their children) by cause or motivation.[12] Combining these classifications, these killings may be grouped as follows: (1) battering deaths; (2) homicides committed by the mentally ill; (3) infanticide/neonaticide; (4)

retaliation homicides; (5) killings of unwanted children; and (6) mercy killings.

Mercy killings, infanticide/neonaticide, and killings of unwanted children are examined in other chapters of this volume. Child abuse deaths of the sort examined in this chapter generally fall into one or more of the following categories: battering deaths, homicides committed by mentally ill parents, and retaliation homicides.

Battering Deaths

Most child abuse killings fall into the category of battering deaths. Occasionally, a parent will deliberately kill his or her child. For example, there are recorded cases in which parents have intentionally killed their children to collect life insurance proceeds. But most child abuse killings seem to result from misguided, albeit sometimes brutal, efforts to discipline, punish, or quiet children.

In many of these cases, the parents have already been abusive to the child killed and have been reported to and/or investigated by child protective authorities. In some of these cases, the children have even been removed from their abusers but returned by courts and child welfare authorities, only then to be beaten to death.

Often the perpetrators in battering deaths are individuals who have never learned any way other than physical abuse to discipline their children. In many instances, the ultimate killing might best be characterized as corporal punishment run amok. The parent tries to discipline the child physically, loses control, and ends up beating the child to death.

Not surprisingly, researchers have identified two particular developmental "triggers" of fatal child abuse among young children: toilet training difficulties among toddlers and colic among infants.[13]

Toilet training a toddler, even in the best of circumstances, requires patience and perseverance. Many parents lack both of these qualities when it comes to training their children. Moreover, many parents seem to have unrealistic expectations about when and how quickly toilet training can be accomplished. As a result, these parents try unsuccessfully to force training upon a youngster who is not developmentally ready to be trained.

The inevitable frustration in such cases leads some parents to become physically and psychologically abusive to their children. In some cases, such as that of Kevin Mikell described earlier, this abuse turns deadly.

Colicky infants cry without apparent cause and often create great distress for parents and others around them. An unfortunate response among some parents is shaking the infant in an effort to quiet him or her. As in the Sulsona case described earlier, the result may be serious internal injury or death from Shaken Baby syndrome.

Shaken Baby syndrome—first described in 1972 by pediatrician Dr. John Caffey—is the single most common cause of brain damage in infants.[14] The syndrome occurs when the baby's body is shaken so vigorously that the head is repeatedly jerked from front to back, thereby causing internal bleeding and swelling in the brain, brain stem, and/or spinal cord. The results of such injury can include loss of hearing and sight, paralysis, seizures, neurological dysfunction, cerebral palsy, mental retardation, and, in some cases, death. Twenty to 25 percent of those babies suffering from the syndrome die as a result.[15]

In some instances of Shaken Baby syndrome, parents claim they did not realize they were injuring the child. Many experts, however, believe that to cause the syndrome, shaking must almost always be violent, and should always be considered a serious form of child abuse.

Homicides Committed by Mentally Ill Parents

Defined broadly, "mental illness" probably accounts, at least in part, for many child abuse fatalities. To put it another way, many, perhaps most, parents who beat their children to death suffer from one or more diagnosable mental disorders.

One clear example of such a case seems to be the brutal killing of Elisa Izquierdo. Even though the perpetrator, Awilda Lopez, was a crack cocaine addict who had previously battered Elisa, Lopez apparently suffered from psychotic delusions that Elisa was possessed by the Devil.

A number of researchers and clinicians have written of psychotic parents who kill their children, but those cases seem to present a rather small and distinct minority. Psychotic infanticide and filicide perpetrators are most likely to be women suffering from postpartum psychosis. Parents who batter their children to death seem more likely to suffer from nonpsychotic mental illnesses such as personality disorders, impulse control disorders, mood disorders, anxiety disorders, and/or substance abuse disorders.

Many who batter their children to death also probably qualify for a diagnosis of antisocial personality disorder.

Retaliation Homicides

The final and perhaps most unusual kind of battering filicide is the so-called retaliation killing. As Pitt and Bale have explained, in these cases "aggression directed at the child [is] displaced from the spouse."[16] And, as they note, the Greek myth of Medea is often used as an example: "Medea killed her two sons after discovering her husband's infidelity. She then told him, 'Thy sons are dead and gone. That will stab thy heart.' "[17]

Undoubtedly, many if not most of the perpetrators in these cases suffer from diagnosable mental disorders. However, the killing most often appears to result more from a desire to inflict harm upon the child's other parent than from any underlying psychopathology.

The case of José Davila cited earlier is perhaps a classic example. Prior to murdering his two young sons, he phoned their mother and told her that if she did not go back with him, she would never see her children again. At one point following his arrest, Davila was found to be mentally disturbed and incompetent to stand trial. However, once his competence was restored, a jury rejected his claim that the killings were the result of mental illness.

CHAPTER ✦ EIGHT

Parricide

✦ For more than 20 years, Lonnie Dutton had been the town bully in Rush Springs, a farming community of 1,700 people, southwest of Oklahoma City. As a youngster, he assaulted a hitchhiker and then urinated on the man. As a grown man, he brutally abused his wife and children, stabbed and shot at his father, and terrorized his neighbors. A hard-drinking, drug-abusing, 200-pound brute with a shaved head and menacing mustache, Dutton routinely carried a 9 mm. pistol in the bib of his overalls and threatened anyone who got in his way.

For years, Lonnie Dutton beat his wife. He even forced his young children to strike, bite, and throw darts at her. When, after 14 years of abuse, she left him, Lonnie branded her an unfit mother and convinced a court to give him custody of their four children. For the next 4 years, he kept the children in an isolated trailer with no electricity, no phone, and no running water. They were allowed to go to school but nowhere else. All visitors were forbidden—and for good reason. Behind closed doors, Lonnie beat the children with rubber hoses, fists, and two-by-fours, slapped them, and kicked them in the groin.

At times Dutton sent his children out to shoplift and gave a beating to the one who came back with the least loot. Other times, he made them play "William Tell," a "game" in which he got drunk and then lined them up against the wall and ringed their heads with bullets. On still other occasions, he locked them out in the cold.

During Lonnie Dutton's reign of terror, neighbors reported hearing the children screaming and pleading at all hours of the day and night. One neighbor made more than 50 complaints to law enforcement and child protective authorities. On at least six occasions, officials visited the trailer, the walls and ceilings of which were riddled with bullet holes. When the children denied being abused, the authorities dropped their investigations.

For their part, Dutton's children were quiet, studious, and well behaved. They caused no trouble and stood out at school only because of the odd way they seemed to cling to one another and the fact that they often showed up with bruises and other injuries. In fact, the two older children loved school so much that when they missed the bus they would walk the 5 miles to get to school.

Lonnie Dutton's abuse of his children ended abruptly on July 12, 1993, when his two older boys shot him in the head with a deer rifle while he slept. Fifteen-year-old Herman held the barrel to his father's head while 12-year-old James pulled the trigger. Moments earlier, the boys had learned from their 10-year-old sister, Alicia, that Lonnie had sexually abused her.

After the shooting, Herman, James, Alicia, and their 8-year-old brother jumped into the family pickup truck and drove to the nearby home of relatives, where the two older brothers told a cousin they had just killed their father. One of the boys later asked if they had done the right thing.

Although the boys were charged with first-degree murder and conspiracy, within days of the killing more than 200 Rush Springs residents rallied in a local school auditorium, pledging support for the boys and urging authorities not to punish them. Ultimately, the prosecutor agreed to allow Herman and James to plead no contest to manslaughter charges. A juvenile court judge accepted the pleas and agreed to dismiss the charges altogether if the boys remained law abiding until April 1996. The boys and their two younger siblings were then placed in therapeutic foster homes. ❖

❖ Brenda Freeman of Pennsylvania feared her two sons, 17-year-old Bryan and 15-year-old David, who abused drugs and alcohol, shaved their heads, associated with neo-Nazis, and repeatedly threatened their parents. One day at dinner, the two, each of whom stood more than 6 feet tall, showed up with tattoos on their foreheads. One tattoo read "Seig Heil" and the other "Berserker."

Mrs. Freeman called psychologists and other mental health professionals and even contacted the Anti-Defamation League in her efforts to understand and control her sons. When she spoke to the director of the ADL, Mrs. Freeman sounded desperate. According to Barry Morrison, who took her call, Mrs. Freeman thought it was just a matter of time before something terrible happened.

Morrison recommended psychological counseling. When he called back later to follow up on the situation, he repeatedly got a busy signal. The next day, February 27, 1995, he learned just how desperate Mrs. Freeman was and how accurate her forecast had been. The day before, authorities had found the bodies of Mrs. Freeman, her husband, and their 11-year-old son, Erik. All three had been brutally stabbed and bludgeoned.

A knife had been driven 5 inches into Mrs. Freeman's back and a pair of shorts shoved into her mouth, apparently to stifle her screams. Mr. Freeman and Erik were found dead in their beds, Mr. Freeman's face beaten beyond recognition. Scattered throughout the home were the bloody weapons: a knife, a baseball bat, a metal bar from a weightlifting machine, and the handle of a pickax. Missing from the home were Bryan and David.

Three days later, the Freeman brothers were arrested along with a cousin in Hope, Michigan. They were charged with murder and returned to Pennsylvania to stand trial. Before trial, however, both boys pleaded guilty to murder and were sentenced to life in prison without parole. Both had previously been examined by a psychologist and a psychiatrist, whose conclusions did not support a defense of insanity. ❖

❖ Four days after the Freeman brothers murdered their parents, their small Pennsylvania community was rocked by yet another double parricide. On March 2, 1995, just a 10-minute drive from the Freeman home, 16-year-old Jeffrey Howorth shot and killed both his parents.

After writing a note to his brother in which he said he wanted a movie made about him after he had killed everyone, Jeffrey used the family's .22 caliber rifle to ambush his parents as they arrived home at around 5 p.m. Jeffrey fired nine shots into his father and five into his mother before taking off in their Chevrolet Lumina. A day later, police located the car in Missouri. Nearby they found Jeffrey. In his possession at the time were one .22 caliber rifle, a shotgun, and some 600 rounds of ammunition.

The community was shocked to learn that Jeffrey had killed his parents. Unlike the Freeman brothers, Jeffrey had never been in any trouble. Prior to the killing, Jeffrey had been an above-average student. He was a Boy Scout, took some honors courses, belonged to the high school swim team, and was active in his church. What friends, neighbors, and others did not know, however, was that the shy youngster had a learning disability, suffered from major depression, had long struggled with feelings of inferiority, and, according to a forensic psychologist who examined him, lacked the ability to cope.

Jeffrey's distress was compounded by academic woes: The day before the killings he received his SAT scores, which were below average. On the day of the killings, he received an "F" on a quiz in Spanish. A psychiatrist who subsequently examined him reported that Jeffrey had intended to go home from school that day and kill himself. Instead, the psychiatrist said, he turned his rage on his parents.

Prosecutors claimed that the killing was inspired by the earlier Freeman murders; defense attorneys claimed Jeffrey Howorth's acts were the product of mental illness. After a hard-fought trial, jurors deadlocked twice before ultimately finding Jeffrey not guilty by reason of insanity. ❖

INCIDENCE AND
PREVALENCE OF PARRICIDE

Each year in the United States, more than 300 parents are killed by their children.[1] Annually, since 1976, between 1.5 percent and 2.5 percent of all homicides in the United States have been parricides.[2]

Generally available data such as the FBI's Uniform Crime Reports do not go much further in specifying the nature of these crimes. However, Dr. Kathleen Heide recently analyzed the FBI Supplementary Homicide Report (SHR) data for the decade between 1977 and 1986 and reached a number of conclusions about the nature of parricide in the United States: (1) Murdered parents and stepparents are "typically white and non-Hispanic"; (2) on average, victims tend to be in their late 40s and 50s, with stepparents younger than parents; (3) the majority of perpetrators are White, non-Hispanic males; (4) more than 70 percent of those who killed fathers, stepfathers, or stepmothers are younger than 30; and (5) nearly 70 percent of those who killed mothers are between 20 and 50.[3] Heide also found that among parricide victims "15 percent of mothers, 25 percent of fathers, 30 percent of stepmothers, and 34 percent of stepfathers were killed by sons and daughters under 18."[4]

Although the percentage of parricides committed by juveniles is relatively low, it is significantly higher than the percentage of all criminal homicides committed by juveniles. In recent years, in the United States, only about 10 percent of all criminal homicides have been committed by youngsters below the age of 18.[5]

ABUSED CHILDREN
KILLING ABUSIVE PARENTS?

Parricide is not a subject that has been well researched. Most of the professional literature on the subject consists of case studies and analyses of small samples of convenience—generally cases of perpetrators evaluated and/or treated by the author, who is usually a psychologist or psychiatrist. Although relatively few in number, however, these reports emphasize a common theme: "Youngsters who kill a parent have generally been severely victimized by that parent."[6]

Paul Mones, an attorney and author who has made a specialty of defending children who kill their parents, believes that most of these youngsters have been severely abused by the parent(s) they killed. Mones paints a chilling profile of the typical adolescent parricide offender—a profile that certainly fits the case of Herman and James Dutton described above:

> They are raised in homes where chaos and persecution are the order of the day. These children exist on the extreme end of the child abuse spectrum, most being victims of what I call "poly-abuse." Not only have they typically been physically, mentally, and often sexually abused since they were very young (oftentimes since infancy), but they have witnessed the repeated abuse of other family members as well.[7]

Heide, a criminologist, concurs with Mones. Although she notes that some young parricide offenders are severely mentally ill and/or dangerously antisocial, she reports that

> the severely abused child is the most frequently encountered type of adolescent parricide offender. . . . In-depth portraits of such youths have

frequently shown that they killed because they could no longer tolerate conditions at home. These children, typically adolescents, were psychologically abused by one or both parents and often witnessed or suffered physical, sexual, and verbal abuse as well.[8]

OTHER FACTORS IN PARRICIDE

In her own study of juvenile killers, Heide included seven cases of parricide. Six of the seven were boys; all were White; and they ranged in age from 12 to 17. These seven offenders had killed six fathers, three mothers, and one brother. All killings were committed with guns, which Heide described as "readily available."[9] Six of the seven youthful parricide offenders had been abused by their parents, five severely. The single female offender had been sexually abused and forcibly raped by her father. All six abuse cases also included evidence of "confirmed alcoholism or heavy drinking in the home."[10]

Finally, after reviewing her own study and those of others, Heide identified 12 characteristics associated with adolescents who kill their parents:[11]

- ❖ A pattern of violence in the family
- ❖ Failed efforts by the adolescents to get help
- ❖ Failed efforts by the adolescents to escape from the family situation
- ❖ Isolation and fewer social outlets among these adolescents
- ❖ A family situation that became increasingly intolerable
- ❖ Increasing feelings of helplessness on the part of these adolescents
- ❖ Inability to cope with increasing stress, leading to a loss of self-control
- ❖ Adolescents with little if any prior involvement with the criminal justice system
- ❖ Ready availability of a gun as a major factor in the homicide
- ❖ Alcohol abuse and/or alcoholism in the home
- ❖ Evidence that the adolescent offender may have been in a dissociative state at or near the time of the killing
- ❖ Evidence that the adolescent offender and other family members felt relieved by the victim's death

FAMILY CONSPIRACY?

With regard to this last characteristic—family feelings of relief at the death of the victim—it should be noted that Sargent, Ewing, and others have observed what has been called a "family conspiracy" in some cases of adolescent parricide.[12] In a classic article on this issue, Sargent speculated that "sometimes the child who kills is acting as the unwitting lethal agent of an adult (usually a parent) who unconsciously prompts the child so that he can vicariously enjoy the benefits of the act."[13] Sargent cited a number of cases in support of this hypothesis, including one in which an 8-year-old shot and killed his abusive father after the boy's mother repeatedly wished aloud that the father would die.

Ewing cites two such cases.[14] In the first, a 16-year-old initially refused his mother's request that he kill his abusive father but then agreed and shot the man to death when the mother threatened to kill herself unless the boy killed his father. In the second case, a 17-year-old was charged with accessory to the murder of his stepfather, a man who had repeatedly abused him and his mother. This boy's mother had told him that she would give $50 to have her husband killed. The boy conveyed this "offer" to a friend, who passed it on to another youth, a 19-year-old who took the offer seriously and gunned down the stepfather. The boy, his mother, and the shooter all pleaded guilty to various homicide charges.

Ewing also notes that "even where there is no 'conspiracy,' explicit or implicit, between parent and child, the killing of one parent to protect the other parent is not an uncommon scenario in juvenile parricide."[15]

Again, Ewing cites two cases as examples. In the first, a 3-year-old boy watched as his intoxicated father beat his mother and threatened her with a pistol. When the man laid the pistol on a table, the boy grabbed it and shot him to death. Later, the boy told authorities, "I killed him. Now he's dead. If he would have hit my mother, I would have shot him again."[16] In the second case, a 15-year-old shot and killed his stepfather, who had abused the boy's mother for 14 years. At the time of the killing, the man was slamming the boy's mother into a metal door. The youth grabbed a gun and shot the man. Wounded, the stepfather released his wife and ran, but he was chased by the boy and shot three or four more times.

Occasionally, "family conspiracies" do not involve parents but siblings. As Ewing has observed, "When juveniles conspire with siblings to kill their fathers, the family dynamics generally seem to fit the typical patricidal pattern of paternal abuse."[17] Ewing refers to a case in which three brothers, ages 15, 13, and 10, conspired to kill their father, who forced them to live in squalor and treated them with "extreme cruelty."[18] Another such example, of course, can be found in the killing of Lonnie Dutton cited at the beginning of this chapter.

MENTAL ILLNESS AND PARRICIDE

Although juveniles who kill their abusive parents often suffer from emotional problems secondary to the abuse they have suffered, most are not seriously mentally ill. Nor are these youngsters usually antisocial. Indeed, many youngsters who kill their abusive parents appear to be "good kids." For the most part, they are conforming, do well in school, stay out of trouble, and give no evidence of psychopathology. Their homicidal acts result not from mental illness or personality disorder but, rather, as a response to the brutal abuse they have endured at the hands of those they ultimately kill.

Still, a small percentage of parricide perpetrators do seem to fit into other classifications. Heide has identified two other types of parricide offender: the "severely mentally ill" and "dangerously antisocial."[19] Maloney refers to the subtypes as "psychotic offenders"[20] and "psychopathic parricides."[21]

Although much of the professional and clinical literature on parricide has emphasized the seriously mentally ill offender, only a very small percentage of juveniles who kill their parents—or anyone else for that matter—are psychotic or otherwise seriously disturbed.

For example, among the seven parricidal youths examined by Heide, only one fit the profile of the "severely mentally ill child."[22]

In most of the cases fitting this "severely mentally ill" profile, the perpetrator has an extensive history of psychiatric impairment and treatment. As Maloney reports,

> First, these individuals almost always have a previous history of treatment for a serious mental disturbance. The history is usually corroborated by formal reports from mental health professionals, psychiatric hospitals or the like. Second, they are psychotic at the time of the offense. . . . Third, these individuals are usually overtly delusional at the time of the killing of their parents. . . . A fourth characteristic of these homicides is that the act of killing, itself, is bizarre.[23]

The case of "J"—a parricide offender in his late 20s—fits this pattern well. "J" killed his father and was seen by Maloney for a psychological evaluation. This young man had been treated for a psychotic episode after graduating from high school and had "serious psychological problems before that time."[24] Even though he had graduated from college, he had never been able to support himself independently and had been living with his father at the time of the killing. "J" also had a history of substance abuse, including the use of marijuana, LSD, PCP, cocaine, and alcohol.

In explaining why and how he killed his father, "J" first gave Maloney a long, rambling, and disorganized narrative about the Devil, baseball, the ocean, and evil. "J" said he believed that his father was "a great evil for living with me so long and lying to me and hiding my goodness from other people."[25] "J" then told Maloney that after his father ignored his request to commit suicide, "I went and got a knife and cut his head three-quarters off and cut a cross on his back."[26]

Heide describes a similar case in which the parricide offender was also clearly psychotic and delusional at the time of the killing. Nineteen-year-old Jonathan stabbed his mother 40 times, slit her throat, and tried to cut off her left hand "to demonstrate his allegiance to Satan."[27] Mental health experts who examined Jonathan concluded that he was extremely delusional, suffered from paranoid schizophrenia, and had acted in response to auditory hallucinations commanding him to kill his mother.

Interestingly, despite this evidence, Jonathan had been declared competent to stand trial and ultimately pleaded guilty to avoid putting his family through the stress of a trial.

Although in most cases involving psychotic or otherwise seriously disturbed parricide offenders, there is clear evidence of mental illness prior to the parricide, that is not always so. In some cases, even when parricide offenders are identified as psychotic or seriously mentally ill, they have no history of serious mental illness prior to the killing, and the diagnosis is made only after the parricide. This does not imply that the posthomicidal diagnoses in these cases are inaccurate, only that the perpetrator's mental illness may not have been apparent to others around him and/or may have become acute only immediately prior to the killing.

One classic example is the case of Jeffrey Howorth described above. Prior to killing both his parents and being acquitted by reason of insanity, Jeffrey had been an above-average student, member of the high school swim team, and maintenance worker at his church. He had never before been in any serious trouble. After the killings, Jeffrey was examined by mental health experts, who concluded that he suffered from severe depression when he killed his parents.

These experts maintained that, as a result of his depression and other emotional problems, Jeffrey had been unable to cope with increasing stress at school. They concluded that low SAT scores and an "F" on a Spanish quiz were among the stresses that drove Jeffrey to become suicidal and then homicidal.

ANTISOCIAL OFFENDER?
OR ABUSE VICTIM?

❖ Fifteen-year-old Gerard McCra III, known as Gerry, had been in trouble on and off since he was 6. According to his mother's half-brother, by that age Gerry was riding his bicycle in front of cars and throwing things at passing drivers. Another family member recalls that by age 11 Gerry had been banned from most nearby stores as a result of his shoplifting. In junior high school, Gerry was suspended for fighting and stealing a yearbook. In high school, he was suspended for carrying a knife and bringing a gun to school.

Gerry was finally admitted to a school for troubled youngsters near his Massachusetts home. But his problems did not cease. He ran away from home, stole cars belonging to a neighbor and his parents, continued shoplifting, and stole and fraudulently used a credit card belonging to one of his mother's friends. During an argument, Gerry shoved another youth to the ground, fracturing his skull. While the boy lay unconscious, Gerry continued to punch him.

Gerry's parents made excuses for his behavior and stood by him until October 9, 1993, the day Gerry broke into his grandparents' home, stole a gun, and then used it to kill his mother, father, and 11-year-old sister. After shooting each of his victims in the back of the head, Gerry hid the bodies, mopped up behind himself, and changed clothes. Within half an hour he was in a taxi on his way to pick up his girlfriend, who spent the night with him in his parents' home. The two had sex in a bedroom just across the hall from the room in which Gerry had hidden his mother's body.

Charged with first-degree murder, Gerry raised a defense based on claims of years of physical and psychological abuse and long-term use of Ritalin, a medication prescribed for hyperactivity in children.

Three relatives testified that they had seen Gerry abused by his parents. Gerry's grandmother testified that she saw Gerry's father slap his hand once when he was just 2 years old. On two other occasions, she said she saw Gerry's father hit his son in the chest and slap him on the mouth.

Gerry's uncle told the jurors he witnessed a late 1993 incident in which Gerry struck his sister with a broom handle. Gerry's father grabbed the handle and broke it over the boy's shoulder. According to the witness, Gerry shouted that he hated his father. His father replied that if he felt that way he should get a gun and shoot him.

After just over half an hour's deliberation, a jury convicted Gerry of three counts of first-degree murder, and the judge sentenced him to life in prison without parole. ❖

On the surface, both Gerard McCra III and the Freeman brothers might appear to fit what Heide and Maloney call the "dangerously antisocial" or "psychopathic" parricide offender. After making it clear that he is using the term "more in a colloquial than a technical psychological or psychiatric sense," Maloney describes the "psychopathic" offender as follows:

> In general, they do not have a history of child abuse, but there may be some deficit in terms of their early bonding and early relationship with their parent [which] may result in impairment in feelings of empathy and compassion for other persons. . . . These defendants are not grossly mentally disturbed. Conversely, upon psychological evaluation, their mental status appears to be essentially normal. Although there may be a history of drug or substance abuse, usually there is no history of treatment for serious mental disturbance. There may be some referral to counseling during the adolescent years primarily for lack of application in school or having conduct problems.[28]

It must be noted, however, that in the McCra and Freeman cases, as well as others in which there is a history of antisocial behavior on the part of the parricide perpetrator, the label "antisocial" or "psychopathic" (even if warranted) usually does not tell the entire story. Even in these cases, claims of child abuse should not be rejected out of hand in the search for causes of parricide. For example, as Heide notes,

> Children who have been abused and neglected may adopt an antisocial way of responding to life as a means of psychic, if not physical, survival. Antisocial behavior can focus their attention away from the problems at home that are too difficult to handle. When faced with an APO [adolescent parricide offender] with any history of acting out, the question whether the adolescent is truly sociopathic (that is, lacks a conscience), or whether he or she has adopted a pattern of acting out to maintain his or her fragile mental health is one best reserved for the mental health professional.[29]

Mones, the attorney who has represented several hundred adolescent parricide offenders, says of these young offenders, "They may try to cover up what is really going on. But when you scratch the surface, you find a significant history of abuse and other family dysfunction."[30]

All three experts, Heide, Maloney, and Mones, make it clear that many youthful parricide offenders do not fall neatly into a single classification. Many apparently antisocial offenders have been abused and/or neglected by their parents as have many mentally ill offenders. Still, all three agree that the most frequent common denominator in cases of parricide is a history of child abuse.

GREED AS A MOTIVE
FOR PARRICIDE?

Although most children and teenagers who kill their parents are victims of child abuse and kill their abusers to avert future abuse and/or avenge past abuse, occasionally individuals who kill their parents have another motive: greed. Rare, but not unheard of, are cases in which children kill their parents in the hope of gaining an early inheritance. In the words of Mones, these "infinitesimal few" parricide offenders are "hell bent on prematurely wrenching the family fortune from Mom and Dad."[31]

Not surprisingly, those who kill their parents for money are often children of the wealthy. Their crimes seem especially horrible not only because they are children of great wealth and privilege but because the money they kill for would eventually have been theirs anyway. The Menendez brothers, whose case was described in Chapter 1, are perhaps the best known parricide offenders alleged to have killed their parents to inherit their wealth. But they are not alone. Consider, for example, the cases of Martin Tankleff and Nicole Yesconis:

❖   Martin Tankleff was 16 years old when he bludgeoned and stabbed both his parents to death in their Long Island, New York home and then tried to pin the killings on his father's business partner.

Although he was raised in it and allegedly killed for it, Martin Tankleff was not born to wealth. His natural mother, who was going through a divorce, gave Martin up the day he was born, August 29, 1971. As fate would have it, a previously arranged adoption fell through at the last minute because the would-be adoptive mother became pregnant. Authorities scrambled, but only briefly, to find another home for the newborn.

When Martin was 4 days old, Seymour and Arlene Tankleff, a wealthy couple from Long Island, New York, adopted him and named him after Seymour's late brother. Seymour had suffered testicular cancer; Arlene had undergone a hysterectomy. Unable to have children of their own, the Tankleffs saw the adoption as a dream come true.

For the next 16 years, Seymour and Arlene showered Martin with attention and just about all the material things any youngster could ask for. Wherever his parents went—whether to formal dinners with other couples, business meetings, racetracks, or European vacations—Martin went too. Friends were always impressed by how devoted and close the Tankleffs were to their son. The family lived in a $700,000 home overlooking Long Island Sound, drove luxury cars, threw lavish parties, and belonged to exclusive yacht and country clubs. An only child, Martin got almost everything he asked for—whether it be an all-terrain vehicle or thousands of dollars worth of baseball cards.

On September 7, 1988, at about 6 a.m., what had once seemed like a dream come true became the worst of all nightmares. Asleep in her bed, 54-year-old Arlene was beaten and stabbed. Her throat was slit. Minutes later, 62-year-old Seymour was bludgeoned and stabbed as he sat working in his den after an all-night poker game.

At 6:15 a.m., Martin dialed 911 and told the operator he had awakened and found his mother apparently dead and his father barely clinging to life. Minutes later, he ran barefooted to the responding police car and greeted the officers, waving his bloody hands and screaming that someone had murdered his parents.

Detectives quickly became suspicious of Martin, despite his immediate efforts to blame his father's business partner for his parents' murders. Picking up on several relatively minor inconsistencies in Martin's accounts of what he had done that morning, investigators took him to police headquarters for further questioning. Once at the police station, investigating officers used a trick to get Martin to confess to the killings.

Although Seymour Tankleff did not die until a month after he was assaulted, he never regained consciousness. After questioning Martin and getting nowhere, Detective James McCready staged a telephone conversation in front of the teenager, pretending to hear that Seymour Tankleff had regained consciousness and had identified Martin as his assailant.

Martin Tankleff responded to McCready's ruse by confessing that he had set his alarm clock for 5:35 a.m., awakened, got up, stripped off his clothing, crept naked into his mother's bedroom, bludgeoned her with a barbell and slashed her throat, and then went to the study, where he did the same to his sleeping father. According to his confession, he then showered and called 911.

Why did Martin kill his mother and father? Police officers say he told them he was tired of driving the family's old Lincoln and wanted a newer and sportier car. Witnesses later testified that before the killings Martin had casually told them he could have any car he wanted if his parents were to die. Indeed, shortly after his father died, other witnesses said Martin bragged about an inheritance and promised to chauffeur them to a rock concert in a limousine.

Martin Tankleff maintained his innocence, went to trial, and testified that he loved his parents and had nothing to do with their deaths. According to one juror, the jury disregarded Tankleff's alleged confession because they believed the police had violated the boy's rights. Still, after 8 days of deliberations, the jury convicted Tankleff, and he was sentenced to 50 years to life in prison.

One juror explained that the guilty verdict was based largely on Martin's own testimony. The juror, a psychiatric nurse, said jurors did not concern themselves with the question of why Tankleff killed his parents. ❖

❖ On January 29, 1994, Robert Yesconis and his wife, Aletha, were looking forward to celebrating their fifth wedding anniversary less than a week away. That evening, they had invited 20-year-old Jennifer Nicole Yesconis, Robert's daughter by a previous marriage, to dinner. Nicole, as she was called, was to bring along her live-in boyfriend, 18-year-old Jeremiah Lee Wetmore.

Nicole never arrived. Instead, as the Yesconises prepared dinner, they were confronted by Wetmore and another youth, 17-year-old Michael Heath. Wetmore used a 9 mm. pistol to shoot Robert Yesconis twice in the head at close range. He then shot Aletha Yesconis once in the back as she tried to escape from the kitchen into an attached garage. The youths fled, and the bodies were not found until 2 days later.

Wetmore and Heath both admitted their involvement in the killings, pleaded guilty, and were sentenced to prison. At the same time, however, both men implicated Nicole in the murders, supporting the prosecution's contention that she masterminded the killings in an effort to collect on a $140,000 insurance policy on her father's life. Authorities claimed that Mr. Yesconis had supported Nicole for the previous several years and had even bought her a new car but had been planning to stop his financial contributions to her.

Nicole denied her alleged role in the killings and went to trial, where she testified that her father had sexually abused her as a child from age 4 to age 10. Nicole did, however, acknowledge that she stood to benefit financially from her father's death, that Wetmore had spoken about killing Mr. and Mrs. Yesconis, and that she had once told a friend she would pay him $30,000 to kill Mr. Yesconis. She added that this had not been a serious offer and that she was simply expressing her frustration.

After a lengthy deliberation, a Texas jury concluded that Nicole Yesconis had solicited the murder of her father and stepmother and convicted her of capital murder. ❖

As these and other similar cases make clear, at least some cases of parricide are arguably motivated by greed. But even in cases where the perpetrator had a clear economic motive to kill his or her parents, the quest for money, by itself, rarely if ever provides a fully satisfactory causal explanation. Undoubtedly, some of these young killers are abused children, acting out long-standing rage against their parents. Witness, for instance, the claims of Lyle and Erik Menendez that they were brutally abused by their millionaire father and Nicole Yesconis's allegation that her father sexually abused her for years.

Still other "greedy" parricide perpetrators appear to fall into the category Heide calls "dangerously antisocial."[32] Their homicidal acts, although immediately motivated by a desire to speed up their inheritances, are really a manifestation of their antisocial personalities.

Finally, of course, some "greed" parricides are committed by offenders who are both antisocial personalities and victims of abuse.

CHAPTER NINE

Fratricide and Sororicide

❖ Armstead Hollins, a Louisiana man, died on his 51st birthday May 5, 1996. His death was the result of a stab wound inflicted by his sister, 39-year-old Carol Sue Anderson. After following her brother to the home of a friend, where he was celebrating, Anderson argued with Hollins. Shoving and shouting at each other, the siblings, who lived together, ended up in the kitchen, where Anderson grabbed a small knife and thrust it into her brother's neck. Following the fatal stabbing, Anderson turned herself in to local police. ❖

❖ On December 30, 1995, 38-year-old Delbert Joy returned to the Northern California home of his 26-year-old brother, Gerald. Delbert, who was living with Gerald temporarily, had been drinking and was armed with a stick. Gerald asked him to leave. When Delbert refused and challenged his brother to a fight, Gerald grabbed a piece of lumber and struck Delbert on the upper arm and the side of the head. Delbert died from his injuries. Authorities concluded that Gerald had killed his bother in self-defense. Thus, no charges were brought against Gerald Joy. ❖

❖ LaVon Davis, a 39-year-old Omaha man, was also exonerated by reason of self-defense in the July 30, 1995 fatal shooting of his 49-year-old brother, Barry. Moments earlier, Barry had shot and killed another brother, 40-year-old Todd Davis. The killings followed a dispute at the home the brothers shared with their mother. The dispute arose when family members began to haul away junk that Barry Davis had stored in the house and garage. Investigators declined to press charges when they concluded that LaVon Davis shot his brother to prevent him from firing again at other family members. ❖

❖ To a neighbor who witnessed it, the July 3, 1995 squabble appeared to be nothing more than the usual brotherly argument. But it was an argument that ended with the death of two Detroit men: Richard Gibson, a 38-year-old water serviceman, and Allen Gibson, a 41-year-old barber.

The brothers had both moved back in with their father and often quarreled about sharing household chores. In the days leading up to their deaths, they argued about building a backyard barbecue pit. Richard planned to build the pit by himself, but Allen said that Richard could never do it on his own.

During a final heated argument on the front porch, Richard drew a .25 millimeter pistol, shot his brother, and then turned the pistol on himself. Both men died of gunshot wounds to the head. ❖

❖ Dana and Cary Jokela, who lived with their mother for years after their parents' divorce, frequently quarreled over who was in charge in their father's absence. On October 26, 1995, 18-year-old Dana beat 20-year-old Cary to death with a baseball bat after an argument about playing a video game. A few weeks earlier, Dana had dropped out of high school and moved out, but he was allowed to return to the family's Ohio home a week before the killing on the condition that he find a job. The county prosecutor allowed Dana to plead guilty to a reduced charge of manslaughter because of the history of violence between the two brothers. ❖

❖ Fraternal twins Dorothea and Mary Margaret Beck lived together in the same house in Alton, Illinois for all of their 68 years until, 2 days before Thanksgiving in 1995, Dorothea killed her sister. Responding to a call from Dorothea, police found Mary Margaret, clad in a nightgown, lying dead on the kitchen floor. Mary Margaret's body was covered with bruises, cuts, scrapes, and other signs of trauma from head to toe. Dorothea admitted beating her twin sister to death, apparently after an argument over Mary Margaret's refusal to eat. ❖

INCIDENCE AND PREVALENCE
OF FRATRICIDE AND SORORICIDE

Of the 8,063 murder cases in large urban counties recently surveyed by the U.S. Department of Justice, 123 (or 1.5 percent) were sibling killings.[1] More than 80 percent of the perpetrators and victims in these sibling homicides were adults (i.e., above the age of 19). The same study also revealed that roughly 85 percent of these killings were committed by males, while only 73 percent of the sibling victims were males. In 69.3 percent of these cases, the perpetrator and victim were of the same sex; 45.1 percent of female perpetrators killed sisters, and 73.6 percent of male perpetrators killed brothers. Approximately 65 percent of both victims and perpetrators were Black. Somewhat less than 40 percent of these killings were committed with firearms.

The Department of Justice report also found that more than a third of the perpetrators were unemployed when they killed siblings, 3.3 percent were classified as homeless, and 71 percent had prior criminal records (arrest(s) and/or conviction(s)).[2]

WHY DO SIBLINGS KILL?

Like many homicides, looked at solely in terms of the immediate precipitant, sibling killings often appear almost senseless. Why, for example, would one adult brother kill another over who was better qualified to build a backyard barbecue pit? Why would a quarrel over a video game result in a brutal beating with a baseball bat? Or why would two brothers die in a disagreement over the removal of junk from their mother's garage?

The answer may lie in the nature of the sibling bond and the long-standing rivalries and conflicts that so often mark the relationships between perpetrators and victims in cases of fratricide and sororicide.

Sibling Rivalry, Stress, and
Unresolved Conflicts

Of all the various familial relationships, those between siblings are undoubtedly the most competitive. From early childhood, siblings nearly always find themselves vying not only for parental attention and affection but also for status, power, and space within the home and family. Normally, by adulthood, sibling rivalries subside or at least are limited as brothers and sisters leave home and establish families of their own.

In some instances, however, especially where adult siblings end up living together and/or under the same roof as their parents, competition among them may continue if not intensify. Even though few adult siblings kill one another, it should come as no surprise that many who do—like Carol Sue Anderson, Gerald Joy, LaVon Davis, Richard Gibson, Dana Jokela, and Dorothea Beck—were living with their sibling-victims at the time of the killings. In these and similar cases, conflicts over space and/or control seem to have been major issues—conflicts that were never fully resolved between the siblings or were rekindled when they resumed living together.

In many adult sibling homicides, perpetrators are dealing not only with unresolved childhood conflicts and the stress of living with a brother or sister but often trying to cope with a variety of other problems in living. Indeed, in many cases, these other stressors—such as unemployment, divorce, substance abuse, and illness—have forced the perpetrator into a situation of being financially dependent on parents and/or the sibling who is eventually killed. In these cases, the event that precipitates the killing is often merely the "straw that breaks the camel's back."

Mental Illness

Still other cases of fratricide and sororicide seem clearly the result of long-standing and severe mental illness. Among the 123 sibling murders considered in the Justice Department study cited above, 17.3 percent involved perpetrators with a history of mental illness.[3] Consider, for example, the following New Jersey case in which a 35-year-old paranoid schizophrenic brutally murdered his 31-year-old pregnant sister.

On January 15, 1993, Terrance O'Brien followed his sister to a local post office, where, in front of a number of horrified onlookers, he repeatedly stabbed her with two serrated steak knives. Noreen O'Brien was stabbed at least 20 times from her eyes to her knees. Although witnesses pleaded with Terrance to stop stabbing his sister, he continued until confronted by an off-duty police officer who threatened to shoot him if he did not put down the knives.

At the time of the stabbing, Terrance O'Brien was on parole, having served a prison term for another stabbing a decade earlier. In that assault, O'Brien stabbed a man whose sister had spurned his advances.

Four days prior to stabbing his sister, O'Brien had been released from a psychiatric hospital and returned to his parents' home. O'Brien, who had a lengthy history of psychiatric hospitalizations, apparently realized that he was decompensating because on the very day he stabbed his sister he called the police and asked to be transported to a local mental health facility where he had previously been treated. O'Brien told the police that he was having dreams, hearing voices, and fearful that he could hurt someone.

While waiting to be seen, just 10 hours before the stabbing, O'Brien became impatient and left the mental health facility against medical advice after telling the staff that he was neither suicidal nor homicidal.

After stabbing his sister, O'Brien was taken to a nearby hospital, where surgeons struggled in vain to save Noreen's life. While waiting to hear the results of his sister's surgery, Terrance O'Brien told a police official that he felt he had to stop his sister because she was pregnant by a foreigner and would have given birth to a sick child. Later, when told that his sister was dead, O'Brien reportedly said that he was pleased.

Although both prosecution and defense attorneys agreed that O'Brien was mentally ill when he killed his sister, the jury rejected his insanity plea and convicted him of murder. He was sentenced to a term of 25 years to life in prison.

Alcohol and Other Substance Abuse

Like many nonfamilial homicides, intrafamilial killings often involve the abuse of alcohol or other substances. Among the sibling killings examined in the Justice Department report cited earlier, more than half the perpetrators and nearly 35 percent of the victims had been using alcohol at the time of the killing.[4] Although the data do not specify what percentage of these sibling homicides involved perpetrators and victims under the influence of substances other than alcohol, many adult sibling homicides appear to be motivated at least in part by abuse of drugs. Indeed, in many instances, both alcohol and other substances are implicated in the same case.

Consider, for example, the killing of a Utah man by his younger brother.

One of 13 children, 33-year-old Michael Dilello had a habit of getting drunk and assaulting family members. When he drank too much at a Mother's Day party and was ordered to leave his older brother Dino's home, he responded by giving Dino a concussion. At a later family celebration, Michael got drunk and punched his younger brother hard enough to send him to the emergency room.

Finally, on November 7, 1993, during yet another family get-together, after abusing a combination of whiskey and amphetamines, Michael slugged his girlfriend and yanked a fistful of hair from her head. His younger brother Joe, who witnessed this assault, fled the scene with Michael's girlfriend and drove her to his own home, where he armed himself with a loaded rifle and waited for Michael to show up.

Four hours later, Michael kicked in the door to Joe's mobile home. Joe responded by firing 14 bullets at his brother. The first shot fatally severed Michael's aorta, two struck him in the front of his body, and another seven ended up in his back. In a plea bargain, murder charges were dropped. Joe Dilello admitted acting recklessly and was sentenced to serve up to 10 years in prison.

Mad or Bad: Mental Illness? Or Antisocial Conduct?

❖ On December 12, 1995, an Arizona probation officer finished his report on 15-year-old Christopher McLeod, who had already been before the juvenile court on a variety of charges including running away, truancy, stealing a check, beating his mother with a belt, purse snatching, and twice stealing his mother's car. In his disposition report to the court, the probation officer recommended detention, saying he feared that Christopher would get into even more serious trouble unless the court took swift action to stop him.

Describing Christopher as a moderately dangerous youngster who liked to defy authority and break rules, the probation officer concluded that giving him more time to shape up would not be helpful.

Christopher was scheduled to appear in court again on December 14, 1995, when in all likelihood the judge would have followed the probation officer's recommendation and ordered the 15-year-old to detention. Unfortunately, the court's action was too late.

The night before his scheduled court date, Christopher was left at home to tend to himself and his sisters, a 3-year-old and a 10-year-old, while his mother went off to work. When his mother returned the next day, she learned that the 10-year-old, Seleana, a straight "A" student in the fourth grade, had never made it to school that day. The mother called the police, and they began a search for the missing girl.

Ten hours later, a police officer lifted the lid on a plastic trash can on the back porch. Inside he found Seleana's body. Christopher, who had taken off in his mother's car after telling her he had dropped Seleana off at school that morning, was apprehended by police the next day. Christopher told authorities that he had strangled Seleana with a telephone cord, dragged her body into a hallway, and raped her, all while his 3-year-old sister slept nearby. After the killing, he bathed the body, tossed it into the trash, and covered it with two plastic bottles and the head of a broom.

Asked whether he was sorry for what he had done to his sister, Christopher reportedly said he was not. Later, he told his mother that he had been using a drug, crystal methamphetamine, near the time of the killing. ❖

❖ On July 14, 1993, just two weeks before her 14th birthday, Hillary Norskog left her suburban Chicago home to party with some friends. When Hillary had not returned home the next morning, her mother made some inquiries and learned that she was last seen with 17-year-old Steven Pfiel. Hillary's mother, Marsha Norskog, called Steven, who claimed he had dropped the girl off at home the night before. Disturbed by Steven's attitude over the phone, Mrs. Norskog called back and was told by Steven's mother to leave her son alone.

Meanwhile, as dozens of searchers combed the area looking for the missing girl, police went to the Pfiel home, where they found Steven scrubbing away at red stains in the interior of his 1988 Chevrolet. Steven claimed that the stains were simply from a packaged fruit drink mix. Skeptical police officers searched the boy's home and found a number of bloody items, including a hunting knife. That same day Hillary Norskog's body was found in a field; she had been stabbed 13 times.

Steven Pfiel, the son of a meatpacking executive, was arrested, charged with first-degree murder, and ordered jailed pending trial. In October 1993, the court set bail at $1 million. On October 8, Steven's parents purchased a $100,000 bail bond and secured his release on bail.

When the Pfiels announced their intention to move to a neighboring state to avoid publicity and the negative reaction of the community, the court agreed and set stringent controls on Steven's behavior. The move was quashed, however, by a petition signed by more than 600 residents from the new neighborhood, protesting Steven's proposed presence in their small rural community. Instead, the family moved to another suburban area in Illinois, 30 miles from their original home.

On March 17, 1994, Steven's parents left their new home for the night, drove 50 miles to Chicago, and attended a St. Patrick's Day party. While they were out, Steven and his 19-year-old brother, Roger, celebrated by drinking. When Roger went to bed at about 3 a.m., Steven smoked some marijuana and then picked up a baseball bat and beat his sleeping brother to death, pausing to slit his throat with a meat cleaver. After killing his brother, Steven then attacked and raped his younger sister before fleeing the home in a pickup truck loaded with guns and camping equipment. Five and a half hours later, Steven turned himself in at the Town Hall.

Steven Pfiel ultimately pleaded guilty to two counts of murder and was sentenced to life in prison in a plea deal that allowed him to avoid any chance of the death penalty. Before and after his sentencing, a profile of Steven emerged from probation reports and the comments of his friends.

According to the probation report, Steven had not been abused and had gotten along well with his parents. As regards the brother he killed and the sister he raped, the report indicated that Steven described a good and close relationship with both siblings. Steven's probation report also indicated that he had been seen by a psychiatrist at the age of 9 and treated with Dilantin, an antiseizure medication. The report further indicated that Steven had begun drinking at age 11 and that by 14 was using alcohol three or four times a week. As for other drug abuse, the report revealed that Steven had acknowledged using marijuana, LSD, and several other substances.

According to one of Steven's friends, several months before stabbing Hillary Norskog, Steven showed him a hunting knife and talked about using it to stab someone in the head. Still other friends and acquaintances described how Steven abused drugs and alcohol, tried to run down animals with his car, and engaged in self-destructive, sometimes potentially lethal behavior. One youngster told of how Steven and others took turns hanging onto the hood of a car being driven at a speed of 80 miles per hour. Another described a so-called test in which Steven and other boys would hold lighted cigarettes between their arms to see who would pull away first. As a result, Steven reportedly had numerous burn marks on his arms.

In a lawsuit filed against Steven's parents in 1996, Hillary Norskog's mother alleged, among other things, that at the age of 7 Steven brutally beat a playmate, at 8 dropped bricks off an overpass onto vehicles passing below, and at 9 chased another child with an ax. Seeking to hold Steven's parents legally responsible for the murder of her daughter, Mrs. Norskog also alleged that while Steven was in junior high school he not only abused drugs and alcohol but developed a fascination with Hitler, shaved his head, joined a skinhead group, and was suspended from school at least seven times. ❖

❖ On October 11, 1994, 15-year-old Heather Gavette disappeared from the Burlington, Connecticut home she shared with her mother and 18-year-old brother, Derek. Her brother told police that Heather left the house while he was napping. According to Derek, Heather thereafter twice called home, asking for her mother.

For 9 days after Heather's disappearance, local police scoured the area around her home, using dogs, divers, and even an airplane to search for the missing teen. Schoolmates, neighbors, and family members were interviewed. Derek was even given a polygraph test, which he reportedly passed.

Stymied, police finally decided to look for clues in an unregistered car that was sitting on the Gavette property. Unable to locate a key to open the trunk of the car, they used a flatbed truck to haul the vehicle to police headquarters. Two days later, evidence technicians tore the back seat out of the car, gained access to the trunk, and were shocked to find the nude body of Heather Gavette. Heather had been shot in the back of the head and had apparently died instantly.

Questioned again, Derek Gavette confessed that he deliberately shot his sister while she was playing a video game. Derek told police that he then had sex with her body, burned her clothes, and dumped her corpse into the trunk of his car. After Derek confessed, his father revealed that the teenager had been sexually abused by a family member at the age of 8 and had been counseled extensively for mental health problems. ❖

Intentional sibling homicides generally occur in dysfunctional, frequently abusive families and are often committed by juveniles who are psychologically disturbed. Published clinical reports often emphasize the role of child abuse and neglect as causal factors in juvenile fratricide and sororicide. Dr. Kay Tooley, for example, has described two young children who made "murderous attacks" on siblings.[5] Six-year-old "Mary" had been left to baby-sit her younger brother beginning when she was 4 years old and had been sexually abused by her mother's boyfriend. Six-year-old "Jay" had been "neglected by a childish, self-centered mother and beaten by an immature and brutal young father."[6]

Similarly, Dr. Gregory Leong has described a case in which 16-year-old "Thomas" shot and killed his 14-year-old sister, "Jody," reportedly at her request.[7] Prior to the killing, "Thomas" had been physically abused by his mother and "shuttled back and forth" between his divorced parents as they fought for custody.[8] The 16-year-old had both a personal and a family history of depression, had been treated with antidepressant medication, and had previously tried to kill himself with assistance from his sister.

Clearly, in some intentional juvenile sibling homicides, the perpetrator is mentally ill, but the clinical literature on this phenomenon also includes many reports in which the perpetrators—like Christopher McLeod, Steven Pfiel, and Derek Gavette—were "ordinary," apparently normal youngsters with no evidence of serious psychopathology. Moreover, even where there is evidence of psychological disorder in such cases, often the perpetrator qualifies for a diagnosis of conduct disorder, which is sometimes the precursor to a later diagnosis of antisocial personality disorder.

"Accidental" Killings

Children who accidentally kill their siblings are sometimes mentally ill or conduct disordered, and many appear to come from dysfunctional abusive homes. Still, the major factors leading to accidental sibling killings appear to be parental neglect, the presence of firearms in the home, and substance abuse.

Many accidental sibling killings result from fires set by children playing with matches and lighters. For example, as early as 1959, Dr. Lauretta Bender reported on six cases of "evidently unintentional deaths" caused by fires set by the victims' siblings, who ranged in age from 5 to 12 years.[9] Although it is not clear that these children were neglected or given inadequate supervision, in other cases that appears to have been so. For example, Ewing has reported a case in which an 8-year-old boy was charged with homicide in the death of his sister, who died in a fire the boy set while playing with a lighter. At the time of the fatal fire, the boy was already under psychiatric care because he refused to stop playing with matches.[10]

By far, the most common accidental sibling killing is one that results from careless handling of a firearm, usually a gun found by the young perpetrator in the family home. In a number of these cases, parental neglect or failure to supervise is also a factor.

Consider, for example, the January 19, 1996 case in which an 8-year-old Illinois boy shot and killed his 7-year-old brother while playing with a .38 caliber semiautomatic pistol he found in the bedroom of his home. Four other children (all under the age of 8) were in the home at the time of the killing and were apparently unattended. Earlier, a neighbor had reported the children as neglected, and the family had been the subject of review by welfare authorities. Following the killing, a prosecutor filed juvenile court petitions alleging inadequate supervision and failure to protect the children. Thereafter, a judge ordered the children removed from the home and placed into protective state custody.

In another recent fatal sibling shooting, a 9-year-old Oregon fifth grader used his father's hunting rifle to kill his 5-year-old sister. Brandon Roses, who was baby-sitting, shot the younger child on June 23, 1995 when she refused his order to return to her room and take a nap.

The youngest person in Oregon history to be charged with murder, Brandon eventually pleaded guilty to manslaughter, which the law defines as reckless and not intentional homicide. Brandon was made a ward of the state, removed from the home, and ordered to undergo counseling. In sentencing the boy, the judge concluded that although Brandon was no murderer, the killing had not been merely an accident.

Another more recent case illustrates how substance abuse may also play a significant role in cases in which juveniles unintentionally kill their siblings with firearms. On March 21, 1996, 14-year-old James Gilligan shot and killed his 2-year-old half-brother in their Massachusetts home. According to the police, James, who was baby-sitting, smoked marijuana, drank beer, and then shot the younger boy in the back of the head while playing with a loaded revolver.

Although family and neighbors agreed that James adored his little brother and must have killed him accidentally, the prosecutor resisted the claim that the shooting was a simple accident. James, a high school athlete with no prior criminal record, was tried in juvenile court, entered a plea to delinquency charges, and was given a suspended sentence.

CHAPTER TEN

Familicide

❖ December 28, 1987: Except for the inevitable post-Christmas letdown, things seemed pretty much as they always did on Monday mornings in Russellville, Arkansas, a sleepy town of 15,000 about 80 miles northwest of Little Rock. Things stayed that way until just after 10 a.m. Thereafter, life in Russellville would never be the same.

Shortly after 10 a.m., Ronald Gene Simmons, a 47-year-old Vietnam veteran, walked into a local law office. Without saying a word, he pulled out a .22 caliber pistol, walked up to the receptionist, 25-year-old Kathy Kendrick, and shot her five or six times in the head. Then, just as calmly and quietly as he had entered, he left.

Minutes later, Gene, as Simmons was known, showed up at the Taylor Oil Company, about a mile from the law offices. Simmons threw open the door, burst in, and shot James Chaffin, a 33-year-old part-time employee, point-blank in the face. Before leaving, he also shot the owner, 38-year-old Russell Taylor.

From Taylor Oil, Gene went to a nearby convenience store. He had worked at the store, owned by Taylor Oil, until the week before, when he quit, complaining of low wages. Once in the store, Gene drew his weapon and fired repeatedly, wounding the manager and a clerk.

From the convenience store, Gene Simmons headed toward what turned out to be his final destination. Within 10 minutes, he shoved his way into the Woodline Motor Freight Company—another place he had once worked—and again started shooting. Gene shot and wounded one woman and took another hostage. Gene told the hostage not to fear because he had already done what he had set out to do.

The police, who had been one step behind Gene since the law office shooting, made it to the freight company just minutes after his arrival. Russellville's chief of police, Herbert Johnston, and his assistant chief, Ron Stobaugh, walked in and found Gene behind a glass door, holding two guns on his female hostage.

Chief Johnston asked Gene to give up. Simmons did so immediately and without a struggle. Forty-five minutes, two killings, and four woundings later, the deadly rampage was over.

Ronald Gene Simmons was calm and remained calm, even as he was booked, jailed, and charged with two murders and four attempts. He said nothing, did nothing, and responded to nothing. Indeed, police said he was completely mute and almost catatonic.

Putting the pieces together as best they could, police identified Gene Simmons and quickly figured out why Kathy Kendrick had been killed. Investigators learned that Gene had long been infatuated with Kendrick, a 25-year-old divorcée and former teenage beauty queen. Kendrick, who had earlier worked with Simmons at the freight office, had rebuffed his many advances and complained to their supervisor that Gene was harassing her. When the boss had reprimanded him, Gene abruptly quit the job.

The shootings at the oil company, convenience store, and freight office were not as easy to figure. Police surmised that they all had to do with Simmons's anger at former employers. Simmons had quit jobs at both the store and the trucking company, leaving hard feelings behind at both places.

Gene Simmons's catatonic-like state was almost but not quite complete. Police interrogators noticed very quickly that the one thing that got any response from him was asking about his family. Whenever they asked him how they could contact his family, his lip quivered.

The officers were not sure what that meant and not sure they wanted to find out. Still, after identifying Gene Simmons and learning the location of his remote, rural home, the police went there in search of more answers. Within hours of the morning's rampage, officers found themselves confronted with the results of an even more horrifying scenario.

Entering the house, situated on 14 acres of land about 15 miles from town, police found a decorated Christmas tree and numerous wrapped gifts. They also found five dead bodies: Gene's son and daughter, their spouses, and his 6-year-old granddaughter. The four adults had been shot to death and the 6-year-old smothered. All five appeared to have been killed sometime after Christmas Day.

Unable to account for six other members of the Simmons family, and fearing the worst, police resumed their search the next day. What they found was worse than what they had feared. First, they found a shallow grave covered with barbed wire and sheet metal. In the grave were seven dead bodies: Gene Simmons's wife, Becky, two of his sons, three of his daughters, and his 3-year-old granddaughter. Nearby, in the trunks of two junked cars, police found the bodies of Gene's two grandsons—21 months old and 20 months old—each one wrapped in a garbage bag.

The adults had been shot to death and the teenagers and children strangled or smothered. Authorities concluded that all nine had been killed a day or two before Christmas.

On Monday morning, Ronald Gene Simmons was just another Vietnam vet who had run amok. But by Tuesday afternoon, he had become known as the perpetrator of the largest family mass murder in the history of the United States. After finding the last nine bodies, police charged Gene with 16 counts of first-degree murder and 4 counts of attempted murder. From the start, the prosecutor made it known that he would seek the death penalty for Simmons. And from the start, everyone suspected that Ronald Gene Simmons was insane.

While Simmons was quickly remanded to the state hospital for a 30-day psychiatric examination, police and prosecutors sifted through the physical and psychological rubble he had left in his wake. What emerged was not a pretty picture but at least one that provided some clues as to why a man would so brutally murder his entire family and then terrorize their small town.

The first clues hit the police as soon as they entered the driveway to the Simmons property, even before they found any bodies. The isolated homesite—really nothing more than two mobile homes stuck together—was surrounded by a wall of cinder blocks, barbed wire, and "no trespassing" signs.

Later, police would learn that the wall, wire, and signs were erected by Gene Simmons not just to keep strangers out but also to keep his family in. Through interviews with neighbors and relatives, investigators discovered that Ronald Gene Simmons had been abusing his wife and children for years.

Gene not only beat his wife but virtually imprisoned her in the fortress he had constructed in the Arkansas woods. Becky Simmons was rarely, if ever, allowed outside the walls that surrounded the property. In a letter found after her death, she had written to her son that living with Gene was like being in prison.

Gene Simmons refused to allow the family to have a telephone or to receive mail. He had all mail delivered to a post office box, to which he alone had access. And he carefully monitored and censored all contacts with outsiders, especially family.

Their younger children attended school and, although described as unduly quiet and shy, actually did quite well academically. But they, too, were virtually prisoners in their own home. Gene ordered them to keep to themselves and refused to allow them to associate with other children. He drove them to the school bus stop, watched them as they waited for the bus, and then even followed them.

As the investigation continued, police learned part of what lay behind his obsession with privacy. Relatives told the authorities that Simmons was a fugitive from justice. He had moved his family to Arkansas in 1981 to avoid arrest and prosecution on incest charges in another state. The district attorney in Alamogordo, New Mexico, where the Simmons family had previously lived, confirmed that in August 1981 Gene Simmons had been indicted for having sexual intercourse with and impregnating his then 15-year-old daughter.

According to the DA, the sexual abuse had been reported to authorities by Simmons's son. The victim, Gene's pregnant daughter, confirmed the abuse but blamed herself. She then refused to testify before a grand jury and finally did so only when threatened with jail for contempt of court. After his daughter's reluctant testimony, Gene Simmons was indicted on multiple counts of incest.

As soon as the indictment was handed down, a warrant was issued for his arrest. Deputies went to his home to serve the warrant and arrest Gene, but it was too late. The house was abandoned. Unknown to the authorities, Gene Simmons had already fled with his family to the woods of Arkansas. The warrant was entered into the FBI's nationwide crime computer but never served because Gene never came to the attention of the law—never, that is, until he was arrested and charged with killing 16 people, including the daughter he had raped and impregnated and the child born of that incestuous union.

While Gene Simmons was at the state hospital undergoing psychiatric examinations, police also discovered that at the time of the killings Becky Simmons had been making plans to leave her husband.

Piecing all the evidence together, investigators concluded that Gene Simmons had somehow become aware of his wife's plans to leave him and possibly take the children with her. Police and prosecutors said that his fear of losing his family may have been what ultimately led Gene Simmons to kill them all.

After undergoing extensive psychiatric and psychological evaluations, Gene was found competent to stand trial. Refusing to plead insanity, he went to trial twice. In the first trial, he presented no defense, was readily convicted of killing two nonfamily members, and was sentenced to die.

Although Simmons publicly announced that he wanted to be executed before being tried for familicide, the state did not oblige. A little more than a year after he annihilated his family, Gene Simmons went to trial on 14 counts of murder. Although he again presented no defense and did not testify, Gene did give the jury a chance to see him in action. Toward the end of the trial, he jumped from his seat and punched the prosecutor, sending jurors and spectators ducking for cover. The next day, the jury convicted him of the additional murders and again sentenced him to die.

At 9:02 p.m. on June 25, 1990, after refusing to appeal his convictions or sentences and pleading for a swift execution, Ronald Gene Simmons was strapped to a gurney and given a lethal injection. Seventeen minutes later, the man who committed the worst family massacre in U.S. history was pronounced dead. ❖

❖ Until 1989, Robert Lynch had been a reasonably successful small business owner. His strip-mall bicycle shop netted him $20,000 to $30,000 a year, enough to pay for a home in a nice suburb of Cleveland and to support himself, his wife, and their three sons. But when nearby competitors with larger stores began to cut into the local bicycle market, Robert's income took a nosedive, and he began to look for someone to buy him out.

No longer able to keep up the payments on their ranch house, the family of five was forced to move first into a rented house and then into a two-bedroom apartment alongside a major highway. It was there that Robert's wife, Joy, learned that she was pregnant. Robert insisted that she have an abortion, but she refused to do so.

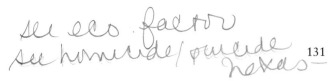

At about 2 a.m. on March 8, 1990, Karen Smith, who lived in the apartment next door to the Lynches, heard what she thought was a argument between Robert and Joy, followed by five loud noises.

Fifteen hours later, at about 5 p.m., the apartment complex manager learned of the incident and called the police. When officers entered the apartment, they found all five members of the Lynch family dead from gunshot wounds. Joy and the boys lay in their beds, and Robert was found slumped on a sofa in the living room, still holding the gun in his hand. On a table at the end of the sofa, they found a penciled suicide note bearing Robert Lynch's signature. ❖

❖ Just seven hours after the Lynch familicide-suicide, the same thing happened in another family less than 20 miles away. At about 9 a.m. the same day, in Painesville, Ohio, Bruce Clinton, an unemployed security guard, shot and killed his live-in girlfriend, Angela Green, and their two children before turning the gun on himself. Bruce, who had recently been released from a hospital where he was receiving psychiatric care, had learned a week earlier that Angela planned to leave him and take the children with her. At the time of the killings, Angela was in the process of moving out. ❖

❖ Willits, a quiet, rural California town of 5,000 residents, lies 150 miles north of San Francisco. By January 1994, the town's unemployment rate had reached 14 percent, nearly 50 percent higher than the state's overall jobless rate. For years, lumbering had been the town's economic mainstay. But when the lumbering industry died, so did most of the town's jobs. And so did the members of two of the town's families.

In August 1993, 21-year-old Ronald Trevor Harden, a local laborer who had pleaded guilty to being an accessory after the fact to murder, was free on $15,000 bail, living with his parents, and awaiting sentencing. Authorities alleged that Ronald provided first aid and fresh clothes to his brother, Troy, and helped his brother hide a bloody knife after Troy slit a man's throat.

As 22-year-old Troy Harden sat in jail awaiting trial on murder charges, his younger brother ingested a large quantity of an amphetamine known on the streets as "crank" and then killed his family and seriously wounded his best friend before committing suicide. Armed with a 12-gauge shotgun, Ronald Harden entered his family's home in Willits at 7:30 on a Monday morning and shot everyone in sight. After killing his mother, father, sister, and 16-month-old niece with shotgun blasts and nearly killing his best friend in the same manner, Ronald turned the 12-gauge on himself. ❖

❖ Six months after the Harden familicide-suicide, police were called to the home of Bruce and Barbara Sweazy by Mrs. Sweazy, who complained that her husband, a laid-off logging employee, had locked himself in a storage shed and was threatening to kill himself. After concluding that Bruce was not irrational, posed no immediate danger to himself or others, and could be cared for by his wife, the responding officers left.

The next time the police were summoned to the Sweazy home was less than 3 months later. Police were called by relatives who reported that they had not seen the couple or their children for 2 days and that no one answered the door at the Sweazy home even though the family's vehicles were parked in the driveway.

When police officers forced in the door of the Sweazy's well-kept home, they found the bodies of 33-year-old Bruce, 32-year-old Barbara, and their three sons: 12-year-old Joshua, 9-year-old Jacob, and 11-month-old Zechariah. From the physical evidence, police readily concluded that Bruce Sweazy had hacked his family to death with a single-bladed, long-handled ax and then shot himself in the chest with a pistol. At the time of the killings, Bruce had just returned to his job and had a prescription for, but apparently was not taking, Prozac, a widely used antidepressant medication. ❖

❖ Far from being unemployed laborers, Thomas Angst and Anthony Paul were, to all outward appearances, both highly successful professionals in Philadelphia—one an attorney, the other a physician.

Tom Angst, a 31-year-old attorney who specialized in handling the estates of deceased clients, lived with his wife, Cynthia, and 3-year-old son in a lavishly furnished $200,000 suburban home. The couple drove new cars and in June 1994 donated $10,000 to support the campaign of the Democratic candidate for governor.

But appearances can be deceiving, and all was not well with Tom Angst. On September 28, 1994, he told colleagues that he was being investigated by the state's legal disciplinary board. At the same time, apparently unknown to Angst, the local district attorney was looking into allegations that Tom had embezzled $700,000 from the estates of three clients.

After telling other lawyers in his firm that he would be giving up his law license for awhile and taking some time off to straighten out his affairs,

Tom left work, never to return. The following morning, after breakfast, he penned a suicide note, grabbed his .22 revolver and a handful of ammunition, shot his wife at least nine times, pumped five bullets into his son, and then shot himself in the head. ❖

❖ Like Tom Angst, Dr. Anthony Paul was also a well-respected professional in the greater Philadelphia area. A specialist in the treatment of intestinal cancer, the 49-year-old physician shared a life with his 48-year-old wife—a child psychiatrist suffering from severe arthritis—their 17-year-old severely retarded daughter, and a 12-year-old son until using his medical skills to commit familicide.

After leaving his secretary a sealed photocopy of what turned out to be a suicide note, Dr. Paul left his office at 4 p.m. on Monday, July 16, 1990. As he left, he instructed the secretary not to deliver the envelope to his office assistant until the next day. Anthony Paul then went home and sedated his wife and children; as they slept, he administered a deadly intravenous solution to each and then to himself.

At about 10 a.m. the next day, the physician's office assistant read the note left for her the day before and contacted the police. When police officers forced their way into the Paul home, they found each of the family members lying on a mattress with their arms attached to intravenous bottles. On a nearby nightstand, officers found the original copy of Dr. Paul's suicide note:

> I am writing this so that no blame should fall on anyone except me.
>
> I cannot go on with the present situation. There's only one solution. It must end with my death.
>
> Unfortunately, I cannot leave my wife and children to suffer at the hands of the "state." So they must join me too. As in life, in death we will be together.
>
> My wife has suffered incredible pain over the last five years due to arthritis of her spine with nerve compression which resulted in physical dependence on prescription pain medicine. I have supplied her with pain medicine because I could not bear to see her suffer because I love her so much. However she would not look upon it in the same light. They would point a finger at her and say that she is an addict. However there is medical evidence to prove what I say and she has been under the supervision of a specialist in physical therapy, who can prove that my wife was ill physically.
>
> My wife has recently become mentally unhinged by her pain, attempting suicide and being unable to sleep for the last seven days. This must stop!

My 17-year-old daughter is a brain-injured child who's been attending a special school all her life. She has the mentality of a one year old. She is also a severe asthmatic requiring medication around the clock. . . . Theodur 300 mg. every six hours. Brethine. Five milligrams every six hours.

I write this in case she's a survivor and I am dead.

My son is a gifted child but without two parents to care for him, his will be a life with frustration in foster homes, unloved, uncared for and ending up a misfit in society. I feel the most for him. It would be very hard dealing with his death.

I have no regrets! I have lived a good life, I have hurt nobody, I have loved my wife and children to the point that I was willing to sacrifice my career and my life for them.

Enough has been said. This is a suicide pact with three unsuspecting victims. But as in life, we must be together in death. All my personal papers are filed in a filing cabinet in my office at the Fox Chase Cancer Center. . . .

I am making a duplicate of this note and I am leaving it with one of my friends so there won't be any misunderstanding as to what happened. ❖

CIRCUMSTANCES AND MOTIVES IN FAMILICIDE

Familicides are almost invariably committed by men and nearly always followed by suicide. The typical familicide perpetrator is a White male in his 30s or 40s who reacts to extreme stress by killing his wife and child(ren) and then himself. Usually, the killings are committed with a firearm that belongs to the perpetrator and has been present in the home for some time.

As Dr. Peter Marzuk and his colleagues have written, "Typically the senior male who is depressed, paranoid, or intoxicated kills every member of his family, including his spouse, children, other relatives, and sometimes pets. The victims are usually shot, stabbed or strangled."[1]

Although homicidal motivation varies among men who kill their families, many if not most of them seem to share a number of personality characteristics that make them more prone than others to resort to familicide when under extraordinary stress. They are men who expect to be—and usually have been—in control. They appear to be have been overcontrolling and yet overly dependent on family members. They are men who have always perceived themselves as being at the center of the family and have viewed their families as extensions of themselves.

At the same time, however, they are likely to be men who view their families as having been at the center of their lives. Typically, they have an idealized or romanticized notion of family and strive to make their own families fit that image. When family members cooperate with or accede to their expectations, they are able to maintain the kind of "front" reported by friends, relatives, neighbors, and others after the killings—the close and loving, though perhaps overly closed and secretive, family. But when people, events, or some combination thereof alter the family portrait they have painted in their minds, and shaped through their control, they begin to feel threatened, if not overwhelmed.

Some clinicians and researchers have stressed the "dependent-protective" motives of men who kill their families and then kill themselves.[2] As Marzuk et al. put it, the familicide-suicide perpetrator often "commands a relationship in which he perceives that only he can satisfy the needs of the victims. When this relationship is threatened, he erupts in a frustrated homicidal-suicidal rage."[3]

In some familicides, the dynamics are similar to those of cases in which abusers kill their abuse victims. The abuser cannot or will not relinquish control. His domination of the family is threatened—often by family members' threats to leave and/or report his abuse to others—and he resorts to homicidal violence in a misguided effort to maintain his control and prevent a complete rupture of the family unit. The murders committed by Ronald Gene Simmons and Bruce Clinton may well have been such cases.

Most familicides, however, do not seem to fit such a pattern. While control is certainly a dynamic in most if not all familicides, the typical family killer is more likely to have been concerned about losing control over more than just his wife and/or family. His concern is more often with losing control over all aspects of his life, or at least those that he most values. He is a man who, in his own eyes, is, or is about to become, a failure.

The more common pattern among familicide-suicides is that seen in the cases of Robert Lynch, Bruce Sweazy, Thomas Angst, and Anthony Paul. Each of these men was, at least at one point, a hard-working, apparently solid citizen and good provider for his family. But each, in his own way, had also suffered a significant reversal of fortune that threatened his ability to continue caring for his family, at least in the way to which he and they had become accustomed. Robert Lynch saw his business fail, his income drop, and his family lose their home. Bruce Sweazy had been laid off in a town where job opportunities were rapidly dwindling and the overall economic future had grown exceedingly bleak. Thomas Angst had gotten himself in over his head financially, relying on what appear to have been stolen funds, and was about to suffer the disgraceful loss of his professional career if not his freedom. For his part, Anthony Paul could see that even with heroic efforts he could no longer meet the needs of his crippled wife and brain-damaged daughter.

Faced with such overwhelming threats to their roles as providers, controllers, and central figures in the lives of their families, each of these men became desperate, depressed, suicidal, and homicidal.

Even though Dr. Paul's final note obviously speaks directly to his own situation, his final words provide a rare, clear, and candid glimpse into the kind of person who kills his entire family and the sort of desperation that leads him to do so. In many ways, Dr. Paul's suicide note paints a graphic portrait of the typical perpetrator of familicide-suicide.

Like Dr. Paul, the man who kills his family and then himself is, first and foremost, generally a deeply distressed and depressed individual who is at the end of his emotional rope. He can see no alternative to suicide: "I cannot go on with the present situation. There's only one solution. It must end with my death."

He blames no one but himself for his misfortune: "No blame should fall on anyone except me." But his distorted view of the family as an extension of himself, his inflated conception of his importance to them, and his need to control them all lead him to conclude that they will be better off dead than alive without him: "Unfortunately, I cannot leave my wife and children to suffer at the hands of the 'state.' So they must join me too. As in life, in death we will be together. . . . As in life, we must be together in death."

Ultimately, he convinces himself that familicide followed by suicide is not just the only way out but the honorable and right thing to do: "I have no regrets! I have lived a good life, I have hurt nobody, I have loved my wife and children to the point that I was willing to sacrifice my career and my life for them."

JUVENILE FAMILICIDE

❖ On April 23, 1991, 15-year-old Bruce Brenizer called the police in his rural Wisconsin town to report that his family was missing. His father, stepmother, and three sisters, he said, had never returned from a trip to the nearby Twin Cities of Minneapolis-St. Paul to buy building materials. Police in both Wisconsin and Minnesota searched without success, and rumors quickly spread that the family had either skipped town, leaving Bruce behind, or had been murdered by a satanic cult.

Two weeks after the missing persons report was filed, a fisherman stumbled upon a burned-out car containing the partially cremated remains of Rick Brenizer, his wife, and their three daughters, ages 10, 7, and 5. All five had been shot, cut up, and then burned. Police investigators learned soon thereafter that Bruce Brenizer had done the killings and then called a teenaged male relative to help him dismember and incinerate the bodies.

After extensive examinations of Bruce, a psychologist and a psychiatrist concluded that the killings were triggered by a lifetime of physical and psychological abuse inflicted on the boy by his father. The mental health experts also concluded that when Bruce killed his sisters, after first slaying his father and stepmother, he was legally insane.

In a plea bargain, Bruce accepted responsibility for killing the two adults and was found not guilty by reason of insanity in the deaths of the three girls. He was sentenced to two consecutive life terms with the proviso that he begin serving his time in a state mental hospital and would be eligible for parole in 27 years. ❖

❖ The Brenizer case was not the only, nor the first, case of teenaged familicide to occur along the border between Minnesota and Wisconsin. Three years before Bruce Brenizer killed his family, 16-year-old David Brom did the same in his rural Rochester, Minnesota home.

On the evening of February 18, 1988, David Brom told a teenaged friend of his plan to take his family's van and move to Florida and encouraged her to come with him. When the girl asked what his parents would think of that, David replied that they would not be able to object. Later the same night, David used an ax to kill his father, mother, 9-year-old brother, and 14-year-old sister.

Charged with four counts of first-degree murder, David pleaded insanity. At trial, a psychiatrist testified that David had been psychotic and depressed when he killed his family. Even the psychiatrist who testified for the prosecution conceded that David was mentally ill and killed his family to keep from killing himself.

After 21 hours of deliberation, a jury convicted David Brom on all four murder counts, and he was sentenced to three consecutive life terms. As a result, he must serve at least 52 years in prison before becoming eligible for parole. ❖

❖ On New Year's Day 1987, 16-year-old Sean Stevenson called his 15-year-old girlfriend and told her he thought he had just shot his family. Sean then asked the girl if she wanted to go to Mexico with him. Later that morning, when approached by a police officer, the Washington youth said he had just killed three members of his family.

When police went to Sean's home, they found his mother and stepfather, Margaret and James Butler, lying dead on the floor in their bedroom. In another room, they found the body of Sean's sister, lying on a bed. Eighteen-year-old Amy Stevenson was naked from the waist down, and semen was clearly visible in her pubic area. All three victims had been shot in the head at close range with a high-powered rifle.

Sean was tried on three counts of murder. Even the prosecutor told the jury that Sean was mentally ill when he killed his family. Still, Sean was convicted of two counts of first-degree murder in the killings of his mother and stepfather and one count of aggravated murder for killing his sister, on the theory that he had raped her as well. Apparently responding to pleas that Sean was mentally disturbed, the jury spared him the death penalty and sentenced him instead to life in prison with no hope of parole. ❖

When familicide is committed by a juvenile, both the dynamics and circumstances surrounding the crime often differ.

Like the adult familicide perpetrator, the youngster who kills his nuclear family is almost always male; familicides perpetrated by girls are almost unheard of. Unlike the adult family killer, however, the juvenile familicide perpetrator rarely follows his homicides with suicide. Instead, the juvenile who kills his entire family usually flees the scene of the homicides before being apprehended or turning himself over to the police.

Also like his adult counterpart, the juvenile family killer is nearly always propelled toward his homicidal act by some form of overwhelming stress. But unlike the adult familicide perpetrator who acts out in the face of a relatively acute crisis, the juvenile who kills his family is usually responding to a combination of long-term stress and chronic mental illness.

In perhaps the majority of cases, the juvenile family killer is responding to a long history of abuse at the hands of one or both parents. Although such young killers are rarely suffering from a long-standing major mental illness such as schizophrenia, they nearly always have a prefamilicidal history of involvement with and diagnosis by mental health professionals. When they do not have such a history, it is usually only because they have somehow managed to mask the psychopathology from which they suffer. Indeed, many of these youngsters, though severely troubled and depressed, initially present not as "disturbed" but "disturbing"—for example, as substance abusers and/or troublemakers.

CHAPTER ELEVEN

Mercy Killings

❖ After nearly 40 years of marriage, Roswell Gilbert retired as an engineer and moved with his wife, Emily, to Spain. Their dream retirement was spoiled, however, when Emily began to lose her memory, become confused, and complain of severe back pain.

In 1978, after just a few years in Spain, the Gilberts returned to the United States, settling in a condominium in Ft. Lauderdale, Florida. Over the next 7 years, Emily became increasingly disabled. She was in constant physical pain that did not respond to painkillers. Her mental state deteriorated, and she was diagnosed as suffering from Alzheimer's disease. Ultimately, she became completely dependent on Gilbert, who had to bathe and dress her.

Sadly, the more time Roswell spent caring for Emily, the less time he had for friends and others who might have been supportive. Eventually, he became socially isolated and overwhelmed with the task of caring for his beloved wife of more than 50 years.

On March 4, 1985, Roswell Gilbert, then 76 years old, loaded a pistol and shot 73-year-old Emily twice in the brain. Two months later, a Florida jury convicted Roswell of first-degree murder, and a judge sentenced him to 25 years in prison without hope of parole. Although the case received national media attention, it was not until August 2, 1990 that the governor of Florida granted clemency and allowed the seriously ill 81-year-old man to be released from prison. ❖

❖ Married nearly 60 years, Cecil and Jean Brush were still a close couple who shared a life in their small, well-kept home in Hamilton, Ontario. In 1994, 80-year-old Cecil began to hallucinate, a symptom of Alzheimer's disease. Over the following months, his condition worsened; he became paranoid and accused Jean of plotting against him. Sometimes, he wandered off. Before long, his vision and hearing were failing, he was incontinent, and at times he did not even recognize his wife.

Jean finally managed to place Cecil in a nursing home, hoping for a temporary break from the demands of his care. Jean's respite proved all too short, however, as Cecil refused to eat, wandered the home, and acted out toward the staff. On August 18, 1994, two weeks after his admission, Jean signed Cecil out for lunch and took him home. There, he not only refused to eat but declined to return to the nursing home.

After a brief discussion in which the couple agreed to die together, Jean used a 5-inch hunting knife to help Cecil stab himself, severing a major artery. Jean then shoved the knife five times into her own abdomen. When the couple's daughter arrived some 5 hours later, she found Cecil dead and Jean barely living.

After surgeons managed to save her life, 81-year-old Jean Brush was charged with murder. Fearing she would be unable to make it through a trial, Jean pleaded guilty to a reduced charge of manslaughter and was sentenced to 18 months' probation by a judge who noted that she had already been punished enough by the loss of her husband. ❖

❖ Like Cecil Brush, Marjorie Faile, a 69-year-old retired schoolteacher, suffered from Alzheimer's disease. Also like Cecil, Marjorie had a long marriage and a supportive, loving spouse who cared for her throughout her illness. Finally, like Cecil Brush, Marjorie Faile was killed by that same loving spouse.

In March 1996, family members became alarmed when they had not heard from 71-year-old Hilliard Faile. Police officers were dispatched to the Failes' home in California. When they entered the house, they found the bodies of Marjorie and Hilliard. Both had been fatally shot in the head.

Marjorie, who was still in bed, appeared to have been shot while sleeping. Hilliard's body was found on a sofa. His right index finger was on the trigger of .32 caliber handgun. A spent shell casing was found nearby. Based on the physical evidence, police theorized that Hilliard shot his ailing wife and then turned the gun on himself. ❖

❖ By age 87, Tom Grentz had lived more than half his life with his sister, 85-year-old Eleanor Simpson. Following their retirement, the two lived together for more than 25 years in the same house near Baltimore. Tom did the grocery shopping and driving, and Eleanor cooked. Together, they tended to the house and yard.

For years Tom had battled emphysema and heart trouble; he had a pacemaker and used oxygen. Still, he managed to care for his sister, who had her own ailments. Already suffering from hypertension, Eleanor suffered a stroke in 1994 and fractured her hip in January 1995. Later that same year, she fell again and thereafter found it increasingly difficult to remain mobile. Indeed, she was unable to even get out of bed without Tom's help.

On January 3, 1996, Tom Grentz put an end to the suffering—his own and that of his sister. First he shot Eleanor. Then he called the police to report hearing shots in the house. He told the police operator to send help immediately. When she asked if he had been shot, he replied in the affirmative, adding that he had been shot in the head. With the telephone still in hand, Tom then turned the gun— a .25 caliber pistol from the early 1900s—on himself. When police officers arrived minutes later, they found that Tom and Eleanor had each been shot a single time in the right temple. Tom was dead. Eleanor was rushed to the hospital but died less than an hour and a quarter later. ❖

MERCY KILLING
AMONG THE ELDERLY

Although advances in medical technology have greatly increased life expectancy, they have also increased the likelihood and duration of disabilities and chronic illnesses associated with old age. In short, people are living longer and are thus at greater risk of developing age-related infirmities.

But the costs of living longer are not limited to physical illness and disability, nor are they borne solely by the elderly themselves. Many elderly individuals find that they have outlived their occupational and familial roles as well as their friends and other sources of social support. Moreover, with increasingly serious health problems and declining mental functioning, many elderly people are rationally concerned about the burdens they place (or will place) on family and society.

One result of these trends has been an increase in the number of intrafamilial murder-suicides and assisted suicides among America's elderly population. Hard data on the subject are rare, but one study done in Florida, a mecca for retired senior citizens, has documented this increase.

Gerontologist Dr. Donna Cohen and her colleagues found 60 cases of murder-suicide among elderly couples in West Central Florida from 1988 to 1994.[1] According to Cohen, the number of such cases doubled over that period of time, ultimately accounting for 20 percent of the homicides of people over the age of 55.

The cases in Cohen's study closely parallel those of the Gilberts, Brushes, Failes, and Grentzes described above. The typical pattern among these cases involved an ill and debilitated elderly woman killed by her husband, who then attempted or succeeded in committing suicide. Typically, these couples had struggled for years (sometimes as long as 15 years) with illness, disability, and caretaking and had become increasingly hopeless prior to the killing.

All the homicides in Cohen's sample were committed by men, 40 percent of whom were reportedly suffering from depression. Ninety-six percent of the killings occurred in the couple's home, and 95 percent were committed with firearms, primarily handguns. Cohen et al. also report that while about half of the women in their sample had experienced recent declines in their health, approximately two-thirds had expressed no desire to die.

The fact that all the perpetrators in Cohen's sample were men and all the victims women comes as little surprise, at least to those who have studied murder-suicide among the elderly. As suicidologists Osgood and Eisenhandler indicate,

> The majority of victims of assisted suicide in this country are women. Compared to men, women are also much more likely to be the victims in murder/suicides, in which the man kills his wife and then himself. When a love pact suicide is committed and husband and wife commit suicide together, women who die with their spouses often are not as physically sick or mentally impaired as the man, but they still die with him.[2]

Osgood and Eisenhandler see both ageism and sexism at work here. They point out that, compared with elderly men, older women are disadvantaged both economically and socially; have less status, power, and authority; are more likely to be viewed as passive and dependent; are more likely to be negatively stereotyped; and, as a result, are more likely "to feel dejected, degraded, devalued, useless, and worthless."[3]

AN END TO WHOSE SUFFERING?

❖ Hospitalized 6 weeks for liver cancer, 80-year-old Alice Rowbottom could not eat, drink, or move her arm without excruciating pain. The dying British widow was being treated with an intravenous morphine drip, but it was not enough to make the pain bearable.

On April 12, 1996, fed up with weeks of watching his mother suffer, 44-year-old Derek Rowbottom decided to do something about it. Reaching out at her hospital bedside, he pressed the button on the IV mechanism until the entire syringe of painkiller had emptied into Alice Rowbottom's arm. Then, after asking a nurse to replenish the morphine, he repeated what he had done. This time a nurse saw what he was doing and directed him to stop. When he refused, she called security.

Derek Rowbottom readily told authorities what he had done, making it clear that he felt he had done nothing wrong. His case was forwarded to the Crown Prosecution Service for a decision as to whether he should be charged criminally.

As this case illustrates, occasionally elderly individuals suffering from debilitating and/or fatal illnesses are killed by their grown children. As in cases where such individuals are killed by their spouses, the motive is often essentially a desire to relieve suffering and allow a loved one to die with dignity. In these cases, however, the perpetrator is less likely to be dependent on the person killed and thus less likely to follow the killing with suicide. ❖

❖ Although 12 years old, Tracy Latimer had never learned to talk, walk, or even sit up by herself. Daily, she vomited and had seizures. Severely disabled since birth and afflicted with cerebral palsy, Tracy weighed just 38 pounds. Incontinent, she had to be diapered. Her body parts were constantly dislocating, she could not sleep, and she seemed to be in pain most of the time. Her parents, Canadian farmers Robert and Laura Latimer took care of her around the clock.

On October 24, 1993, while others in the family attended church services, Robert Latimer put Tracy in his truck, rigged a piece of hose from the exhaust to the cab, and ended his daughter's life with carbon monoxide. Latimer then placed the dead child in her bed and claimed that she had died in her sleep. Later, when an autopsy found massive amounts of the deadly gas in Tracy's body, Latimer confessed to killing his daughter.

Latimer was convicted of murder and sentenced to serve at least 10 years in prison. Although an intermediate-level appeals court denied him a new trial, the court's chief judge concluded that "while the killing was a purposeful one, it had its genesis in altruism and was motivated by love, mercy and compassion or a combination of those virtues, generally considered by people to be life-enhancing and affirmative."[4] Further appeals are pending. ❖

❖ In November 1994, Gloria Christianson, mother of a disabled child, warned a Canadian government official that another case like the death of Tracy Latimer could easily happen in Ontario as a result of the province's failure to provide sufficient home-based care for handicapped children. As it turned out, her prediction was accurate. On December 5, 1994, Cathie Wilkieson placed her disabled son, Ryan, in a car in his grandparents' garage and turned on the engine, killing her son and herself with carbon monoxide.

Ryan Wilkieson was born small and sickly after a difficult pregnancy. He was kept in the hospital for 2 weeks after his birth. Four months later, he underwent his first surgery aimed at correcting his partial blindness. By age 2, he was diagnosed as deaf and suffering from cerebral palsy. Several years later, he developed a debilitating bone disorder that left him wheelchair-bound.

Despite his multiple handicaps, Ryan was a bright, charming boy with a good sense of humor. Assisted by hearing aids and special glasses, he learned sign language for the deaf-blind and eventually learned to speak.

At the time of his death, Ryan was receiving only 12 hours a week of in-home nursing care, with his parents forced to assume responsibility during the other hours he was not in school. Ryan had recently begun attending high school, and apparently the school was unable to meet his special needs.

According to Christianson, who was a friend of Ryan's mother, Cathie Wilkieson had once referred to the Tracy Latimer case, saying that she would never leave Ryan alone in a running car but would sit with him. ❖

❖ On October 24, 1984, 2½-year-old Joy Griffith was watching cartoons at the home of her grandparents. Suddenly, the child's neck became trapped between the footrest and seat of her grandfather's recliner. When she was finally freed from the mechanism, some 10 to 25 minutes later, Joy was unconscious. Although still alive, she had lost virtually all her brain functions.

Doctors declared that Joy would never recover, but her father, Charles Griffith, refused to give up hope. For months, he sat by her bedside, reading and singing to her. He argued with the nursing staff over her medications and feeding and claimed to see signs of recovery that others could not detect. Eventually, Joy did improve: She was no longer comatose but in a vegetative state with no chance of recovery.

Despite his faith that his daughter would one day recover, Charles Griffith eventually came to see that her situation was hopeless. The child was alive legally but had only minimal brain activity. She was fed though a stomach tube and breathed though a tracheotomy hole. Reluctantly, he signed a "do not resuscitate" order for the child, but his estranged wife refused to sign, so the order never took effect.

When Joy's condition worsened, she began to have seizures and suffered a broken shoulder. Charles became increasingly depressed, had trouble sleeping and eating, and increased his use of alcohol and marijuana. He sought counseling at a mental health center and was given a prescription for Valium.

In June 1985, 8 months after Joy's accident, the 25-year-old father rode his motorcycle to the hospital, armed with a rusty .32 caliber revolver. He entered his daughter's room and inserted 100 mg. of crushed Valium into her feeding tube. He then held a nurse at bay with the gun and begged her to allow Joy to die. After a 1-hour standoff, Charles shot Joy twice in the chest and then collapsed.

Charles Griffith was charged with first-degree murder, convicted, and sentenced to serve a minimum term of 25 years, with a potential maximum of life in prison. Charles sought clemency from the governor but withdrew his petition after his former wife told the clemency board that he had abused her, beating her even while she was pregnant with Joy.

After 10 years in prison, Charles finally had the charge against him reduced, was allowed to plead guilty to the lesser charge, and was released on probation. ❖

❖ Although the leniency ultimately granted Charles Griffith was controversial, it was far from unique. Indeed, in several other similar cases, legal authorities have either refused to press charges or declined to imprison parents who have killed their disabled children.

For example, on May 11, 1987, Irene Bernstein, a 41-year-old Philadelphia mother, shot and killed her son Eric, who was then 2 years and 10 months old. Eric was born 9 weeks premature and suffered from a lack of oxygen that caused brain damage. After conventional therapies failed to improve the boy's condition, his parents turned to a controversial and exhausting regimen called patterning. Patterning involved, among other things, rhythmically simulating crawling every 20 minutes, 12 hours a day.

Although some 70 volunteers assisted with the patterning, Irene devoted herself full-time to her son's care and rehabilitation, often working with him 16 hours a day, 7 days a week. When Eric showed little improvement despite months on the patterning regimen, his distraught mother shot him once in the head and once in the back. She later told police she had wanted to shoot herself but was unable to do so.

Charged with first-degree murder, Irene Bernstein pleaded no contest to a reduced charge of third-degree murder. Although the prosecutor demanded a prison sentence, citing the need to deter others, the judge sentenced Irene to 5 years' probation and 750 hours of community service. ❖

❖ More recently, a Chicago grand jury declined to indict a father who held hospital personnel at bay with a gun while he disconnected his infant son's life support system.

By all accounts, Rudy Linares, a 23-year-old house painter, was the loving father of three young children. On August 2, 1988, Samuel, then less than a year old, somehow inhaled or swallowed a small object, thought to be part of a balloon. The object choked the infant, cut off his oxygen, and left him irreversibly brain damaged. Rudy Linares carried the boy to a nearby fire station, but efforts to revive him were unsuccessful. Later, against the wishes of the parents, physicians tried for 12 hours to resuscitate the baby.

Ultimately they were unsuccessful, and Samuel lapsed into a persistent vegetative state. Partially brain dead, he had no chance of recovery and was kept alive only by continuous mechanical life support.

In December 1988, Rudy Linares went to his son's bedside in the pediatric intensive care unit and disconnected the boy's life support. After a struggle with hospital security officers, the respirator was reconnected and Samuel continued in his vegetative state.

Hospital officials refused the parents' request to terminate the life support, citing Illinois law forbidding such action except where a patient was brain dead. In April 1989, Rudy and his wife were notified of the hospital's plan to transfer Samuel to a long-term care facility. Around the same time, the couple learned that government payments for their son's costly care were to be terminated.

On April 26, 1989, Rudy and Tamara Linares stood at their son's hospital bedside and discussed the planned transfer. After Tamara left, Rudy produced a .357 magnum pistol, directed hospital personnel to leave, and then disconnected Samuel's life support system. Rudy made it clear that he had no intention of hurting anyone, and he never pointed the gun at anyone. He did, however, ask how long it would take before his son would die without life support.

For approximately 40 minutes, the tearful father held his son in his arms. When Rudy finally handed Samuel over to the staff, the boy was declared dead.

Although the district attorney charged Rudy Linares with first-degree murder, a grand jury heard the evidence and refused to indict. Subsequently, the medical examiner changed the cause of Samuel's death from undetermined to accidental, concluding that Samuel had been legally dead at the time he was admitted to the hospital. Following these actions, Rudy pleaded guilty to a misdemeanor charge of unlawful possession of a weapon. ❖

❖ Even more recently, a Louisiana grand jury refused to indict a father who smothered a child suffering from a rare, fatal hereditary disorder. When she was 21 months old, Yvonne Hensley suffered her first seizure. Doctors quickly diagnosed Tay-Sachs disease and told her parents she would be unlikely to live past the age of 2. Nine years later, as a result of excellent care, Yvonne was still alive. But the disease had robbed her of the ability to walk, talk, or exercise other motor functions. The illness had also left her in excruciating pain—pain physicians declined to treat with powerful narcotics for fear that such medications would hasten her death. Her sister, a year younger, was afflicted with the same illness and was also deteriorating.

On March 24, 1991, 35-year-old Michael Hensley felt he could no longer stand by and watch his daughter. Yvonne had undergone stomach surgery and been in severe pain for nearly a year. Michael tried to calm himself first by taking several Valiums and then by drinking cooking wine. Later, he took a pillow, held it over Yvonne's face for less than half a minute, and suffocated her. When his wife discovered what he had done, she called 911.

Michael confessed to killing Yvonne and was arrested, but the grand jury that heard the case declined to indict him. ❖

After the deaths of Tracy Latimer, Ryan Wilkieson, Joy Griffith, Eric Bernstein, Samuel Linares, and Yvonne Hensley, legal, medical, and psychological professionals as well as members of the general public struggled to make sense of these tragedies. Although rare, such cases raise a host of deeply troubling moral issues, most of which can never be fully resolved.

Not surprisingly, public and professional response to these cases was mixed and often ambivalent. Many sympathized with the plight of these parents, who had long struggled against sometimes seemingly hopeless odds to care for and raise their severely disabled and well-loved children. Even though few if any commentators fully supported the parents' actions in these cases, many felt that they were best understood as acts of desperation devoid of any selfish or otherwise culpable motives.

Others, however, saw these parents as blameworthy despite their desperate situations. From this viewpoint, these cases were seen as setting a dangerous precedent—one that might lead to similarly tragic deaths of other disabled children unable to protect themselves from being killed by their understandably distraught parents.

Still others sought to distinguish the cases, seeing greater excuse if not justification for some parents while condemning others. Some, however, could find no justification or rationale for any case in which a parent killed a child. For example, one American commentator even went so far as to liken the Tracy Latimer killing to the Susan Smith case.[5] Smith, a young South Carolina mother, deliberately drowned her two young sons, lied about it to authorities and the media, and was convicted of first-degree murder and sentenced to life in prison. According to that analyst, the only significant difference between the cases was that Smith's boys were viewed as healthy and having a right to live, whereas Tracy Latimer was disabled and thus better off dead.

In analyzing these cases and others like them, it is virtually impossible to divorce one's reasoning from one's immediate and visceral response. Consideration of the dynamics of these cases will undoubtedly be colored by one's moral, religious, and/or ethical views regarding the sanctity and meaning of life.

For present purposes, suffice it to say that parental motives in rare cases such as these are complex and not as easily reduced to simple explanations as some commentators appear to believe. Whatever else may be said of them, as each of these cases amply demonstrates, mothers and fathers who kill their handicapped children are likely to be devoted and loving but long-suffering and desperate parents who have found themselves pushed to extremes most people could not even imagine.

Indeed, their situations appear so extreme as to render most other generalizations about them meaningless. Perhaps the most that can be said is that these cases must always be examined individually in the context of their own peculiar, troubling, and compelling facts.

CHAPTER TWELVE

Preventing
Family Homicide

Intrafamilial homicide has been a part of the human condition at least since Cain rose up in the field and killed his brother Abel. As the preceding chapters make clear, the problem is still with us and likely to be so for a long time to come.

Although it is difficult to foresee a time when family members no longer kill one another, it is not impossible to envision steps that a sane society might take to decrease the number of "fatal families."

Prevention of any problem requires first an understanding of the roots of that problem. Although very little systematic research has been directed toward the etiology of intrafamilial homicide, it is not difficult to see the more obvious causal factors. Anyone who has read the preceding chapters of this volume should already be familiar with the major factors that contribute to intrafamilial homicide in contemporary American society.

The more difficult question is what can and will society do to eradicate or at least reduce the toxic impact of these underlying social problems that lead family members to kill each other?

151

THE ROOTS OF FAMILY HOMICIDE

Among the most obvious causal factors in intrafamilial homicide are (1) domestic violence, (2) overwhelming social stress, (3) mental illness, (4) alcohol abuse, and (5) the ready availability of firearms.

Domestic Violence

Intrafamilial homicide is not only a form of domestic violence but often a product of domestic violence. For example, when abusers kill or are killed by their abuse victims, the homicide is frequently the culmination of a long-standing pattern of child and/or spousal abuse.

There are no reliable data as to how many spouse killings are the result of domestic violence, but in a recent federal study of spousal murder in large urban counties, 44 percent of wives who killed and 10 percent of husbands who killed had been assaulted by their spouse-victims "at or around the time of the murder."[1]

Similarly, in cases where children kill or are killed by their parents, it is impossible to determine exactly how many of these youngsters were earlier victims of domestic violence. But available data and estimates suggest that the number is large. For instance, recent data indicate that nearly half of all maltreatment fatalities involve families with previous child protective services contact—that is, families who have been the subject of allegations of abuse and/or neglect.[2] In its study of homicide in large urban counties, the U.S. Justice Department found that "among offspring murder victims who were under the age of 12, before their death 79 percent had suffered abuse by the assailant."[3]

Although comparable data are not available for parricide cases, it has been estimated that as many as 90 percent of juvenile perpetrators in these cases have been abused by the parents they kill.[4]

Despite recent reforms, in many jurisdictions police officers, judges, prosecutors, and other criminal justice officials continue to respond slowly and ineffectively to instances of nonlethal intrafamilial violence.

Similarly, despite many highly publicized "horror stories," many if not most child protective agencies continue to be underfunded, overworked, and inadequately staffed. Thus, many cases of nonlethal child abuse are either undetected, uninvestigated, or otherwise improperly handled. But even where child protection professionals are able to function effectively, their efforts may go for naught because courts are often unwilling and/or legally unable to adequately protect children from their abusive parents. Finally, even where abused children are removed from their abusive parents, there are all too many cases in which they end up being abused by foster parents or others charged with their continuing care.

Overwhelming Social Stress

The term *stress* has become a cliché in modern American society. Being "stressed out" is said to be an almost constant state for many people, and "stress" is not only blamed for a host of deviant behaviors but frequently invoked to excuse antisocial conduct.

Still, the lives of many Americans are genuinely stressful, and stress is clearly a contributing factor to many if not most intrafamilial killings. Perhaps the clearest example is the person who, overwhelmed by the suffering of a loved one afflicted with a horribly debilitating handicap and/or terminal illness, commits what is commonly referred to as a mercy killing. Similarly overwhelming stress appears to play a role in many cases in which young mothers kill their newborn infants.

Outside of mercy killings, perhaps the single most readily identified stress related to intrafamilial homicide is that stemming from unemployment. In the U.S. Justice Department's study of murder in large urban counties, 29.1 percent of those charged with killing family members were unemployed. These unemployed killers included 25.0 percent of those who killed spouses, 28.9 percent of those who killed offspring, 33.6 percent of parricide offenders, and 34.9 percent of those who killed siblings.[5] Even considering that these data are derived from urban areas where unemployment may be higher than the norm, and that many of those who killed parents and siblings were probably juveniles, the overall unemployment rate among family killers is significantly higher than that found among the general population.

Mental Illness

Clearly, many women who kill their children are mentally ill, suffering from postpartum depression or Munchausen syndrome by proxy. But mental illness is implicated in many other family killings as well. For example, in the Justice Department's study of homicide in large urban counties, a history of mental illness was found among 12.3 percent of those who killed spouses, 15.8 percent of those who killed offspring, 25.1 percent of those who killed a parent, and 17.3 percent of those who killed a sibling.[6]

Alcohol Abuse

Research indicates that alcohol consumption is associated with virtually all types of homicide, except for killings committed by children.[7] Some studies indicate that as many as half of all homicide offenders had been drinking at the time of the offense.[8] Other drugs, especially crack cocaine, have also been associated with lethal violence in many cases.

Intrafamilial homicide is no exception. For example, studies of battered women who killed their abusers have consistently found that many of these women were alcohol abusers at the time they killed.[9] These studies have also found that a large percentage, if not the vast majority, of batterers in these cases were serious alcohol abusers, many of whom were intoxicated at the time they were killed.[10]

Similar findings emerged from the Justice Department's urban murder study. Among defendants charged with killing family members, 47.6 percent were drinking at the time of the killing. "Alcohol use at the time of the murder" was reported among 54.4 percent of those who killed spouses, 29.8 percent who killed their children, 28.4 percent who killed a parent, and 53.9 percent who killed siblings.[11]

Ready Availability of Firearms

In its recent study of murder in large urban counties, the Department of Justice found that 41.6 percent of intrafamilial homicide victims were killed with firearms, primarily handguns. Firearms were used by 58 percent of wives who killed husbands and 50 percent of husbands who killed wives. Firearms were also used by 20.6 percent of parents who killed their children, 33.9 percent of children who killed their parents, and 38.3 percent of those who killed siblings.[12]

An FBI analysis of homicides committed nationwide in 1992 concluded that "62 percent of murder victims known to have been killed by intimates were shot to death."[13] The FBI report also concluded that firearms were used to kill 69 percent of wives and ex-wives, 61 percent of husbands and ex-husbands, 60 percent of girlfriends, and 41 percent of boyfriends.[14]

An earlier study by Ewing of 100 battered women who killed their abusers found that "among the 95 cases in which the woman killed the batterer herself, a gun was used in 69 (73 percent) of the cases," and that in most of these cases, the gun appeared to have been present in the home prior to the killing.[15]

There can be little doubt that many intrafamilial killings are committed in the heat of passion and would never have occurred but for the perpetrator's immediate access to a firearm. To put it another way, in all probability, but for the ready availability of a gun, many of these homicides would have been, at worst, cases of serious assault.

PREVENTING FAMILY HOMICIDE

Any efforts to prevent intrafamilial homicide generally must begin with an awareness of the overall social context in which these killings occur. We live in a society in which a great deal of violence is not only tolerated but also viewed as acceptable, even entertaining; a society rife with gender, racial, and class inequality; and a society in which vulnerable groups such as the young, the elderly, and the handicapped have been increasingly marginalized.

Like most of our nation's major social ills, intrafamilial homicide is unlikely ever to be substantially reduced until we begin to successfully address these pervasive toxic aspects of contemporary culture. But as a practical matter, we cannot wait for the revolution. There are smaller steps that can and should be taken now that would at least contribute to some reduction in the number of fatal families.

Domestic Violence

Obviously, the major thrust in any effort to curb intrafamilial homicide must be directed toward reducing the incidence and prevalence of domestic violence.

First, there is a need to further develop, fund, and implement programs aimed at better identifying domestic violence in its early stages and calling such violence to the attention of the legal authorities. Frontline personnel likely to confront incipient abuse (e.g., emergency room staff, teachers, day care providers, police officers) need to be better trained in both spotting and providing a helpful initial response to cases of suspected domestic violence.

Many of these personnel are already mandated reporters—that is, they are required by law to report reasonable suspicions of child abuse.[16] But rarely are they under any mandate to report other forms of domestic violence, such as spousal abuse or elder abuse.

There also is a clear need for laws mandating reports of all forms of domestic violence that come to the attention of these personnel.

Additionally, there is a need for a stronger and more effective second-line response to identified cases of family violence. If there is any lesson to be learned from this volume, it should be that individuals identified as victims of domestic violence should always be considered potential homicide victims. As such, their plight should always be taken extremely seriously, and they should be entitled to our utmost efforts to protect them.

Together with the need for more shelters for battered women, more and better foster care placements for abused children, and a tougher law enforcement stance against those who abuse family members, there is a need for better ways to identify which victims of domestic violence are at greatest risk for additional injury or death. One promising development is a new computer program created by violence expert Gavin DeBecker.

Using DeBecker's "Mosaic-20" protocol, law enforcement personnel ask domestic violence victims a series of questions related to issues such as alcohol abuse, presence of guns, and children in the home.[17] They are then able to use the computer program to compare the characteristics of the particular case of domestic violence with more than 4,000 others that have resulted in homicides. The result should be the identification of those high-risk cases in which immediate and powerful intervention may prevent a family killing.

Although DeBecker's program deals with spousal abuse, it might be feasible to adapt that program or to develop other similar approaches to predicting the risk of lethal violence in child and elder abuse situations as well.

Stress

Recognition of the stress of modern life has led to the creation of all sorts of stress-reducing technology, from biofeedback to psychotropic medications. But little has been done to reduce the specific stresses that so often give rise to the kind of family violence that culminates in homicide.

Many child abuse deaths could undoubtedly be prevented simply by identifying parents at risk of abusing their children and making parenting less stressful for them. At a minimum, there is an obvious need for more and better educational programs aimed at teaching young people how to parent, for such programs could significantly reduce the number of child abuse deaths in this country by teaching and reinforcing alternatives to corporal punishment.

Young and inexperienced parents, who often pose the greatest risk of harm to their children, would also most assuredly benefit from the kinds of home visitation programs recently implemented in other countries as well as some parts of the United States. This approach involves identifying parents at risk of abusing their children—for example, unmarried, disadvantaged, teenaged mothers—and providing them with periodic home visits from public health nurse-educators and/or other child care specialists.[18]

Many so-called mercy killings might be avoided by efforts to reduce the overwhelming stress so often felt by family members of individuals who are either mortally ill but suffering horribly or severely handicapped by chronic or progressive conditions. Efforts to provide ongoing counseling and respite services to such family members are a step in the right direction but are not nearly as available or as extensive as they should be.

Here, as in most preventive efforts, early identification is the key. Since virtually all cases of "mercy killing" involve individuals who have recently been (or are still) under medical care, health care providers should be better trained to assess the stress experienced by family members of their patients and the likelihood that such stress may lead to a homicide. Here, too, implementation of the visiting nurse-educator model might be effective.

Mental Illness

Far from all family killers suffer from diagnosable mental illnesses. And not all who do ever come to the attention of a professional who could make that diagnosis. Still, many individuals who kill family members are not only mentally ill but have sought mental health treatment prior to the killing or are in such treatment at the time of the killing. As a result, mental health professionals are often in a position to predict and possibly prevent lethal family violence.

At a minimum, mental health professionals should evaluate the domestic violence history of every patient they see. The evaluation should encompass the patient's experiences, if any, as both a victim and perpetrator. Where there is reason to suspect that the patient is a victim and/or perpetrator, careful efforts should be made to assess the risk of future domestic violence. Protocols for such assessments are available and should be used in appropriate cases.[19]

Mental health professionals should also always be alert to factors that may suggest the possibility of family homicide. Where patients make clear or even veiled threats to harm a family member, those threats must be taken seriously and investigated carefully. Where a threat is directed at an identified or readily identifiable individual, the mental health professional may have a legal duty to take steps to protect the threatened party.[20]

But even where threats are not made, mental health professionals may play a role in preventing family homicide by simply paying close attention to diagnosis. Obviously, where the mother of a newborn demonstrates symptoms of postpartum depression, a careful assessment of the potential for lethality is called for. Similarly, where the diagnosis or suspected diagnosis is Munchausen syndrome by proxy, such an assessment is probably even more critical, although perhaps more difficult to accomplish.

But aside from these obvious diagnostic clues, mental health professionals need to be cognizant of other factors that may indicate a patient's potential for lethality to family members. For example, when dealing with depressed men, mental health professionals should pay careful attention to recent or pending losses in their patients' lives—particularly losses that significantly threaten the stability or viability of each patient's nuclear family, such as employment, bankruptcy, impending divorce, and child custody disputes.

Alcohol Abuse

The relationship between alcohol and violence, including lethal family violence, although obvious, is not well understood.[21] It does seem clear, however, that abuse of alcohol is a substantial risk factor in intrafamilial homicide and that awareness of and response to that risk factor may in some instances prevent family homicides.

At the very least, those who assess domestic violence situations and attempt to determine the potential they hold for lethal violence should give careful consideration to the degree of alcohol consumption by both the perpetrator and the victim. The association between alcohol abuse and domestic violence (including intrafamilial homicides) suggests that alcohol abuse may be a major risk factor for serious, sometimes lethal violence, particularly in families where there is also evidence of ongoing abuse.

Additionally, family violence perpetrators who abuse alcohol should be closely monitored by the professionals involved with them. These perpetrators should be steered (mandated, if possible) to alcohol abuse treatment programs, but it is important to keep in mind that successful treatment of the drinking problem will not necessarily prevent further violence.

Firearms

Traditional methods of gun control seem to have had little if any impact on the use of firearms in homicides, either within or outside the family. More recent enactments, such as the Brady Law imposing up to a 7-day delay in gun purchases and the federal ban on certain types of automatic and semiautomatic weapons, appear to have had some success in reducing the incidence of homicides in general. But these laws are likely to have little if any significant effect on intrafamilial killings, which are most often committed with firearms that have been present in the home long before they were used to kill.

More promising is the recently enacted amendment to the federal Gun Control Act of 1968. The amendment, which took effect on September 30, 1996, prohibits anyone who has been convicted of a misdemeanor involving domestic violence from owning or possessing a firearm or ammunition.[22] Persons convicted of felonies had already been banned from gun ownership and possession.

The 1996 amendment provides no time limits, no statute of limitations, and no exceptions, even for police or military personnel. Violation of the new ban is punishable by up to 10 years in federal prison and a fine of $250,000. It has been estimated that this law already applies to hundreds of thousands of Americans.[23]

If enforceable, this law would undoubtedly reduce the number of family homicides, for it would take guns out of the hands of many of those who pose the greatest risk for intrafamilial homicide—that is, persons who have abused family members and been convicted for doing so. The problem is that the new law is difficult to enforce and is being challenged by the National Rifle Association, police organizations, and others concerned with its breadth.[24]

Enforcement of the new law is difficult because there is no requirement that state or federal agencies seek out convicted abusers who may be in possession of guns. State officials have already complained that they lack the resources to run background checks on all gun owners and would-be gun owners.[25] Moreover, even if these agencies were to undertake such a task, many computerized criminal justice databases do not list misdemeanors, and those that do often fail to specify whether a conviction was for a domestic violence crime.[26]

The 1996 amendment may have some deterrent effect, assuming it becomes widely known and survives court challenges. What is needed, however, is some legally enforceable and practical mechanism whereby those with criminal records for domestic violence may be readily identified, contacted, and required to divest themselves of any firearms and ammunition in their possession. The initial costs of implementing such a mechanism would undoubtedly be extremely high, but once in operation, convictions could be routinely listed, notifications made, and costs decreased substantially.

One solution that would both cut costs and answer many of the critics of the new federal law would be to repeal the retroactive aspects of the law and make the gun ban applicable only to those convicted of domestic violence crimes after a certain date.

Alternatively, those previously convicted of domestic violence could be required to identify themselves to the authorities, much the way convicted child sex offenders in some jurisdictions are now required to report their whereabouts to local law enforcement officials. Creating a public list of known domestic violence offenders would not only enhance enforcement of the new federal gun ban but would also make it easier for police, courts, and others to determine whether or not a given individual has a history of domestic violence.

CONCLUSION:
HOPE FOR THE FUTURE?

With the exception of a substantial decrease in the number of women killing their husbands and boyfriends, the annual incidence of intrafamilial homicide in the United States has been relatively stable for nearly two decades.[27] The fact that the annual number of family homicides has not increased substantially would be good news except that during this same time period there has been a growing and concerted effort in this country to recognize and combat domestic violence, one of the major contributing factors in intrafamilial homicide.

It may be that this effort, while apparently successful in reducing the overall level of domestic violence, will have no substantial impact on lethal family violence other than to reduce the number of spouse killings committed by women. However, an alternative explanation is that even though society has become more sensitive and responsive to the problem of domestic violence, it has also become less sensitive and responsive to other factors that seem to contribute to intrafamilial homicide.

For example, gun ownership and access have reached all-time highs over the past decade. Alcohol and other substance abuse continues to be a growing and serious problem, especially among young people. The availability of mental health services has dropped considerably in recent years with the virtual abandonment of the community mental health center concept, increasing deinstitutionalization of severely ill psychiatric patients, and implementation of harsh cost controls on insurance reimbursement for psychotherapy. Finally, the significant increase in social ills such as unwed teenaged motherhood, homelessness, family poverty, and urban decay has been met with an equally significant decrease in government programs aimed at ameliorating these problems.

Given these trends, it is all the more critical to continue efforts to curb domestic violence by whatever means possible. The overall prognosis for reducing the incidence of intrafamilial homicide still appears bleak, but without continuing and vigorous efforts to combat spousal, child, and elder abuse, the number of fatal families in America is unfortunately bound to grow.

References
and Notes

CHAPTER 1:
ALL IN THE FAMILY

References

Christine Lane: *People v. Lane,* 600 N.Y.S. 2d 848 (1993); Deborah Homsher, *From Blood to Verdict: Three Women on Trial* (Ithaca, NY: McBooks, 1993); United Press International (UPI), Jury Finds Lane Guilty in Child-Killing, Nov. 8, 1990; UPI, Mother on Witness Stand in Murder Trial, Oct. 30, 1990; UPI, Opening Arguments in Child Killing Trial, Oct. 16, 1990; UPI, Prosecutor Says Bush Autopsy Going to Grand Jury, Feb. 27, 1990; Associated Press (AP), Mother Made Up Abduction Story; Said She Panicked After Child Died, *Bergen Record,* Feb. 18, 1990, p. A-13; Wayne T. Price, Missing Aliza Found Dead; Mother Arraigned, Gannett News Service, Feb. 16, 1990; UPI, Police: Mom Buried Her Two-Year-Old and Reported Her Missing, Feb. 16, 1990; Offer of Leniency for Kidnapper Seeks Return of a Missing Girl, 2, *New York Times,* Feb. 14, 1990, p. B-2; UPI, Toll-Free Line Set Up in Probe for Missing Girl, Feb. 9, 1990; UPI, Mom Receives Package with Missing Girl's Mitten, Feb. 8, 1990; Kathy Hovis, Few Leads on Missing Tot, Gannett News Service, Feb.

5, 1990; UPI, Search Continues for Missing Two Year Old in Tompkins County, Feb. 4, 1990; UPI, Rescue Workers Search for Missing Child, Feb. 3, 1990.

Charles Stuart: Doris Sue Wong, Matthew Stuart Reports for Prison Term, *Boston Globe,* Nov. 24, 1992, p. 56; Sean P. Murphy, No Trial, No Testimony, No Verdict Leaves Stuart Case Forever Open, *Boston Globe,* Nov. 11, 1992, p. 25; Mike Barnicle, Stuart Case Defies Ending, *Boston Globe,* Nov. 3, 1992, p. 21; Fox Butterfield, New Doubt as Jury Takes Up Stuart Case, *New York Times,* Feb. 4, 1990, p. 1-32; Margaret Carlson, Hero, Suspect, Suicide; A Bizarre Murder Inflames Racial Tension in Boston, TIME, Jan. 15, 1990, p. 30; Keith Botsford, Murder with Extreme Prejudice, *The Independent,* Jan. 13, 1990, p. 29; Peter J. Howe, From Nightmare to Reality, a City Is Reeling; The Stuart Murder Case, *Boston Globe,* Jan. 7, 1990, p. 1; Kevin Cullen et al., Stuart Dies in Jump Off Tobin Bridge after Police Are Told He Killed His Wife, *Boston Globe,* Jan. 5, 1990, p. 1; Montgomery Brower et al., A Dark Night in the Soul of Boston, TIME, Nov. 13, 1989, p. 52; Dolores Kong et al., Infant of Shooting Victims Dies of Respiratory Failure, *Boston Globe,* Nov. 10, 1989, p. 1; Christopher B. Daly, Pregnant Woman's Murder Shakes Boston's Image; Ruthless Shooting Prompts New Debate on Crime, Death Penalty, Racism and Taxes, *Washington Post,* Nov. 2, 1989, p. A-3; Peter J. Howe and Jerry Thomas, Reading Woman Dies After Shooting in Car; Husband, Baby Termed Critical, *Boston Globe,* Oct. 25, 1989, p. 1.

Erik and Lyle Menendez: Tracey Venegas, Menendez Brothers Convicted of Murder, UPI, March 20, 1996; Robert Reinhold, Brutal Plot Is Rated R (For 'Real') by Police, *New York Times,* Mar. 14, 1990, p. A-20; Joseph Poindexter et al., A Beverly Hills Paradise Lost; They Were Ambitious Sons in Their Father's Image; Now Lyle and Erik Menendez Stand Accused of Their Parents' Murder, PEOPLE, Mar. 26, 1990, p. 66; Rorie Sherman, Parricide Case Hinges on Search, *National Law Journal,* Apr. 2, 1990, p. 3; Michael D. Harris, Coroner: Beverly Hills Couple Murdered by 15 Shotgun Blasts, UPI, May 15, 1990; Ronald L. Soble and John Johnson, Menendez Gun Link Pursued, *Los Angeles Times,* May 16, 1990, p, B-3.

Notes

1. U.S. Department of Justice, Bureau of Justice Statistics, *Murder in Families,* July 1994.

2. Federal Bureau of Investigation, *Crime in the United States: Uniform Crime Reports, 1990* (Washington, DC: U.S. Government Printing Office, Aug. 1991).

3. Federal Bureau of Investigation, *Crime in the United States: Uniform Crime Reports, 1993* (Washington, DC: U.S. Government Printing Office, Dec. 1994).

4. Federal Bureau of Investigation, *supra* note 2.

5. Based upon estimates for 1977-1992 from United States Department of Justice, Bureau of Justice Statistics, *Violence Between Intimates,* Nov. 1994.

6. U.S. Department of Justice, *supra* note 1.

7. National Center on Child Abuse and Neglect, *Child Maltreatment, 1992* (Washington, DC: U.S. Department of Health and Human Services, 1994).

8. Presidential Task Force on Violence and the Family, *Violence and the Family* (Washington, DC: American Psychological Association, 1996).

9. Feb. 8, 1993, Researchers Say Child Abuse Deaths Underreported, UPI.

10. M. Levine, C. Compaan, and J. Freedman, Maltreatment-Related Fatalities: Issues of Policy and Prevention, *16 Law & Policy,* 449 at 455.

11. U.S. Department of Justice, *supra* note 1.

12. *Id.*

13. See, generally, Adam Dobrin et al., *Statistical Handbook on Violence in America* (Phoenix: Oryx Press, 1996) and Federal Bureau of Investigation, *Crime in the United States: Uniform Crime Reports* (1990-1995).

14. Charles Patrick Ewing, *When Children Kill: The Dynamics of Juvenile Homicide* (Lexington, MA: Lexington Books, 1990).

15. U.S. Department of Justice, *supra* note 1.

16. *Id.*

17. *Id.*

CHAPTER 2:
BATTERERS WHO KILL

References

Lisa Bianco: Mary Dieter, Simpson Case No Surprise to Mother of Slain Hoosier, *Courier Journal,* June 30, 1994, p. 1-B; Matheney v. State of Indiana, 583 N.E. 2d 1202 (1992); Nancy Gibbs, 'Til Death Do Us Part, TIME, Jan. 18, 1993, p. 38; Death Penalty Upheld for Inmate Who Killed Ex-Wife, *Chicago Tribune,* Jan. 10, 1992, p. 3; Indiana Inmate Guilty in Furlough Murder, *Chicago Tribune,* April 12, 1990, p. 3; Karen Tumulty and Stephanie Chavez, Domestic Abuse Laws; Victims Find Little Safety in System, *Los Angeles Times,* Sept. 4, 1989, p. 1; Shiela Weller, Till Death Do Us Part; Violent Attacks on Women by Their Ex-Husbands, REDBOOK, Aug. 1989, p. 112; Dick Polman, Dead Right, *Chicago Tribune,* April 21, 1989, p. 1; Janice C. Simpson, Beware of Paper Tigers; A Brutal Indiana Killing Raises Questions about the Limits of Court Protection for Battered Women, TIME, March 27, 1989, p. 104.

Pamela Nigro Dunn: SJC Upholds Conviction in Slaying of Battered Wife, *Boston Globe,* July 4, 1990, p. 23; Commonwealth v. Paul Dunn, 556 N.E. 2d 30 (Mass. 1990); Shiela Weller, Till Death Do Us Part; Violent Attacks on Women by Their Ex-Husbands, REDBOOK, Aug. 1989, p. 112; Jerry Berger, Judge Fined $75,000 for Misconduct, UPI, March 14, 1989; Associated Press, Judge Censured for Rudeness to Woman in Massachusetts, *New York Times,* Oct. 2, 1988, p. 51; Man Sentenced to Life Term for Killing Wife, UPI, May 20, 1987; Joan Meier, Battered Justice, WASHINGTON MONTHLY, May 1987, p. 37.

Maria Navarro: Associated Press, Killer of Four Women Given Life Term Without Parole, *Los Angeles Times,* May 9, 1991, p. B-3; John Kendall and Tina Anima, Husband Admits Killing Wife, 3 Others at Party, *Los Angeles Times,* March 13, 1991, p. B-1; David Freed, System Overflows with a Flood of Probationers, *Los Angeles Times,* Dec. 21, 1990, p. A-1; Sheriff's Dept. Sues Over Handling of Slayings, *Los Angeles Times,* July 14, 1990, p. B-2; Louis Sahagun, Claims Filed in Shooting; 911 System Faulted, *Los Angeles Times,* Sept. 27, 1989, p. 2-3; Shiela James Kuehl, 911 Must Bring Protection, Not Just a Post-Mortem, *Los Angeles Times,* Aug. 31, 1989, p. 2-7; David Ferrell and Louis Sahagun, Dispatcher's Actions Defended After Killings, *Los Angeles Times,* Aug. 31, 1989, p. 2-1; Stephanie Chavez, Restraining Orders—Desperate People Seek Protection, *Los Angeles Times,* Aug. 30, 1989, p. 2-1; Louis Sahagun and David Ferrell, 4 Women Killed When Gunman Invades Party, *Los Angeles Times,* Aug.

29, 1989, p. 1; Stephanie Chavez and Laurie Becklund, A Family Torn; Survivors Try
to Comprehend Loss, *Los Angeles Times,* Aug. 29, 1989, p. 3.

April Lasalata: Marilyn Goldstein, The Bail Didn't Fit the Crime, *Newsday,* July 29, 1994,
p. A-8; Ann Jones, *Next Time She'll Be Dead: Battering and How to Stop It* (Boston:
Beacon Press, 1994); Paul Vitello, Boy's Grief for Mom: 'If Only . . .', *Newsday,* June
17, 1993, p. 8; Shiela Weller, Till Death Do Us Part; Violent Attacks on Women by
Their Ex-Husbands, REDBOOK, Aug. 1989, p. 112; John Rather, Justice for Whom?
Wife Fears for Safety, *New York Times,* Feb. 26, 1989, p. 12-1; Donald Mace Williams
et al., When Love Is Twisted Into Terror, *Newsday,* Jan. 8, 1989, p. 4; Kathy Bocela,
Latest Victim Mourned with Tears, Anger, *Newsday,* Jan. 8, 1989, p. 4; Kinsey Wilson
and Joshua Quittner, Wife-Slay Suspect Found Dead; Police Call It Suicide, *Newsday,*
Jan. 7, 1989, p. 5; Dan Fagin et al., A 'Sense of Futility'; Cops Shaken by Murder in
Brentwood, *Newsday,* Jan. 5, 1989, p. 3; Dan Fagin, The Domestic Violence Debate;
At Issue: When Arrest Is Warranted, *Newsday,* March 15, 1988, p. 7.

Anna Alfaro: Ann W. O'Neill, Alleged Killer Portrayed as Manipulator of the Justice System,
Los Angeles Times, Aug. 17, 1994, p. B-4; Michael Connelly, Woman's Calls Buried
by 'So Many Cases,' *Los Angeles Times,* Jan. 1, 1990, p. B-3; Inhumanity on the Home
Front, *Los Angeles Times,* Dec. 30, 1989, p. B-6; Tracey Kaplan and Michael Connelly,
Fugitive Ex-Boyfriend Charged with Murder, *Los Angeles Times,* Dec. 29, 1989; Steve
Padilla and Michael Connelly, Shooting Victim Had Told Police of Threat, *Los Angeles
Times,* Dec. 28, 1989, p. B-1; Steve Padilla and Michael Connelly, Fear and Confusion
Haunt Family of Slain Woman, *Los Angeles Times,* Dec. 28, 1989, p. B-3; Michael
Connelly and Steve Padilla, Police Protect Family of Slain Reseda Woman, *Los Angeles
Times,* Dec. 27, 1989, p. B-1; Ex-Boyfriend Sought in Fatal Shooting, *Los Angeles
Times,* Dec. 26, 1989, p. B-6.

Notes

1. Susan Yocum, Police Can't Prevent Domestic Killing; It's Naive and Deadly to Expect a
Response to Most Threats, *Los Angeles Times,* Oct. 4, 1989, p. 2-7.

2. Presidential Task Force on Violence and the Family, *Violence and the Family* (Washington,
DC: American Psychological Association, 1996).

3. Arnold P. Goldstein, *Violence in America* (Palo Alto, CA: Davies-Black, 1996).

4. Martha Mahoney, Legal Images of Battered Women: Redefining the Issue of Separation,
90 *Michigan Law Review* 1 (1991).

5. Charles Patrick Ewing, Violence, Custody and Visitation. In Elizabeth K. Carll (Ed.),
Violence in the Workplace, Home and Community (Boston: Allyn & Bacon, in press); Charles
Patrick Ewing, *Battered Women Who Kill: Psychological Self-Defense as Legal Justification*
(Lexington, MA: D. C. Heath, 1987).

6. *Id.* See also Lenore Walker, *Terrifying Love: Why Battered Women Kill and How Society
Responds* (New York: Harper & Row, 1989).

7. *Id.* See also Ewing, *supra* note 5.

8. Lenore M. J. Simon, A Therapeutic Jurisprudence Approach to the Legal Processing of
Domestic Violence Cases, 1 *Psychology, Public Policy and Law* 43 (1995).

9. Ronald M. Holmes and Stephen T. Holmes, *Murder in America* (Thousand Oaks, CA: Sage,
1994) at 27.

10. Walker, *supra* note 6; Daniel Sonkin et al., *The Male Batterer* (New York: Springer, 1985).

11. Walker, *supra* note 6; Sonkin et al., *supra* note 10.

CHAPTER 3:
BATTERED WOMEN WHO KILL

References

Leslie Emick: Charles Patrick Ewing, *Battered Women Who Kill: Psychological Self-Defense as Legal Justification* (Lexington, MA: D. C. Heath, 1987); *People v. Emick,* 481 N.Y.S. 2d 552 (1984); Sentence in Emick Case Is Fair, Compassionate, *Buffalo News,* April 15, 1985, p. B-2; Emick Gets Probation in Manslaughter Case, *Buffalo News,* April 11, 1985, p. C-5.

Judy Norman: *State of North Carolina v. Judy Ann Laws Norman,* 378 S.E. 2d 8 (N.C. 1989); *State of North Carolina v. Judy Ann Laws Norman,* 366 S.E. 2d 586 (N.C. App. 1988).

Evelyn Humphrey: Claire Cooper, Beaten Woman Who Killed Boyfriend Copes with Freedom, *Sacramento Bee,* Sept. 17, 1996, p. A-1; Pablo Lopez, She Could Stay Silent, But Pain That Runs Deep Won't Let Her, *Fresno Bee,* Sept. 15, 1996, p. A-1; *People v. Evelyn Humphrey,* 921 P.2d 1 (Cal. 1996).

Donna Bechtel: *Donna Lee Bechtel v. State of Oklahoma,* 840 P.2d 1 (Okla. Crim. App. 1992); Lenore Walker, *Terrifying Love: Why Battered Women Kill and How Society Responds* (New York: Harper & Row, 1989).

Notes

1. Presidential Task Force on Violence and the Family, *Violence and the Family* (Washington, DC: American Psychological Association, 1996).

2. Charles Patrick Ewing, *Battered Women Who Kill: Psychological Self-Defense as Legal Justification* (Lexington, MA: D. C. Heath, 1987).

3. *Id.*

4. *Id.*

5. Lenore Walker, *The Battered Woman* (New York: Harper & Row, 1979).

6. *Id.*

7. Martin P. Seligman, *Helplessness: On Depression, Development and Death* (New York: John Wiley, 1975) at 74.

8. Ewing, *supra* note 2.

9. *Id.*

10. *Id.*

11. Federal Bureau of Investigation, *Crime in the United States: Uniform Crime Reports, 1994* (Washington, DC: U.S. Government Printing Office, 1995).

12. See Ewing, *supra* note 2.

13. *Id.*

14. See *State v. Kelly,* 478 A. 2d 364 (N.J. 1984).

15. Ewing, *supra* note 2.

16. See Wayne R. Lafave and Austin W. Scott, *Handbook on Criminal Law* (St. Paul, MN: West Publishing, 1972).

17. See *State v. Kelly, supra* note 14.

18. See Ewing, *supra* note 2.

19. *Id.*

20. See Ewing, *supra* note 2 for a detailed description of this theory of psychological self-defense.

CHAPTER 4:
MUNCHAUSEN MOTHERS

References

Martha Woods: *U.S. v. Martha L. Woods,* 484 F.2d 127 (4th Cir. 1973); V. J. DiMaio and C. G. Bernstein, A Case of Infanticide, 19 *Journal of Forensic Sciences* 744 (1974).

Marybeth Tinning: Joyce Eggington, *From Cradle to Grave* (New York: Jove Books, 1990); DA Drops Case Against Tinning, UPI, April 17, 1990; *People v. Tinning,* 536 N.Y.S. 2d 193 (App. Div. 1988); Lena H. Sun, Over Years, Couple Buried 9 Children; Before Probe, Caller Asked: 'How Many More Have to Die?', *Washington Post,* March 1, 1987, p. A-1.

Lori Z.: *In re Jessica Z.,* 515 N.Y.S. 2d 370 (Family Ct. of Westchester Co. 1987).

Priscilla Phillips: *People v. Priscilla E. Phillips,* 122 Cal. App. 3d 69; 175 Cal. Rptr. 703 (1981).

Pamela Walker: Mitch Himaka, Mother Jailed for Trying to Smother Infant, *San Diego Union-Tribune,* Oct. 28, 1987, p. B-1; Mike Konon, Jail Ordered for Attempt to Smother Child, *San Diego Union-Tribune,* Oct. 28, 1987, p. B-1; Munchausen, UPI, April 11, 1987; Mother Held in Attack, *San Diego Union-Tribune,* April 1, 1987, p. B-2.

Karen Sterchi: Andre Jackson, Woman Gets Probation; Injected Filth in Son, *St. Louis Post-Dispatch,* March 31, 1989, p. 7-A; Woman Accused of Injecting Bacteria Into Son's Intravenous Tubes, UPI, March 31, 1989; Mother Allegedly Injected Bacteria Into Young Son, UPI, June 3, 1988.

Milwaukee Mother: Camera Catches Mom Trying to Choke Son, Chicago Tribune, Oct. 22, 1987, p. 3.

Tammie Lynn Smith: Reston Woman Is Sentenced to 8 Years in Prison for Giving Son Mouse Poison, *Washington Post,* April 14, 1990, p. D-7; Mother Guilty of Attempted Poisoning, UPI, Jan. 17, 1990; DeNeen L. Brown, Reston Mother Pleads Guilty to Trying to Poison Son, 2, *Washington Post,* Jan. 17, 1990, p. B-4; Lori K. Weinraub, Mother Charged with Poisoning Son, UPI, Sept. 1, 1989; Pamela Babcock, Woman Said to Have Fed Son Poison, *Washington Post,* Sept. 1, 1989, p. D-1.

Notes

1. V. J. DiMaio and C. G. Bernstein, A Case of Infanticide, 19 *Journal of Forensic Sciences* 744 (1974) at 748.

2. *Id.* at 749.

3. *Id.*

4. *Id.* at 750.

5. *U.S. v. Martha L. Woods,* 484 F.2d 127 (4th Cir. 1973) at 127.

6. *Id.*

7. *Id.*

8. DiMaio and Bernstein, *supra* note 1 at 751.

9. Joyce Eggington, *From Cradle to Grave* (New York: Jove Books, 1990) at 115.

10. *Id.* at 129.

11. *Id.* at 219.

12. *Id.* at 220.

13. *Id.* at 223.

14. See, generally, Bernard Kahan and Beatrice Crofts Yorker, 9 *Behavioral Sciences and the Law* 73 (1991).

15. American Psychiatric Association, *Diagnostic and Statistical Manual of Mental Disorders* (4th ed.) (Washington, DC: American Psychiatric Association, 1994).

16. *Id.* at 474.

17. *Id.* at 472.

18. See Kahan and Yorker, *supra* note 14.

19. American Psychiatric Association, *supra* note 15 at 703.

20. *Id.* at 725.

21. *Id.*

22. *In re Jessica Z.,* 515 N.Y.S. 2d 370 (Family Ct. of Westchester Co. 1987) at 372.

23. *Id.* at 374.

24. *Id.*

25. See, for example, Kahan and Yorker, *supra* note 14.

CHAPTER 5:
POSTPARTUM HOMICIDES

References

Sheryl Lynn Massip: *People v. Sheryl Lynn Massip,* 235 Cal. App. 3d 1884 (1990); Andrea Ford, Judge Won't Confine Massip: Outpatient Therapy Is Ordered, *Los Angeles Times,* March 11, 1989, p. 2-1; Eric Lichtblau, 6-Month Evaluation of Sheryl Massip's Mental State Urged, *Los Angeles Times,* March 7, 1989, p. 2-1; Eric Lichtblau, A Long Road for Massip; Postpartum Psychosis: Recovery Is Torturous, *Los Angeles Times,* Feb. 3, 1989, p. 1-1; Eric Lichtblau, Massip Ruling Seen as Boost for Postpartum Education, *Los Angeles Times,* Dec. 25, 1988, p. 2-1; Eric Lichtblau and Bob Schwartz, Judge Again Affirms His Credentials as a Free Thinker, *Los Angeles Times,* Dec. 25, 1988, p. 2-1; Judge Frees Mother Who Killed Her Child, *Chicago Tribune,* Dec. 25, 1988, p. 29; Nancy Wride and Bill Billiter, Some Jurors in Massip Case Express Surprise, Disappointment, *Los Angeles Times,* Dec. 24, 1988, p. 2-1.

Beverly Bartek: Bartek, UPI, Oct. 25, 1986; Regional News, UPI, Sept. 9, 1986; Bartek Found Not Responsible for Infant Drowning, UPI, Aug. 11, 1986; Regional News, UPI, July 22, 1986; Regional News, UPI, May 27, 1986.

Ann Green: Timothy Clifford, Woman Who Killed 2 Infants Freed After Psychiatric Review, *Newsday,* April 13, 1989, p. 41; Barbara Goldberg, Killer Mom Freed After 37 Days Evaluation, UPI, April 12, 1989; Timothy Clifford, Mom Who Killed Kids Ordered to Mental Facility, *Newsday,* Feb. 9, 1989, p. 8; Peg Byron, Green, Cleared with Post-Partum Depression Defense, Back in Court, UPI, Jan. 13, 1989; Timothy Clifford, Mother "Not Responsible" for Murdering Her Babies, *Newsday,* Oct. 1,

1988, p. 3; Scott Ladd, Verdict Breaks Ground, *Newsday,* Oct. 1, 1988, p. 3; Barbara
Goldberg, Green, UPI, Sept. 30, 1988; Timothy Clifford, Doc Says Illness Made Nurse
Kill, *Newsday,* Sept. 16, 1988, p. 38; Constance L. Hays, Mother Testifies on Murders
of Her Children, *New York Times,* Sept. 15, 1988, p. B-8; Timothy Clifford, Lawyers
Differs on Depression, *Newsday,* Sept. 7, 1988, p. 20; Constance L. Hays, Mother
on Trial in 2 Deaths Had Postpartum Psychosis, Lawyer Says, *New York Times,* Sept.
7, 1988, p. B-4; Barbara Goldberg, Mother Accused of Killing Kids to Plea Post-Birth
Insanity, UPI, Sept. 6, 1988; Kirk Johnson, Nurse Accused of Murdering 2 of Her
Babies, *New York Times,* March 4, 1986, p. B-1; Bernard Cullen, Nurse Charged in
Babies' Deaths, UPI, March 3, 1986.
Michelle Remington: Carl Burak and Michelle Remington, *The Cradle Will Fall* (New York:
Donald Fine, 1994); Molly Walsh, Serious Depression Often Dismissed as Baby Blues,
Sacramento Bee, Sept. 5, 1994, p. A-6; Anastasia Toufexis, The Baby Blues Pressures
on New Moms Lead to Terrifying Resolutions, *Chicago Tribune,* Oct. 16, 1988, p. 9;
Anastasia Toufexis, Why Mothers Kill Their Babies, TIME, June 20, 1988, p. 81.
Angela Thompson: Eric Lichtblau, A Long Road for Massip; Postpartum Psychosis: Recovery
Is Torturous, *Los Angeles Times,* Feb. 3, 1989, p. 1-1; Short Takes: Blood's Thicker . . .,
Los Angeles Times, Jan. 17, 1988, p. 6-2; Ann Japenga, Ordeal of Postpartum
Psychosis Can Have Tragic Consequences for New Mothers, *Los Angeles Times,* Feb.
1, 1987, p. 6-1; Woman Who Drowned Her Infant Son Sues Doctors, Midwife for
Negligence, *San Diego Union-Tribune,* Sept. 7, 1984, p. A-21.

Notes

1. *People v. Sheryl Lynn Massip,* 235 Cal. App. 3d 1884 (1990).
2. See N.Y. Penal Law, Sec. 40.15.
3. See L. A. Callahan et al., The Volume and Characteristics of Insanity Defense Pleas: An
Eight State Study, 19 *Bulletin of Psychiatry and the Law* 331 (1991); R. Simon and D. E. Aaronson,
The Insanity Defense (New York: Praeger, 1988).
4. Anastasia Toufexis, Why Mothers Kill Their Babies, TIME, June 20, 1988, p. 81.
5. When Do New Mom's 'Baby Blues' Become More Serious Illness? *Chicago Tribune,* Nov.
27, 1988, p. 3.
6. *Id.*
7. American Psychiatric Association, *Diagnostic and Statistical Manual of Mental Disorders*
(4th ed.) (Washington, DC: American Psychiatric Association, 1994) at 386.
8. *Id.*
9. *Id.* at 386-387.
10. Eric Lichtblau, A Long Road for Massip; Postpartum Psychosis: Recovery Is Torturous,
Los Angeles Times, Feb. 3, 1989, p. 1-1.
11. Anastasia Toufexis, The Baby Blues Pressures on New Moms Lead to Terrifying Resolutions, *Chicago Tribune,* Oct. 16, 1988, p. 9; Marianne Yen, High-Risk Mothers; Postpartum
Depression, in Rare Cases, May Cause an Infant's Death, *Washington Post,* Aug. 23, 1988, Health
p. 18.
12. Gail Diane Cox, Postpartum Defense: No Sure Thing; Recent Verdicts Split Both Ways,
National Law Journal, Dec. 5, 1988, p. 3.
13. *Id.*
14. *Id.*
15. Sarah Pattee, Maternal Instinct Gone Awry; A Mother Who Kills Her Child Deserves Help,
Not Prison, Psychologist Says, *Los Angeles Times,* Sept. 30, 1989, p. 5-1.

16. Ann Japenga, Ordeal of Postpartum Psychosis Can Have Tragic Consequences for New Mothers, *Los Angeles Times,* Feb. 1, 1987, p. 6-1.

17. Lichtblau, *supra* note 10.

CHAPTER 6:
DISAPPEARING, DISPOSABLE BABIES

References

Paula Sims: Paula Sims Pleads Guilty, UPI, May 1, 1990; Sims' Appeal Denied, UPI, April 30, 1990; Sims Sentenced to Another 11 Years, UPI, March 28, 1990; News Director Quits Amid TV Poll Backlash, *Electronic Media,* March 5, 1990, p. 12; Associated Press, Life Term for Mom in Baby's Death, *Chicago Tribune,* Feb. 2, 1990, p. 3; Marc Magliari, Lawyer: Convicted Baby Killer Wants Death, UPI, Feb. 1, 1990; Michael Tackett, Jury Convicts Alton Mother in Baby's Death, *Chicago Tribune,* Jan. 31, 1990, p. 3; Associated Press, Mother Found Guilty in Death of 'Stolen Baby,' *Los Angeles Times,* Jan. 31, 1990, p. A-4; Marc Magliari, Jury Considers Sims Case, UPI, Jan. 30, 1990; Michael Tackett, Mom Says She Didn't Kill Her Kids, *Chicago Tribune,* Jan. 25, 1990, p. 8; Michael Tackett, Husband Backs Wife's Kidnapping Account, *Chicago Tribune,* Jan. 24, 1990, p. 6; Marc Magliari, Paula Sims Trial, UPI, Jan. 24, 1990; Marc Magliari, Robert Sims Defends Wife in Emotional Testimony, UPI, Jan. 23, 1990; Detective Says Sims Actions Led to Suspicion, UPI, Jan. 22, 1990; Friends Testify in Sims Defense, UPI, Jan. 19, 1990; Prosecution Rests in Sims Trial, UPI, Jan. 18, 1990; Cop Testifies Sims Was Suspect from Outset, UPI, Jan. 17, 1990; Michael Tackett, Story of Kidnapping Portrayed as 'Fairy Tale,' *Chicago Tribune,* Jan. 12, 1990, p. 5; Marc Magliari, Testimony Begins in Sims Trial, UPI, Jan. 11, 1990; Two Times, Too Much, TIME, July 24, 1989, p. 25; Paula Sims Indicted on 2 Counts of Murder, UPI, July 11, 1989; Michael Tackett, Three Years Later, Baby's Death Leads to Charges, *Chicago Tribune,* May 14, 1989, p. 4; Michael Tackett, Alton Mom Charged in First Baby's Death, *Chicago Tribune,* May 13, 1989, p. 3; Michael Tackett, Mother's Account of Kidnap Probed, *Chicago Tribune,* May 10, 1989, p. 3; Associated Press, Illinois Man Implicates His Wife in Deaths of Their Two Infant Girls, *Los Angeles Times,* May 8, 1989, p. 1-16; Steve Whitworth, Police Say Father Suspicious in Infant's Death, UPI, May 7, 1989; Michael Tackett, Slain Baby's Parents Now Prime Suspects, *Chicago Tribune,* May 6, 1989, p. 8; Body Identified as Missing Infant, UPI, May 5, 1989; Associated Press, Pair Again Report Baby Taken; First Found Dead, *Los Angeles Times,* May 2, 1989, p. 1-14; Associated Press, Police Skeptical on Report of Abduction of 2nd Infant, *Los Angeles Times,* May 1, 1989, p. A-2; FBI Joins Search for Missing Child, UPI, May 1, 1989; Baby, UPI, Sept. 10, 1986; Body Identified as Missing Infant, UPI, Sept. 5, 1986; Infant Found Dead Near Home, UPI, June 25, 1986; Abduction, UPI, June 21, 1986; Family of Abducted Infant Seeks Public Help, UPI, June 20, 1986; Abduction, UPI, June 20, 1986; Abduction, UPI, June 19, 1986; No Sign of Two-Week Old Girl, UPI, June 19, 1986; Twelve-Day-Old Girl Abducted, UPI, June 18, 1986.

Kathleen Householder: Todd Spangler, Householder Still Facing Charge in Virginia, UPI, Jan. 6, 1988; W. Va. Woman Who Killed Baby Is Freed, *Washington Post,* Jan. 4,

1988, p. D-6; Mother Who Killed Baby Gives Birth, *Washington Post,* Sept. 19, 1987, p. B-5; Todd Spangler, Householder Gives Birth to Baby Girl, UPI, Sept. 17, 1987; Todd Spangler, Householder, UPI, April 11, 1987; Jefferson County Woman Gets 1-5 Years in Prison for Killing Daughter, UPI, March 11, 1987; Barbara Carton, Guilty Plea in Infant's Death; Mother Said Baby Had Been Kidnapped, *Washington Post,* Jan. 23, 1987, p. C-3; Philip Smith, No Hint of Tragedy in Mother's Past; Kathleen Householder's Recent Troubles Were Prelude to Incident, *Washington Post,* March 2, 1986, p. B-1; Patricia Davis, Mother Threw Rock at Baby, Police Testify, *Washington Post,* Feb. 8, 1986, p. B-1; Missing, UPI, Jan. 25, 1986; Barbara Carton, Mother's Slaying Charge Stuns W. Va. Town, *Washington Post,* Jan. 24, 1986, p. B-1; Barbara Carton, Asphyxiation, Head Trauma Killed Baby, Officials Say, *Washington Post,* Jan. 23, 1986, p. C-5; Associated Press, Mother Charged with Killing Baby She Made TV Plea For, *New York Times,* Jan. 22, 1986, p. A-13; Barbara Carton, Missing Baby's Mother Faces Murder Charge, *Washington Post,* Jan. 22, 1986, p. D-1; Missing, UPI, Jan. 21, 1986; Missing, UPI, Jan. 8, 1986; $15,000 Reward Posted for Baby, *Washington Post,* Jan. 8, 1986, p. D-10; Sandra Sugawara, W. Va. Woman Keeps an Anxious Vigil for Missing Infant, *Washington Post,* Jan. 5, 1986, p. B-1; Two Week-Old Girl Kidnapped, UPI, Jan. 3, 1986.

Tanya Dacri: Judge Denies Tanya Dacri's Bid for New Murder Trial, UPI, March 8, 1990; Phillip Dacri Sentenced in Killing of Infant, UPI, Jan. 18, 1990; Vince Piscopo, Mother Gets Life in Jail for Drowning, Dismembering Baby, UPI, July 13, 1989; Vince Piscopo, Dacri Receives Life Term for Drowning, Dismembering Infant Son, UPI, July 13, 1989; Dacri Hearing Continues, UPI, July 12, 1989; Woman Ignores Legal Advice, Admits Killing Infant Son, *Chicago Tribune,* July 11, 1989, p. 4; Barbara McCabe, Tanya Dacri Pleads Guilty to Murder in Death of Infant Son, UPI, July 10, 1989; Dacri Trial Date Set, UPI, May 23, 1989; Dacri Says She Cannot Endure Trial in Son's Slaying, UPI, May 9, 1989; Brian Mooar, Accused Baby-Killer Ordered to Stand Trial, UPI, Feb. 8, 1989; Battered Infant Buried in Private Funeral, UPI, Jan. 25, 1989; Dismembered Body Had Earlier Broken Bones, UPI, Jan. 19, 1989; Barbara McCabe, Father to Stand Trial for Role in Baby's Death, UPI, Jan. 18, 1989; Barbara McCabe, Baby's Torso Found in Creek, UPI, Jan. 13, 1989; Philadelphia Woman Charged with Infant Son's Murder, Reuters, Jan. 12, 1989; Baby, UPI, Jan. 12, 1989; Police Searching for Kidnapped Infant, Reuters, Jan. 11, 1989; Mother Charged in Murder of Son She Said Was Kidnapped, UPI, Jan. 11, 1989; Kidnap, UPI, Jan. 11, 1989.

Lucrezia Gentile: Patricia Hurtado, Mom Recounts Drowning Baby in Depression: A Daydream of Death, *Newsday,* Nov. 10, 1989, p. 4; Gentile Begins Psychiatric Counseling, UPI, April 27, 1988; Rita Giordano, Parish Prays for Dead Baby's Mom, *Newsday,* April 25, 1988, p. 5; Bob Liff, Tale of Mother's Turmoil in Aftermath of Baby's Death, *Newsday,* April 23, 1988, p. 3; Allison Carper et al., 'Kidnapped' Baby Found Dead, Mother Charged with Murder, *Newsday,* April 22, 1988, p. 5.

Sharon Comitz: *Commonwealth v. Comitz,* 530 A.2d 473 (Pa. Super. 1987); Comitz, UPI, Oct. 25, 1985; Comitz, UPI, June 14, 1985; Around Western Pennsylvania, UPI, Feb. 2, 1985; Comitz, UPI, Jan. 31, 1985; Comitz, UPI, Jan. 28, 1985; Comitz, UPI, Jan. 26, 1985; Mother Charged in Disappearance, Death of 1-Month-Old Son, UPI, Jan. 25, 1985; Comitz, UPI, Jan. 4, 1985.

April Olivia: George James, In Trash, a Brief Life and a Note of Love, *New York Times,* May 1, 1991, p. B-1; Infant Girl's Body Is Found in Bag on a Brooklyn Street, *New*

York Times, April 30, 1991; Curtis Rist, Infant's Body Found, *Newsday,* April 30, 1991, p. 26.

East New York Baby: M.E. Rules Baby Death a Homicide; Mother Arrested, UPI, March 27, 1991; Newborn Boy Found Dead in Trash Bag, UPI, March 26, 1991.

Twelve Year Old Brooklyn Girl ("Tina"): Anemona Hartocollis, Regret for Trashed Lives, *Newsday,* April 15, 1991, p. 6; Patricia Hurtado, B'klyn Mom, 12, Won't be Indicted, *Newsday,* April 5, 1991, p. 7; Report: No Charges for 12-Year Old Mother Who Left Baby in Trash, UPI, April 5, 1991; Michael Specter, Horror Not a Stranger to Project; Only Disposal of Baby Made Child-Mother's Tragic Life Remarkable, *Washington Post,* March 30, 1991, p. A-3; Infant Thrown in Trash by Mother, 12, Is Rescued, *Chicago Tribune,* March 29, 1991, p. 8; Chris Hedges, Mother, 12, Suffered 'Too Much Too Young,' *Memphis Commercial Appeal,* March 29, 1991, p. A-2; Chris Hedges, A Child-Mother in the Jaws of New York, *New York Times,* March 29, 1991, p. A-1; William Douglas and Bob Liff, 'Baby's Dad' Saved From Leap; He's Charged With Statutory Rape of Minor, *Newsday,* March 29, 1991, p. 3; James C. McKinley, Jr., Baby Saved From Compactor, Where Mother, 12, Says She Put Him, *New York Times,* March 28, 1991, p. B-1; William Douglas and Bob Liff, 'A Very Lucky Baby,' *Newsday,* March 28, 1991, p. 1.

"I Love New York" Babies: Melinda Henneberger, Two Infants Left in Trash; Each Found in 'I Love New York' Bag; One Dies, *Newsday,* June 22, 1991, p. 5; Curtis Rist, 2 Trashed Babies, 1 Lives, 1 Dies, *Newsday,* June 20, 1991, p. 35; John T. McQuiston, Two Infants Found in Trash Bins; One Dies, *New York Times,* June 20, 1991, p. B-3; Search for Mothers of Two Newborns Thrown in Trash, UPI, June 20, 1991.

Coney Island Baby: George James, Newborn Is Thrown in Trash and Dies, *New York Times,* Aug. 14, 1991, p. B-3; Curtis Rist, Dead Baby in Garbage, *Newsday,* Aug. 13, 1991, p. 32; Newborn Baby Found in Garbage Disposal, UPI, Aug. 13, 1991; Newborn Baby Found in Garbage Disposal, UPI, Aug. 12, 1991.

Kendra Nowak: Teenager Given Probation in Infant's Death, UPI, July 17, 1990; Teenager Pleads Guilty to Misdemeanor in Newborn's Death, UPI, March 7, 1990; Teenager Ordered to Trial in Newborn's Death, UPI, Nov. 14, 1989; Woman Charged in Death of Baby, UPI, June 9, 1989.

Dawn Chapman: Teenage Mother Charged in Death of Newborn, UPI, July 12, 1988.

Juana Lopez: Jerry Hicks, Girl Who Killed Her Baby Gets Year in Juvenile Hall, *Los Angeles Times,* April 13, 1988, p. 2-14; David Reyes, Release Denied for Girl, 16, Held in Death of Her Baby, *Los Angeles Times,* Oct. 20, 1987, p. 2-4.

Notes

1. George James, Newborn Is Thrown in Trash and Dies, *New York Times,* Aug. 14, 1991, p. B-3.

2. *Id.*

3. Jeff Collins, Infant Abandonment an Act of Fear, Experts Say, *Orange County Register,* Oct. 10, 1993, p. B-1.

4. Michael Kelly, The Psychology of Abandonment, *Bergen Record,* Jan. 25, 1985, p. A-1.

5. Penelope McMillan, Drug Link Studied; Abandoned Babies: Why the Surge? *Los Angeles Times,* Feb. 24, 1989, p. 1-1.

6. Gerry Brailo Spencer, Woman Farm Worker Sought in Baby's Death, *Los Angeles Times,* Aug. 1, 1991, p. B-1; Jane Hulse, Charges Pending in Baby's Death, *Los Angeles Times,* July 31,

1991, p. B-2; Mack Reed, Hospital Cited for Not Reporting Baby's Death, *Los Angeles Times*, July 23, 1991, p. B-6; Body of Newborn Girl Found in Dumpster at Montebello Motel, *Los Angeles Times*, July 5, 1991, p. A-26.

    7. Victor Galvan, Number of Abandoned Infants in Tampa Bay High, UPI, March 11, 1990.

    8. Carolyn Colwell, Death of a Newborn, *Newsday,* March 8, 1991, p. 23.

    9. Temple Terrace, A Gift Abandoned, *St. Petersburg Times,* April 14, 1991, p. 5.

    10. Ronald M. Holmes and Stephen M. Holmes, *Murder in America* (Thousand Oaks, CA: Sage, 1994) at 48-49.

    11. Steven E. Pitt and Erin M. Bale, Neonaticide, Infanticide, and Filicide: A Review of the Literature, 23 *Bulletin of the American Academy of Psychiatry and Law* 375 at 379.

CHAPTER 7:
CHILD ABUSE FATALITIES

References

Awilda Lopez/Elisa Izquierdo: Russ Buettner and Salvatore Arena, Mom Pleads Guilty to Elisa's Murder, *New York Daily News,* June 25, 1996, p. 6; NY Mother Pleads Guilty in Girl's Abuse Death, *Dallas Morning News,* June 25, 1996, p. 3A; Joe Sexton, Mother of Elisa Izquierdo Pleads Guilty to Murder in a Pivotal Child-Abuse Case, *New York Times,* June 25, 1996, p. B-3; Tells of Abuse of Daughter, *Bergen Record,* June 25, 1996, p. A-4; NY Mom Pleads Guilty to Daughter Slay, UPI, June 24, 1996; Murray Kempton, Many Share Blame in Child's Death, *Newsday,* May 1, 1996, p. A-44; Vivian S. Toy, Hospital Ousts Psychologist in Abuse Case, *New York Times,* April 16, 1996, p. B-2; Russ Buettner, Elisa's Death Is System's Shame, *New York Daily News,* April 9, 1996, p. 5; Lizette Alvarez, Report in Wake of Girl's Death Finds Failures in Child Agency, *New York Times,* April 9, 1996, p. A-1; Beth Holland, The Paper Trail: Report Details Horror of Abused Child's Life, *Newsday,* April 9, 1996, p. A-3; Barbara Ross, Sex Abuse of Girl Is Cited in Autopsy, *New York Daily News,* Feb. 1, 1996, p. 19; William Tucker, A Little Girl Murdered, THE WEEKLY STANDARD, Dec. 18, 1995, p. 19; Marc Peyser, The Death of Little Elisa, NEWSWEEK, Dec. 11, 1995, p. 42; David Van Biema, Abandoned to Her Fate; Neighbors, Teachers, and the Authorities All Knew Elisa Izquierdo Was Being Abused but Somehow Nobody Managed to Stop It, TIME, Dec. 11, 1995, p. 32.

Emily Hernandez: Richard Whitmire, Child's Death Moves State Closer to Taking Children from Homes More Quickly, Gannett News Service, April 11, 1996; Tom Condon, 'The Boyfriend Problem' Hard to Counteract, *Hartford Courant,* Feb. 20, 1996, p. A-3; Betsy Rubiner, Violence Claims the Young, *Des Moines Register,* Dec. 30 1995, p. 2; Knight-Ridder Tribune News, Hard Lessons Learned from Rape, Death of 9-Month-Old Girl, *Houston Chronicle,* Dec. 17, 1995, p. A-28; John Lender, Baby's Death Blamed on Adults Who Failed to Protect Her, *Hartford Courant,* April 27, 1995, p. A-1; Maxine Bernstein and Jon Lender, Agency Knew of Family's Abusive Past; Infant Injured Weeks Before Killing, *Hartford Courant,* March 15, 1995, p. A-1.

Kevin Mikell: Ilene Barth, A Boy's Life and Death, *Washington Post,* April 18, 1996, p. C-2; Jorge Fitzgibbbon, Slay-Suspect Dad Abused Others, *New York Daily News,* Feb. 29, 1996, p. 10; Jorge Fitzgibbbon, Bronx Dad Indicted in Beat-Slay of Son, 2, *New York*

Daily News, Feb. 27, 1996, p. 3; Russ Buettner, Dad Abused Before; Hurt Baby in '84, City Records Show, *New York Daily News,* Feb. 23, 1996, p. 5; Wendell Jamieson, Battering of Boy, 2, Detailed, *New York Daily News,* Feb. 22, 1996, p. 8; Often Open and Shut Case, *New York Daily News,* Feb. 22, 1996, p. 5; Joe Sexton, Bronx Judge Defends Ruling in Abuse Case, *New York Times,* Feb. 22, 1996, p. B-1; Man Tells Police He Beat 2-Year-Old Son to Death, *Orlando Sentinel,* Feb. 22, 1996, p. A-8; Associated Press, Dad Held in Killing Son, 2; Toilet Training Cited as Reason for Beating, *Bergen Record,* Feb. 22, 1996, p. A-4; Corky Siemaszko, Son, 2, Beaten to Death, Cops Say Dad Raged Over Toilet Training, *New York Daily News,* Feb. 21, 1996, p. 5; Joe Sexton, Abused Boy Found Dead in the Bronx, *New York Times,* Feb. 21, 1996, p. B-1; Potty Murder, *Phoenix Gazette,* Feb. 21, 1996, p. A-7.

Michael Sulsona: Colleen Mancino, Pompton Lakes Dad Indicted in Shaking Charge Cut to Manslaughter, *Bergen Record,* June 19, 1996, p. N-5.

José Davila: David Polochanin, Chelsea Man Guilty in Murder of Two Sons, *Boston Globe,* Oct. 1, 1994, p. 17; Elizabeth Stankiewicz, Marchers Decry Domestic Violence, *Boston Globe,* Oct. 26, 1992, p. 15; Elizabeth Stankiewicz, Murder Suspect Found Incompetent; DA to Contest Finding in Case of Deaths of 2 Boys in Methuen, *Boston Globe,* Oct. 10, 1992, p. 27; Alexander Reid, DA Says Killer Left Taped Message; Slain Boys' Custody Cited, *Boston Globe,* Sept. 1, 1992, p. 1; Linda Gorov and Zachery R. Dowdy, Chelsea Man Charged in Sons' Deaths, *Boston Globe,* Aug. 31, 1992, p. 1.

Notes

1. Richard Whitmire, Child's Death Moves State Closer to Taking Children from Homes More Quickly, Gannett News Service, April 11, 1996.

2. Bruce Frankel, Safety and Family Clash in Child Welfare Debate, *USA Today,* April 25, 1996, p. A-1.

3. Whitmire, *supra* note 1.

4. Phillip W. McClain, Jeffrey J. Saks, Robert G. Froehlke, and B. G. Ewigman, Estimates of Fatal Child Abuse and Neglect, United States, 1979 through 1988, 91 *Pediatrics* 338 (1993).

5. Murray Levine, Jennifer Freeman, and Cheryl Compaan, Maltreatment-Related Fatalities: Issues of Policy and Prevention, 16 *Law and Policy* 449 (1994) at 458.

6. *Id.*

7. *Id.*

8. J. F. Campion, J. M. Cravens, and F. Covan, A Study of Filicidal Men, 145 *American Journal of Psychiatry* 1141 (1988).

9. See Levine et al., *supra* note 5 at 458.

10. *Id.* at 455.

11. *Id.* at 452-453.

12. See Steven E. Pitt and Erin M. Bale, Neonaticide, Infanticide, and Filicide: A Review of the Literature, 23 *Bulletin of the American Academy of Psychiatry and the Law* 375 (1995) at 377-378.

13. Levine et al., *supra* note 5 at 455-456.

14. Jamie Kritzer, Expert: Many Don't Realize Danger of Shaking Babies, *Montgomery Advertiser,* July 17, 1996, p. B-1; Jamie Talan, Syndrome Symptoms/Docs: Violent Shaking Can Injure and Kill, *Newsday,* April 5, 1996, p. A-3.

15. Robin Topping, When 'Shaken Baby' Abuse Is Suspected, *Newsday,* March 12, 1996, p. A-25.

16. Pitt and Bale, *supra* note 12 at 378.

17. *Id.* at 377.

CHAPTER 8:
PARRICIDE

References

Lonnie Dutton: Dennis Romero, Target: Parents; Stories of Teens Who Kill Their Mothers and Fathers, *Los Angeles Times,* March 21, 1995, p. E-1; Phil Reeves, Why the Boys Killed Daddy, *The Independent,* Sept. 29, 1993, p. 15; Associated Press, 2 Boys Free in Killing of Abusive Father, *Chicago Tribune,* Sept. 15, 1993, p. 18; 2 Boys Get Deal in Dad's Killing, *Memphis Commercial Appeal,* Sept. 15, 1993, p. A-2; Arnold Hamilton, Boys Plead No Contest in Dad's Slaying, *Dallas Morning News,* Sept. 15, 1993, p. 1-A; Associated Press, Boys Who Shot Abusive Father Win Freedom on Plea Bargain, *St. Louis Post-Dispatch,* Sept. 15, 1993, p. 8-A; Mark Potok, Sons' Deadly Defense/Killing of Abusive Dad Unites Okla. Town/Blue Ribbons Everywhere Show Support, *USA Today,* Aug. 26, 1993, p. A-1; Pam Lambert, Killing Dad, PEOPLE, Aug. 16, 1993, p. 87; B. E. Stewart, The Dragonslaying, *Washington Post,* Aug. 15, 1993, p. F-1; Susan Ellicott, When Children Kill Dad, These Americans Cheer, *Sunday Times of London,* Aug. 1, 1993, p. 1; Sam Howe Verhovek, Town Rallies Behind Boys Who Killed Father, *New York Times,* July 25, 1993, p. 1-14.

Bryan and David Freeman: Younger Skinhead Brother Pleads Guilty to Killing Father, Associated Press, Dec. 15, 1995; Debbie Garlicki, David Freeman Pleads Guilty, *Allentown Morning Call,* Dec. 16, 1995, p. A-3; John P. Martin, Freeman Gets Life in Prison; Oldest Brother Admits Murdering His Mother, *Allentown Morning Call,* Dec. 8, 1995, p. A-1; 2 Skinhead Brothers Charged With Killing Family Members, *New York Times,* Dec. 8, 1995, p. A-14; Keith Schneider, Triple Murder Causes Alarm About Hate Groups' Growth, *New York Times,* March 6, 1995, p. A-1; Lorraine Adams, Too Close for Comfort; Two Pairs of Parents Slain by Their Sons, 4 Days and 9 Miles Apart, *Washington Post,* April 2, 1995, p. F-1.

Jeffrey Howorth: Aminah Franklin and Susan Todd, Howorth Verdict Criticized and Backed, *Allentown Morning Call,* Oct. 24, 1995, p. B-1; Thomas Kupper and Megan O'Matz, Call Made to Abolish Insanity Defense, *Allentown Morning Call,* Oct. 24, 1995, p. B-1; Sophia Lezin, Hospital to Determine Howorth's Exact Mental Illness, *Allentown Morning Call,* Oct. 24, 1995, A-1; Debbie Garlicki, Howorth Not Guilty; Teen Judged Mentally Ill, *Allentown Morning Call,* Oct. 23, 1995, p. A-1; Debbie Garlicki, Howorth Jury Is Optimistic, Will Continue, *Allentown Morning Call,* Oct. 22, 1995, p. A-1; Susan Todd, Affection Hid Howorth's Inner Turmoil, *Allentown Morning Call,* Oct. 14, 1995, p. B-16; John P. Martin, Trooper: Howorth Admitted Slayings, *Allentown Morning Call,* Sept. 12, 1995, p. A-1; Susan Todd, Howorth Scribbled of Murder, *Allentown Morning Call,* July 14, 1995, p. A-1; Susan Todd, Howorth Threatened Brother, Court Told, *Allentown Morning Call,* July 13, 1995, p. A-1; Susan Todd, Mental Woes Made Howorth Kill, Experts Say, *Allentown Morning Call,* July 11, 1995, p. A-1; Jennifer Steinhauer, 'I Want a Movie After I Kill Everyone,' *New York Times,* March 5, 1995, p. 1-12; Aminah Franklin, Police Scour Region for Teen Accused of Shooting Parents, *Allentown Morning Call,* March 4, 1995, p. A-3.

Gerard McCra III: Ann E. Dolan, Grisly Murders Led to Tougher Juvenile Laws, *Boston Herald,* Jan. 7, 1996, p. 8; Paul Langner, McCra Is Sentenced to Life in Prison; Convicted in Shooting of Parents, Sister, *Boston Globe,* Oct. 24, 1995, p. 25; Joe Heaney, Teen Gets Life Sentence in Slaying of Family, *Boston Herald,* Oct. 24, 1995, p. 5; Family Killer Convicted in Mass., UPI, Oct. 23, 1995; Paul Langner, Kin Testify on McCra Family Turmoil, *Boston Globe,* Oct. 20, 1995, p. 30; David Weber, Accused Killer's Kin Says Boy Was Abused, *Boston Herald,* Oct. 20, 1995, p. 19; Paul Langner, Relatives Set to Testify in McCra Murder Trial, *Boston Globe,* Oct. 19, 1995, p. 32; David Weber, 'Stupid Argument' Led Boy to Kill Family, Cop Says, *Boston Herald,* Oct. 18, 1995, p. 20; Charles M. Sennott, Violence at Home: Chilling Cases of Slain Parents, *Boston Globe,* March 14, 1995, p. 3.

Martin Tankleff: Tankleff Guilty in Murder of Parents, UPI, June 28, 1990; Carolyn Colwell, Cops Tell of Tankleff Murder Scene, Testify That Son Blamed Deaths on Father's Business Partner, *Newsday,* April 26, 1990, p. 6; Joshua Quittner, Judge OKs Tankleff's Confession as Evidence, *Newsday,* May 9, 1989, p. 4; Joshua Quittner, Detective: How I Tricked Tankleff, *Newsday,* March 9, 1989, p. 5; Shirley E. Perlman and Joseph Demma, A Child of Suburban Wealth: Martin Tankleff's House Was a Place of Luxury, *Newsday,* Dec. 13, 1988, p. 7; Joseph Demma, Tankleff Stands to Inherit Millions, *Newsday,* Nov. 2, 1988, p. 3; Man Charged With Killing Dad, UPI, Oct. 27, 1988; Carolyn Colwell, Reward Offer in Tankleff Case, *Newsday,* Oct. 15, 1988, p. 7; Kinsey Wilson, Seymour Tankleff Dies of Injuries, *Newsday,* Oct. 8, 1988, p. 3; Paul Vitello, One Side Isn't the Truth, *Newsday,* Sept. 21, 1988, p. 3; Carolyn Colwell, Bail Denied to Murder Suspect, 17, *Newsday,* Sept. 16, 1988, p. 6; Natalia de Cuba and Kinsey Wilson, 'We Love You, Marty'; At Funeral, Family Supports Accused Teen, *Newsday,* Sept. 11, 1988, p. 3; Laura Muha, For Suspect's School a New Tragedy, *Newsday,* Sept. 9, 1988, p. 31; Shirley Perlman, Deadly Temper Tantrum, *Newsday,* Sept. 9, 1988, p. 3; Shirley E. Perlman and Laura Muha, Teen Charged in the Stabbing of His Parents, *Newsday,* Sept. 8, 1988, p. 3; Youth Charged with Killing Mother, Critically Wounding Father, UPI, Sept. 8, 1988; Village Police Commissioner Critically Wounded, Wife Slain, UPI, Sept. 7, 1988.

Jennifer Nicole Yesconis: Todd Bensman and Tony Hartzel, Woman, 20, Held in Parents' Slayings; Police Say She Wanted Insurance, *Dallas Morning News,* Feb. 13, 1994, Pg. 27-A; Woman, 22, Convicted of Murder, Faces Life Term in Parents' Death, *Austin American-Statesman,* Oct. 15, 1995, p. B-6; Selwyn Crawford, Tarrant Woman Guilty of Killing Dad, Stepmom; 22-Year-Old Must Serve at Least 40 Years in Prison, *Dallas Morning News,* Oct. 15, 1995, p. 1-A; Selwyn Crawford, No Verdict in Yesconis Trial; Jury to Resume Deliberations Today on Capital Murder Charges, *Dallas Morning News,* Oct. 14, 1995, p. 38-A; Selwyn Crawford, Defendant Testifies She Was Sexually Abused by Father; But She Denies Involvement in Her Parents' Slayings, *Dallas Morning News,* Oct. 12, 1995, p. 23-A; Selwyn Crawford, FW Woman Talked of Killing Parents Months Before Deaths, Witness Testifies; Polygraph Examiner Recalls '94 Conversation, *Dallas Morning News,* Oct. 11, 1995, p. 24-A; Laura Griffin, Woman Plotted Killings, Witness Says, *Dallas Morning News,* Oct. 7, 1995, p. 36-A; Laura Griffin, Yesconis Murder Trial Opens; Prosecutors Talk of Greed; Defense Calls Her Unstable, *Dallas Morning News,* Oct. 6, 1995, p. 39-A; Selwyn Crawford, Trial to Open in Mansfield Slaying of 2; Woman Allegedly Plotted Death of Father, Stepmom, *Dallas Morning News,* Oct. 4, 1995, p. 28-A; Selwyn Crawford, Unraveling the Motives of a Killing; Daughter's Arrest Leaves Victims' Kin Wondering, *Dallas Morning News,* March 28, 1994, p. 1-A; Todd Bensman and Tony Hartzel, Woman, 20, Held in Parents' Slayings; Police Say She Wanted Insurance, *Dallas Morning News,* Feb. 13, 1994, p. 27-A.

Notes

1. Kathleen M. Heide, *Why Kids Kill Parents: Child Abuse and Adolescent Homicide* (Columbus: Ohio State Press, 1992) at 3.

2. Paul Mones, *When A Child Kills: Abused Children Who Kill Their Parents* (New York: Pocket Books, 1991) at 6.

3. Heide, *supra* note 1.

4. *Id.*

5. Charles Patrick Ewing, *Kids Who Kill* (Lexington, MA: Lexington Books, 1990) at 5.

6. Charles Patrick Ewing, *When Children Kill: The Dynamics of Juvenile Homicide* (Lexington, MA: Lexington Books, 1990) at 32.

7. Mones, *supra* note 2 at 12.

8. Heide, *supra* note 1 at 6.

9. *Id.* at 36.

10. *Id.* at 37.

11. *Id.* at 42-43.

12. Ewing, *supra* note 8 at 36-38; D. Sargent, Children Who Kill—A Family Conspiracy? 7 *Social Work* 35 (1962).

13. *Id.* at 35.

14. Ewing, *supra* note 8 at 36-38.

15. *Id.* at 37.

16. *Id.* at 35.

17. *Id.* at 38.

18. *Id.*

19. Heide, *supra* note 1 at 7-11.

20. Michael Maloney, Children Who Kill Their Parents, 16 *Prosecutor's Brief: California District Attorney's Association Journal* 20 (1994).

21. *Id.* at 22.

22. Heide, *supra* note 1 at 36.

23. Maloney, *supra* note 20 at 21.

24. *Id.* at 20.

25. *Id.* at 21.

26. Heide, *supra* note 1 at 8.

27. Id.

28. Maloney, *supra* note 20 at 22.

29. Heide, *supra* note 1 at 11.

30. Telephone interview with Paul Mones, Esq., Jan. 13, 1997.

31. Mones, *supra* note 2 at 15.

32. Heide, *supra* note 1 at 9.

CHAPTER 9:
FRATRICIDE AND SORORICIDE

References

Armstead Hollins: Petula Dvorak and Rochard Boyd, Part Ends in Slaying; Victim's Sister Jailed, *New Orleans Times-Picayune*, May 6, 1996, p. B-5.

Delbert Joy: Hanford Man Cleared in Fatal Fight with Brother, *Fresno Bee*, Jan. 3, 1996, p. B-2.

LaVon Davis: Jennifer Dukes, County Attorney Rules Slaying Is Self-Defense, *Omaha World Herald*, Aug. 4, 1995; Associated Press, Brother Kills Brother and Is Slain by Third,

New York Times, Aug. 2, 1995, p. A-13; Cindy Gonzalez, Police Say Omahan Fired Gun to Defend Family, *Omaha World Herald,* July 31, 1995, p. 9-SF.

Richard Gibson: Kim Trent, Brothers' Spat Ends in Murder, Then Suicide, *Detroit News,* July 4, 1995, p. 1.

Dana Jokela: Debra Dennis, Man Who Beat, Killed Brother Headed to Jail, *Cleveland Plain Dealer,* Jan. 27, 1996, p. B-1; Man Who Killed Brother Sent to Prison, UPI, Jan. 27, 1996; Karen Scholz, Man Admits Beating Brother to Death With Bat, *Cleveland Plain Dealer,* Jan. 4, 1996, p. B-6. Karen Scholz and Debra Dennis, Teen Accused of Killing His Brother, *Cleveland Plain Dealer,* Oct. 28, 1995, p. B-1.

Dorothea and Mary Margaret Beck: Twin Held on Charge of Murdering Sister, *Bergen Record,* Nov. 24, 1995, p. A-29; Alton Twin's Death Ruled a Homicide, *St. Louis Post-Dispatch,* Dec. 14, 1995, p. C-6; Associated Press, 68 Year Old Twin Charged In Sister's Death, Charleston Gazette, Nov. 24, 1995, p. B-7; Charles Bosworth Jr., Woman Is Charged in Death of Her Twin; Alton Police Say She Beat, Kicked Sister, 68, *St. Louis Post-Dispatch,* Nov. 23, 1995, p. 1-A.

Terrence O'Brien: Regional Week in Review, *Asbury Park Press,* May 19, 1996, p. 5; Elaine Silvestrini, Man Guilty of Murder in Stabbing of His Sister, *Asbury Park Press,* May 16, 1996, p. B-1; Elaine Silvestrini, Defendant Knew Stabbing Was Wrong, Doctor Testifies, *Asbury Park Press,* May 15, 1996, p. 1; Elaine Silvestrini, Hospital Sued in Stabbing Death, *Asbury Park Press,* May 11, 1996, p. A-1; Elaine Silvestrini, Man Sought Aid Before Stabbing, Doctor Testifies, *Asbury Park Press,* May 10, 1996, p. B-1; Elaine Silvestrini, A 'Futile' Attempt, *Asbury Park Press,* May 9, 1996, p. B-1; Elaine Silvestrini, Trial Opens in '93 Fatal Stabbing, *Asbury Park Press,* May 8, 1996, p. A-1; Elaine Silvestrini, Murder Defendant's Statements Admissible, *Asbury Park Press,* May 3, 1996, p. B-1; Elaine Silvestrini, Suspect 'Happy' He Killed Sister; Detective Testifies Man Wanted to Kill Pregnant Woman, *Asbury Park Press,* May 1, 1996, p. B-1.

Michael Dilello: Brian Maffly, Family Stands Behind Brother Who Shot Brother, *Salt Lake Tribune,* Jan. 23, 1996, p. B-1; Brian Maffly, Self-Defense Killings Often Probed as Setups, *Salt Lake Tribune,* Sept. 5, 1995, p. A-3; Brian Maffly, Utahan Gets 10 Years for Fratricide—Dilello Fired 14 Bullets Into the Torso of Irate, Drunken Brother, *Salt Lake Tribune,* Aug. 9, 1995, p. D-2; For the Record, *Salt Lake Tribune,* June 29, 1995, p. B-2; T. J. Quinn, Former Wives Oppose Plea in Shooting, *Salt Lake Tribune,* June 23, 1995, p. B-2.

Christopher McLeod: Judi Villa, Teen Details Murdering Half Sister; Mesa Youth to Be Tried as Adult, *Arizona Republic,* March 9, 1996, p. B-1; Judi Villa, Governor Wants Records Opened in Girl's Murder, *Arizona Republic,* Jan. 11, 1996, p. A-1; Judi Villa, Tidal Wave of Juvenile Crime Building in State, *Arizona Republic,* Jan. 12, 1996, p. A-1; Judi Villa, Boy 'Out of Control,' Mom Says; Was to Be in Court Day Sister Was Killed, *Arizona Republic,* Dec. 20, 1995, p. B-1; Richard Ruelas, Mesa Boy Charged in Death of Sibling; Slaying Described as 'Cruel, Heinous,' *Arizona Republic,* Dec. 17, 1995, p. B-1; Judi Villa, Half Brother Quizzed in Slaying, *Arizona Republic,* Dec. 16, 1995, p. A-1; Abraham Kwok, Mesa Girl Found Dead in Trash Can, *Phoenix Gazette,* Dec. 15, 1995, p. B-1.

Steven Pfiel: Pamela Cytrynbaum, Suit Blames Parents for Deadly Son; Slain Girl's Mother Alleges Negligence, *Chicago Tribune,* Jan. 30, 1996, p. 1; Jonathan Eig, A Question of Blame; Child Murder Case Involving Parental Responsibility, *Chicago Magazine,* Nov. 1995, p. 98; Phillip J. O'Connor, Suburb Teen Gets Life Term for Killing Brother, *Chicago Sun-Times,* Oct. 21, 1995, p. 4; Mark Caro, Pfiel Admits Second Murder; Confession Read to Court, *Chicago Tribune,* Oct. 21, 1995, p. 1; Mark Caro,

Drug Question Delays Second Pfiel Guilty Plea, *Chicago Tribune,* Sept. 23, 1995, p. 5; Guilty Plea in Girl's Death, *Chicago Sun-Times,* Aug. 19, 1995, p. 9; Mark Caro, Pfiel Gets 100 Years in Norskog Murder, *Chicago Tribune,* Aug. 19, 1995, p. 1; Mark Caro, Pfiel Set to Admit Killing 2, *Chicago Tribune,* Aug. 17, 1995, p. 1; Sarah Nordgren (Associated Press), As Family Reeled from Tragedy, Fate Was Saving One Final Blow, *Fresno Bee,* May 28, 1995, p. A-8; Cameron McWhirter and Darlene Gavron Stevens, Neighbors in Fear of Accused Killer, *Chicago Tribune,* Jan. 28, 1994, p. 3; Cameron McWhirter, Parents of Murder Suspect Say He Is Innocent of Palos Killing, *Chicago Tribune,* Jan. 27, 1994, p. 4; Paul Sloan, Girl's Killing Still Scars Palos, *Chicago Tribune,* Nov. 3, 1993, p. 4; Paul Sloan and Cameron McWhirter, Girl in a Hurry to Grow Up, But She Never Had a Chance, *Chicago Tribune,* Aug. 24, 1993, p. 1; Paul Sloan and Cameron McWhirter, Prosecution Tells Evidence in Palos Slaying, *Chicago Tribune,* Aug. 11, 1993, p. 4; Philip Franchine, Teen Charged With Stabbing Murder of Palos Hills Girl, *Chicago Sun-Times,* July 21, 1993, p. 5.

Derek Gavette: Bryan T. Morytko, Judge Grants Teen Extension in Case of Burlington Slaying, *Hartford Courant,* Jan. 30, 1996, p. B-1; Michael Greenwood, Mental State of Murder Defendant Raised, *Hartford Courant,* Sept. 26, 1995, p. B-1; Will Tacy, Judge Continues Burlington Murder Case, *Hartford Courant,* Jan. 24, 1995, p. B-1; Daniela Altimari, Murder Suspect at First Said Shooting Accidental, *Hartford Courant,* Dec. 10, 1994, p. B-2; Daniela Altimari, No Death Penalty Charges Filed in Case of Brother Shooting Sister, *Hartford Courant,* Dec. 9, 1994, p. B-13; Hearing Postponed in Gavette Case, *Hartford Courant,* Dec. 2, 1994, p. B-2; Michael Greenwood, Burlington Teen May Face More Charges, *Hartford Courant,* Nov. 3, 1994, p B-1; Michael Greenwood, Man Confesses to Assault of Sister After He Shot Her, *Hartford Courant,* Oct. 27, 1994, p. B-12; Michael Greenwood, Grieving Family, Friends Pay Tribute to Slain Teen, *Hartford Courant,* Oct. 25, 1994, p. A-3; David Owens, Hundreds Gather to Mourn Girl, 15; Brother Charged, *Hartford Courant,* Oct. 24, 1994, p. B-7; John Springer and Michael Greenwood, Police Report Confession in Slaying of Girl, *Hartford Courant,* Oct. 22, 1994, p. A-3; David Polochanin, 18-Year-Old Charged in Slaying of His Sister, *Boston Globe,* Oct. 21, 1994, p. 37; Michael Greenwood, Girl Found Dead; Body Discovered in Trunk of Car; Brother Charged, *Hartford Courant,* Oct. 21, 1994, p. A-1; Daniela Altimari, Tragedy Shocks Torrington Family, *Hartford Courant,* Oct. 21, 1994, p. B-1; Michael Greenwood, Search Continues for Burlington Teenager, *Hartford Courant,* Oct. 20, 1994, p. B-1; Michael Greenwood, Search Is Continuing for 15-Year-Old Girl, *Hartford Courant,* Oct. 18, 1994, p. B-5.

Eight-Year-Old Illinois Boy: Charles Bosworth Jr. and Virginia Baldwin Hick, Boy, 7, Killed as Brothers Play With Pistol, *St. Louis Post-Dispatch,* Jan. 20, 1996, p. B-1.

Brandon Roses: Boy, 10, Sentenced for Killing Younger Sister, Reuters, Jan. 9, 1996; 10-Year Old Pleads Guilty to Fatally Shooting 5-Year-Old Sister With Rifle, *Charleston Gazette,* Nov. 22, 1995, p. C-2; Gary Boerg, Boy, 10, Pleads Guilty in Death of Little Sister, *Chicago Tribune,* Nov. 22, 1995, p. 12; Boy, 10, Faces Trial for Shooting Sister, Reuters, Nov. 20, 1995.

James Gilligan: Boy, 15, Avoids Jail in Brother's Slaying, *Boston Herald,* June 6, 1996, p. 32; Mark Mueller, Pols Urge Gun Safety After Tot's Slaying, *Boston Herald,* March 24, 1996, p. 7; Mark Mueller, 'Loving Brother' Accused in Tot's Slaying, *Boston Herald,* March 23, 1996, p. 1.

Notes

1. U.S. Department of Justice, Bureau of Justice Statistics, *Murder in Families,* July 1994.

2. *Id.*

3. *Id.*

4. *Id.*

5. Kay Tooley, The Small Assassins, 14 *Journal of the American Academy of Child Psychiatry* 306 (1975).

6. *Id.* at 316.

7. Gregory Leong, Clinicolegal Issues for the Forensic Examiner, in E. P. Benedek and D. G. Cornell (Eds.), *Juvenile Homicide* 115, 123 (1989).

8. *Id.* at 125.

9. Lauretta Bender, Children and Adolescents Who Have Killed, 116 *American Journal of Psychiatry* 510, 511 (1959).

10. Charles Patrick Ewing, *When Children Kill: The Dynamics of Juvenile Homicide* (Lexington, MA: Lexington Books, 1990).

CHAPTER 10:
FAMILICIDE

References

Ronald Gene Simmons: Bryce Marshall and Paul Williams, *Zero at the Bone* (New York: Pocket Books, 1991); Associated Press, Killers Are Executed in Arkansas and Texas, *New York Times*, June 26, 1990, p. A-21; Associated Press, Arkansas Man Convicted of Killing 14 Relatives, *Chicago Tribune*, Feb. 12, 1989, p. 20; Associated Press, Arkansan Sentenced to Die for Killing 14 Relatives, *New York Times*, Feb. 12, 1989, p. 29; Accused Mass Killer Punches Prosecutor, UPI, Feb. 10, 1989; Killer Guilty of First 2 in 16 Slayings, *Chicago Tribune*, May 13, 1988, p. 2; Jim Nichols, Arkansan Sentenced to Death in 2 Murders; Alleged Mass Killer Asks Swift Execution, *Washington Post*, May 12, 1988, p. A-3; Defense Drops Insanity Plea for Defendant in 16 Killings, *Chicago Tribune*, May 10, 1988, p. 4; Gary Abrams, Portrait of a Mass Killer, *Los Angeles Times*, Jan. 12, 1988, p. 5-1; Suspect's Slain Wife Wanted to Leave Him, *Chicago Tribune*, Jan. 4, 1988, p. 8; Mass Murder Suspect's Wife: 'I Want Out . . .,' UPI, Jan. 4, 1988; Slain Wife Weighed Leaving Mass-Murder Suspect, *Washington Post*, Jan. 4, 1988, p. A-10; Ron Davis, A Daughter's Letters of Fear, *Newsday*, Jan. 2, 1988, p. 4; Associated Press, Sheriff Reconstructs the Murders of 16, *New York Times*, Jan. 1, 1988, p. 1-32; Arkansas Daughter's Letters Reveal Unhappy Home Life, UPI, Jan. 1, 1988; Six Adults Shot, Others Strangled, UPI, Jan. 1, 1988; John F. Harris, Divorce Plans May Be Motive in Arkansas Killings, Probers Say, *Washington Post*, Jan. 1, 1988, p. A-3; Stephen Franklin, Slaying Suspect Tried to Flee Past, *Chicago Tribune*, Dec. 31, 1987, p. 14; Associated Press, 'It's All Over' Figure in 16 Deaths Quoted as Telling Hostage, *Los Angeles Times*, Dec. 31, 1987, p. 1-4; John F. Harris, A Reign of Intimidation in Arkansas Loner's Refuge, *Washington Post*, Dec. 31, 1987, p. A-1; Stephen Franklin, Toll Hits 16 in Arkansas Shooting Spree, *Chicago Tribune*, Dec. 30, 1987, p. 1; Suspect Built Walls to Keep World Away, *Chicago Tribune*, Dec. 30, 1987, p. 2; J. Michael Kennedy, Slayings of 16 May Have Started Before Christmas, *Los Angeles Times*, Dec. 30, 1987, p. 1-1; UPI, Mass Slayer Abused Wife, Got Daughter Pregnant, In-Laws Say, *Los Angeles Times*, Dec. 30, 1987, p. 1-2; Christmas Massacre Suspect Linked to Sexual Abuse, Reuters, Dec. 30, 1987; Jeff Necessary, Massacre,

UPI, Dec. 30, 1987; John F. Harris, Nine Victims Found at Killing Site, *Washington Post*, Dec. 30, 1987, p. A-1; 2 Killed, 4 Wounded in Shooting Spree in Arkansas, *Chicago Tribune*, Dec. 29, 1987, p. 5; Mary Lenz, Christmas Massacre Death Toll in Arkansas Rise to 16, Reuters, Dec. 29, 1987; Infatuation for Secretary Suspected in Arkansas Killing Spree, Reuters, Dec. 29, 1987; Jeff Necessary, Massacre, UPI, Dec. 29, 1987; Jeff Necessary, 'The Great Unanswered Question Is Why?,' UPI, Dec. 29, 1987; Jeff Necessary, Spree, UPI, Dec. 29, 1987.

Robert Lynch: Michael Matza (Knight-Ridder), Stable Loving Image of Family Takes Only Minutes to Destroy, *Buffalo News*, June 30, 1990, p. E-3; Family of Five Shot to Death, UPI, March 8, 1990; Apparent Murder-Suicides Kill 9, Including 5 Children, UPI, March 8, 1990.

Bruce Clinton: Apparent Murder-Suicides Kill 9, Including 5 Children, UPI, March 8, 1990.

Ronald Trevor Harden: Glen Martin, Willits Family of 5 Slain—Second Such Tragedy in a Year, *San Francisco Chronicle*, May 27, 1994, p. A-1; Mendocine Man Guilty in Slaying, *Sacramento Bee*, Feb. 10, 1994, p. B-3; High Level of Methamphetamine in Willits Mass Killer's Blood, *San Francisco Chronicle*, Sept. 9, 1993, p. A-19; Ron Sonenshine, Police Theory on Willits Killings, *San Francisco Chronicle*, Aug. 25, 1993, p. A-17; Nancy Vogel, A Ticking Time Bomb in Willits, *Sacramento Bee*, Aug. 25, 1993, p. B-1; Ron Sonenshine, 5 in Family Shot to Death in Willits, *San Francisco Chronicle*, Aug. 24, 1993, p. A-1; Toddler, Four from Family Shot in Willits, *Sacramento Bee*, Aug. 24, 1993, p. B-1; Killing in Town was Murder-Suicide, Reuters, Aug. 24, 1993.

Bruce Sweazy: Ron Sonenshine, Man Who Killed Family, Self Was Prozac-Free, Report Shows, *San Francisco Chronicle*, July 9, 1994, p. A-18; Glen Martin, Friends Say Willits Slayer Had Changed, *San Francisco Chronicle*, May 28, 1994, p. A-1; Kevin Leary, Willits Shaken by Details of Slaying, *San Francisco Chronicle*, May 28, 1994, p. A-19; Glen Martin, Willits Family of 5 Slain—Second Such Tragedy in a Year, *San Francisco Chronicle*, May 27, 1994, p. A-1.

Thomas Angst: Knight-Ridder, Problems Cited as Lawyer Kills Family, Self, *Buffalo News*, Oct. 2, 1994, p. A-11.

Anthony Paul: Abigail Trafford, Families Need More Help When Serious Illness Strikes, *Washington Post*, July 31, 1990, p. Z-6; Knight-Ridder, Suicide Note Says Pain Led to the Deaths of 4, *Orlando Sentinel Tribune*, July 19, 1990, p. A-11; Michael deCourcy Hinds, No Hope, Doctor Ends Family's Lives, *New York Times*, July 19, 1990, p. A-16.

Bruce Brenizer: Maureen M. Smith, Even Experts Struggle for Answers in Tragic Killings, *Minneapolis Star Tribune*, Dec. 2, 1993, p. A-21; Richard Mayhew, Death in a Small Town, *Minneapolis Star Tribune*, June 13, 1993, p. B-1; Dad, 4 Others Slain; Son Gets 2 Life Terms, *Chicago Tribune*, June 10, 1993, p. 3; Richard Mayhew, Life Terms for Brenizer in Family Slayings; Will Be Sent First to Mental Facility, *Minneapolis Star Tribune*, June 10, 1993, p. A-1; Wisconsin Teen Faces Sentencing in Family Deaths, *Madison Capital Times*, June 4, 1993, p. B-1; Teenage Murderer Ruled Insane, *Chicago Tribune*, May 8, 1993, p. 4; Mother Says Teen Killer Was Afraid of His Father, *Madison Capital Times*, May 7, 1993, p. A-8; DA Says Mental Hospital May Be Best for Killer of 5, *Madison Capital Times*, May 7, 1993, p. A-8; Attorney: Murderer Can Be Rehabilitated, *Wisconsin State Journal*, May 3, 1993, p. D-3; Associated Press, Wisconsin Teen Admits Killing Father, 4 Others in Family, *Chicago Tribune*, April 23, 1993, p. 8; Richard Mayhew, Brenizer Pleads Guilty, *Minneapolis Star Tribune*, April 23, 1993, p. A-1; Chronology of Brenizer Family Tragedy, *Wisconsin State Journal*, Jan. 22, 1993, p. C-3; Robert Imrie (Associated Press), Teen

Faces Trial in Family Killing, *Madison Capital Times*, May 20, 1992, p. A-5; Wisconsin Teen Charged with Killing 5 in Family, *Chicago Tribune*, April 15, 1992, p. 3; Richard Mayhew, A Year Later, Chilling Details Unfold in Brenizer Killings, *Minneapolis Star Tribune*, April 15, 1992, p. B-1; Kevin Duchschere, Documents Allege Motivations for Brenizer Killings, *Minneapolis Star Tribune*, Sept. 21, 1991, p. A-1; Sheriff Says He Knows What Happened to Missing Family, UPI, May 24, 1991; Rogers Worthington, Rumors Fly but Murders Still a Puzzle, *Chicago Tribune*, May 23, 1991, p. 28.

David Brom: Raj Persaud, Deep Mysteries of Family Cruelty, *The Independent*, Aug. 10, 1994, p. 18; Maureen M. Smith, Even Experts Struggle for Answers in Tragic Killings, *Minneapolis Star Tribune*, Dec. 2, 1993, p. A-21; Chuck Haga, Mentally Ill Inmates, *Minneapolis Star Tribune*, Dec. 27, 1992, p. A-1; Associated Press, Life Term in Ax Slaying, *New York Times*, Oct. 18, 1989, p. A-14; Jury in Murder Case Rejects Insanity Plea, *Chicago Tribune*, Oct. 16, 1989, p. 3; Jury Spurns Insanity Defense in Ax Killings, *New York Times*, Oct. 16, 1989, p. A-14; Jury Finds Youth Sane in Ax Slayings of Family, UPI, Oct. 15, 1989; Martin J. Moylan, Boy Held in Ax Deaths of 4 Family Members, *Chicago Tribune*, Feb. 20, 1988, p. 3; Associated Press, Boy, 16, Charged in Ax Murders of 4 in His Family in Minnesota, Feb. 20, 1988, p. 1-50; Teenager Held in Ax Slayings of Parents, Brother and Sister, UPI, Feb. 19, 1988.

Sean Stevenson: Brett Oppegaard, Sean Stevenson, *The Columbian*, Oct. 2, 1994, p. A-6; Stevenson, Other Escapees Plead Innocent, UPI, April 6, 1988; Stevenson's Life Spared, UPI, May 12, 1987; Teen's Triple-Murder Trial Nears End, UPI, May 6, 1987; Stevenson Confessions Recalled, UPI, April 28, 1987; Teen Held in Slaying of Family Was 'Lonely,' UPI, Jan. 3, 1987; Teen Pleads Insanity in New Year's Slayings of Family, UPI, Jan. 2, 1987.

Notes

1. Peter Marzuk, Kenneth Tardiff, and Charles Hirsch, The Epidemiology of Murder-Suicide, 267 *Journal of the American Medical Association* 3181 (1992).

2. See, e.g., A. L. Berman, Dyadic Death: Murder-Suicide, 9 *Suicidal and Life Threatening Behavior* 15 (1979).

3. Marzuk, *supra* note 1 at 3181.

CHAPTER 11:
MERCY KILLINGS

References

Roswell and Emily Gilbert: Nancy J. Osgood and Susan A. Eisenhandler, Gender and Assisted and Acquiescent Suicide: A Suicidologist's Perspective, 9 *Issues in Law & Medicine* 361 (1994).

Cecil and Jean Brush: Scott Steele, Mercy Killing: An Elderly Woman Goes Free After Taking the Life of Her Ailing Husband, MACLEANS, March 13, 1995, p. 32.

Hilliard and Marjorie Faile: Allison C. Gregory, Lancaster Shooting Called Mercy Killing, *The Herald* (Rock Hill, SC), March 16, 1996, p. A-1; Allison C. Gregory, Couple Found Slain, *The Herald* (Rock Hill, SC), March 15, 1996, p. A-1.

Tom Grentz and Eleanor Simpson: Lowell E. Sunderland, The Final Act; An Old Man
    Caught in the Age of Desperation Kills His Ailing Sister and Then Himself, *Baltimore
    Sun,* March 10, 1996, p. J-1.
Derek and Alice Rowbottom: Steve Boggan, Living: I Couldn't Let Her Suffer, *The
    Independent,* May 23, 1996, p. 6; Lynda Lee-Potter, Why the Law Must Rule Over
    Life and Death, *Daily Mail,* April 17, 1996, p. 13; Crown Gets Mercy Killing File,
    The Guardian, April 15, 1996, p. 5; Steve Boggan, Dozens Confess After Son's 'Mercy
    Killing,' *The Independent,* April 15, 1996, p. 6; Justin Dunn, I Gave My Sick Mum
    Killer Overdose, *Scottish Daily Record,* April 13, 1996, p. 4; Justin Dunn, I Killed
    Mum to Stop Her Suffering, *Scottish Daily Mirror,* April 13, 1996, p. 11; Nigel
    Bunyan, Son Admits Giving Drug Overdose to Mother in Agony with Cancer, *The
    Daily Telegraph,* April 13, 1996, p. 3; James Golden, A Son's Act of Mercy, *Daily
    Mail,* April 13, 1996, p. 15; Police Called in After Woman Suffering from Cancer Is
    Given Morphine Overdose; Son Admits to 'Mercy Killing,' *The Herald* (Glasgow),
    April 13, 1996, p. 3.
Robert and Tracy Latimer: Canadian High Court to Hear Case of Man who Killed
    Handicapped Daughter, Agence France Presse, Feb. 9, 1996; Russell Gibson, Cana-
    dian Farmer Wins Right to Appeal, UPI, Feb. 8, 1996; Dave Eisler, Latimer's Setback,
    MACLEANS, July 31, 1995, p. 22; Brian Hutchinson, Latimer's Choice; Bob Latimer,
    Convicted of Murdering Daughter Suffering from Cerebral Palsy, SATURDAY
    NIGHT, March 1995, p. 38; Father Sentenced in Mercy Killing, *Facts on File World
    News Digest,* Dec. 1, 1994, p. 902. 'An Honor to Have Known Her'; Laura Latimer
    says Tracy's Death 'Brought Us Closer,' MACLEANS, Nov. 28, 1994, p. 22; Patricia
    Chisholm, 'A Blunt Instrument'; The Latimer Case Raises Questions About Canada's
    Rigid Murder Laws, Nov. 28, 1994, p. 24; Ray Corelli, Mercy on Trial, MACLEANS,
    Nov. 21, 1994, p. 48; Associated Press, Father Defends Killing of Ailing Girl as
    Kindness, *Commercial Appeal* (Memphis), Nov. 20, 1994, p. A-20.
Cathie and Ryan Wilkieson: Christie Blatchford, Search for Truth About Mother, *Toronto
    Sun,* April 7, 1995, p. 5; Christie Blatchford, The Loss of Ryan, *Toronto Sun,* April 12,
    1995, p. 5; Joe Warmington, Groups Sorry for Comments; 'Hurt' Families, Volunteer
    Says, *Toronto Sun,* April 11, 1995, p. 14; Christie Blatchford, A Father Lashes Out,
    Toronto Sun, April 4, 1995, p. 5; George Christopoulos, Funeral for Mother, Son;
    What Happened to Ryan 'Not Fair', Pal Says, *Toronto Sun,* Dec. 10, 1994, p. 18;
    Christie Blatchford, Terrible Wishes, *Toronto Sun,* Dec. 8, 1994, p. 5; Robert Benzie
    and Antonella Artuso, Warning Ignored; Silipo Told Latimer-Type Murder Possible,
    Toronto Sun, Dec. 7, 1994, p. 4; Christie Blatchford, One Dark Moment; Mom's
    Frustration Reached Point of No Return, *Toronto Sun,* Dec. 7, 1994, p. 5.
Charles and Joy Griffith: Donna O'Neal, Governor and Cabinet Hear but Don't Act on
    Clemency Cases, *Orlando Sentinel Tribune,* Dec. 9, 1992, p. B-1; Diane Rado, Board
    Deals with Life and Death, *St. Petersburg Times,* Dec. 9, 1992, p. A-1; Mike Williams,
    'This Was Done Out of Love'; Florida Weighs Clemency Plea in Mercy Killing, *Atlanta
    Constitution,* Dec. 8, 1992, p. A-2; Maya Bell, A Tough Call: Reviewing the 'Ultimate
    Act of Love'; Florida's Clemency Board Will Debate the Case of a Man who Killed
    His Daughter Trapped in a Vegetative State, *Orlando Sentinel Tribune,* Dec. 6, 1992,
    p. A-1; Maya Bell, A Father's Torment Over His Severely Injured Daughter Drove
    Him Over the Edge, *Orlando Sentinel Tribune,* Aug. 25, 1991, p. 10.
Irene and Eric Bernstein: David Finkel, A Parent's Desperate Solution / Was Raising
    Brain-Damaged Son Too Much for a Mother to Bear? *St. Petersburg Times,* Sept. 27,
    1987, p. A-1; Itabari Njeri, Patterns of Hope: A Controversial Therapy for Brain-
    Damaged Children, *Los Angeles Times,* Dec. 8, 1987, p. 5-1; Probation Ordered in
    Death of Toddler, *Chicago Tribune,* Nov. 19, 1987, p. 22; Associated Press, Light

Sentence in Slaying of Retarded Son, *San Diego Union-Tribune*, Nov. 19, 1987, p. A-16; Judge Grants Light Sentence to Mother Who Shot Retarded Son, *Reuter Library Report*, Nov. 18, 1987; Bernstein Given Probation Term, UPI, Nov. 18, 1987; Bernstein Pleads No Contest to Killing Son, UPI, Nov. 16, 1987; Judge OKs State Exam for Bernstein, UPI, Sept. 14, 1987; Mother Pleads Innocent in Slaying of Brain-Damaged Son, UPI, July 7, 1987; Woman to Be Tried for Murder of Brain-Damaged Son, Reuters, June 12, 1987; Associated Press, Mother Is Accused of Killing Her 2-Year-Old Retarded Son, *New York Times*, May 14, 1987, p. A-28.

Rudy Linares: John Lantos, Steven H. Miles, and Christine Cassel, The Linares Affair, 17 *Law, Medicine and Health Care* 308 (1989); Laurel Burton, Russell Burck, and Max Douglas Brown, Humane Help for Dying Patients, *Chicago Tribune*, Sept. 5, 1991, p. 27; Ellen Alderman and Caroline Kennedy, Happy Birthday Bill of Rights, REDBOOK, July, 1991, p. 72; Mark M. Hagland, The Top 10 Developments in U.S. Health Care, 64 *Hospitals*, Dec. 20, 1990, p. 38; Illinois Panel Urges Right to Refuse Life-Support, *Los Angeles Times*, April 13, 1990, p. A-23; Kevin Johnson, Mercy Death: Aftermath of 'Ifs,' USA TODAY, April 11, 1990, p. A-3; Life Support Parents Were Told Son Was Dead, UPI, July 17, 1989; Marcia Chambers, Did Lawyers for Hospital Act Properly? *National Law Journal*, June 19, 1989, p. 13; Associated Press, Death of Boy in Coma Spurs Study of Laws, *Los Angeles Times*, May 31, 1989, p. 1-4; Linares: 'I Was Ready to Go to Jail,' UPI, May 23, 1989; Associated Press, Man Who Let Son Die Is Cleared by Coroner, *New York Times*, May 22, 1989, p. A-18; Associated Press, Father Cleared; Pulled Plug on His Baby, *St. Louis Post-Dispatch*, May 21, 1989, p. B-5; Larry Green, Grand Jury Rejects Murder Count; Teary Father Not Charged in Death of Comatose Boy, *Los Angeles Times*, May 19, 1989, p. 1-1; Associated Press, Man Cleared in Death of Son, *St. Louis Post-Dispatch*, May 19, 1989, p. A-18; Jury Refuses to Indict Man Who Cut Son's Life-Support System, *Washington Post*, May 19, 1989, p. A-18; B. D. Colen, Rudy Linares, A Father Betrayed, *Newsday*, May 16, 1989, p. 11; Robert Davis, Partee Says He Must Prosecute Father in Death of Comatose Son, *Chicago Tribune*, May 14, 1989, p. 2; Baby Likely Dead When Admitted, UPI, May 10, 1989; Murder or Mercy? TIME, May 8, 1989, p. 33; Dirk Johnson, Questions of Law Live On After Father Helps Son Die, *New York Times*, May 7, 1989, p. 1-26; Linares Faced Cut Off of Welfare Benefits, UPI, May 5, 1989; Kenneth Vaux, A Tragic Triptych—the Linares Case, *Chicago Tribune*, May 3, 1989, p. 17; Ian Ball, Gunman Takes Son Off Life-Support System, *Daily Telegraph*, April 27, 1989, p. 1; Associated Press, Father Faces Murder Charge in Death of Comatose Infant, *San Diego Union-Tribune*, April 27, 1989, p. A-3; Associated Press, Crying Father Holds Doctors Off So Child in a Coma Can Die, *New York Times*, April 27, 1989, p. A-20; Father Succeeds in Second Effort to Yank Son from Respirator, UPI, April 27, 1989; 'I Loved My Son,' says Father Who Yanked Boy, UPI, April 27, 1989.

Michael Hensley: Does Extreme Suffering Justify the Taking of Life? *Larry King Live*, CNN Transcript No. 298, May 9, 1991; South in Brief: Refusing to Indict, *Atlanta Journal and Constitution*, May 3, 1991, p. 7; No Indictment on Father Accused of Killing Child, *Orlando Sentinel Tribune*, May 3, 1991, p. A-12.

Notes

1. Donna Cohen and Carl Eisdorfer, Homicide-Suicide in Older Persons, *American Association of Suicidology Newslink*, in press; see also John A. Cutter, A Last, Desperate Decision, *St. Petersburg Times*, Nov. 21, 1995, p. D-1; Bard Lindeman, When Death Seems the Only Answer, *Bergen Record*, Nov. 14, 1995, p. H-10.

2. Nancy J. Osgood and Susan A. Eisenhandler, Gender and Assisted and Acquiescent Suicide: A Suicidologist's Perspective, 9 *Issues in Law & Medicine* 361 (1994).

3. *Id.*

4. *Regina v. Latimer,* 99 C.C.C. 3d 481, 126 D.L.R. 4th 203 (Saskatchewan Ct. App. 1995).

5. Wesley J. Smith, Is Our Changing Definition of Death for the Better? / NO: The Death Culture, Once It Is Allowed to Take Root, Grows Like a Weed, USA TODAY, May 18, 1995, p. A-15.

CHAPTER 12:
PREVENTING FAMILY HOMICIDE

Notes

1. U.S. Department of Justice, Bureau of Justice Statistics, *Spouse Murder Defendants in Large Urban Counties,* Sept. 1995.

2. Richard Whitmire, Child's Death Moves State Closer to Taking Children from Homes More Quickly, Gannett News Service, April 11, 1996.

3. U.S. Department of Justice, Bureau of Justice Statistics, *Murder in Families,* July 1994.

4. Kathleen M. Heide, *Why Kids Kill Parents: Child Abuse and Adolescent Homicide* (Columbus: Ohio State Press, 1992).

5. U.S. Department of Justice, Bureau of Justice Statistics, *Murder in Families,* July 1994.

6. *Id.*

7. Ann Goetting, *Homicide in Families and Other Special Populations* (New York: Springer, 1995).

8. *Id.*

9. Charles Patrick Ewing, *Battered Women Who Kill: Psychological Self-Defense as Legal Justification* (Lexington, MA: D. C. Heath, 1987).

10. *Id.*

11. U.S. Department of Justice, *supra* note 5.

12. U.S. Department of Justice, *supra* note 1.

13. U.S. Department of Justice, Bureau of Justice Statistics, *Violence Between Intimates,* Nov. 1994.

14. *Id.*

15. Ewing, *supra* note 9 at 39.

16. See Murray Levine and Howard Doueck, *The Impact of Mandated Reporting on the Therapeutic Process* (Thousand Oaks, CA: Sage, 1995).

17. Daniel B. Wood, L.A. Police to Use Computers to Prevent Domestic Abuse, *Christian Science Monitor,* Oct. 29, 1996, p. 3; Tracey Johnson, Software Assesses Likelihood of Violence in Home, *Los Angeles Times,* Oct. 21, 1996, p. B-1.

18. See Goetting, *supra* note 7.

19. See Jacquelyn C. Campbell (Ed.), *Assessing Dangerousness: Violence by Sexual Offenders, Batterers, and Child Abusers* (Thousand Oaks, CA: Sage, 1995).

20. See, e.g., James C. Beck, The Potentially Violent Patient: Clinical, Ethical and Legal Considerations, in Eric Margenau (Ed.), *The Encyclopedic Handbook of Private Practice* (New York: Gardner Press, 1990) at 697.

21. See Goetting, *supra* note 7.

22. Ann O'Connor and Jim Adams, New Gun Restriction Takes Most by Surprise, *Minneapolis Star Tribune,* Dec. 13, 1996, p. 1-A; Arlene Levinson (Associated Press), Domestic Violence Misdemeanor Now Bar to Ownership, *Chattanooga Free Press,* Dec. 7, 1996, p. A-1.

23. Arlene Levinson (Associated Press), Abusers Could Lose Guns, *Dayton Daily News,* Dec. 15, 1996, p. A-2.

24. Jillian Lloyd, Police Up in Arms Over Revised Federal Gun Law, *Christian Science Monitor,* Dec. 18, 1996, p. 4; Vince Horiuchi, Abusive Utah Cops Will Lose Weapons, *Salt Lake Tribune,* Dec. 17, 1996, p. A-1; June Arney, New Law Aims to Keep Guns Away from Family Abusers; People Will Lose Their Livelihoods, Say Some Who Expect a Court Challenge, *Virginian-Pilot* (Norfolk, VA), Dec. 16, 1996, p. A-1.

25. Levinson, *supra* note 23.

26. Horiuchi, *supra* note 24; O'Connor and Adams, *supra* note 22.

27. U.S. Department of Justice, Bureau of Justice Statistics, *Violence Between Intimates,* Nov. 1994.

Name Index

Subject Index

About the Author

<hr>
<hr>

Charles Patrick Ewing, a forensic psychologist and attorney at law, is Professor of Law and Psychology at the State University of New York at Buffalo, where he has taught criminal law, evidence, juvenile law, and psychology, psychiatry, and law since 1983.

He received his Ph.D. from Cornell University, was a Post-Doctoral Fellow at Yale University, and graduated with honors from Harvard Law School.

Dr. Ewing is author of *Kids Who Kill*; *When Children Kill: The Dynamics of Juvenile Homicide*; *Battered Women Who Kill*; and *Crisis Intervention as Psychotherapy* and coauthor of *Psychology, Psychiatry and the Law: A Clinical and Forensic Handbook*. He has also authored or coauthored more than 50 other publications dealing with issues in forensic psychology.

He is Senior Editor of the journal *Behavioral Sciences and the Law* and serves on the editorial boards of three other journals: *Law and Human Behavior*, *Journal of Child Sexual Abuse*, and *Journal of Emotional Abuse*. He is a Fellow of the American Psychological Association, and a Diplomate in Forensic Psychology of the American Board of Forensic Psychology and the American Board of Professional Psychology.

Dr. Ewing has been selected for listing in *Who's Who in American Law, Who's Who in Emerging Leaders in America,* and the *Best Lawyers in America Directory of Experts.* In 1993, he received the Distinguished Contributions to Forensic Psychology Award, an award presented annually by the American Academy of Forensic Psychology.